Corruption in Tanzania

The Case for Circumstantial Evidence

Edward Hoseah

CAMBRIA
PRESS

Amherst, New York

Printed in the United States of America

Library of Congress Cataloging-in-Publication Data

Hoseah, Edward.
Corruption in Tanzania : the case for circumstantial evidence / Edward Hoseah.
p. cm.
Includes bibliographical references and index.
ISBN 978-1-60497-593-2 (alk. paper)
1. Evidence, Circumstantial—Tanzania. 2. Evidence (Law)—Tanzania. 3. Corruption—Tanzania. 4. Evidence, Circumstantial—United States. 5. Criminal investigation. I. Title.

KTT470.5.H67 2008
347.678'064—dc22

2008048882

Table of Contents

List of Charts and Tables

List of Cases

Adelaide Kumalija and Another v. R. (1982) TLR 115

Agnes Doris Liundi v. R. (1980) TLR 46

Ally Bakari and Pili Bakari v. R. (1992) TLR 10 (CA)

Ally Fundi v. R. (1983) TLR 210

Attorney General v. Shamba Ali Kajembe (1958) EA 505

August Mahiyo v. R. (1993) TLR 117 (CA)

Ben Zuberi Mwamba v. R. (1984) TLR No. 172

Board of Commissioner of Excise v. Backus, 29 Hon. Pr. 33 (N.Y. Sup. Ct. 1864)

Chambers v. Moroney 10 Wend. 30, 304 (N.Y. Sup. Ct. 1833)

Chimera v. R. (1998) LLR 710 (CAK)

Danzig Case (1931) PCIJ Reports, Series A/B No. 44

Daubert v. Merrell Dow Pharmaceuticals Inc. 509 US

Dhalay v. R. (1997) LLR 514 (CAK)

DPP v. Felician Tibakweitira (1973) EA 440

DPP v. Jaffari Mfaume Kawawa (1981) TLR 149

Edom Godgrey Mlinga v. R. (1981) TLR 140

Eggington's Case 2 East's P.C. 666 (1801)

Gaidon Nelson Mapunda v. R. (1982) TLR 318

Grimm v. U.S., 156 U.S. 604 (1895)

Haining v. R. (1970) EA 620

Haji Moledina v. R. (1960) EA 678 (1919) 2 KB 171

Hamidu Mussa Thimotheo and Majid Mussa Thimotheo v. R. (1993) TLR 125 (CA)

Henry Akulo v. R., Cr. App. No. 120 of 1976, High Court (Unreported) (1978)

Hilda Abel v. R. (1993) TLR 246 (CA)

John Kachuri v. R. (1978) LRT No. 27

Joseph s/o Kamiliango and 5 Others v. R. (1983) TLR 186 (CA)

Kata v. U.S., 389 U.S. 347 (1967)

Khanja v. R. (1983) LLR 137 (CAK)

Korba s/o Farah v. R. (1967) HCD 92

Magendo Paul and Another (1993) TLR 220 (CA)

Makungire Mtani v. R. (1983) TLR 179 (CA)

Mariam Siri v. R., Court of Appeal Tanzania, Criminal Appeal No. 3 of 1990, Dar Es Salaam Registry (Unreported)

Mayagila s/o Sima v. R. (1967) HCD 62

Mkendeshwo v. R. (2002) LLR 3700 (CAK)

Mohamed Rafiq al Baghdad and 6 Others, Economic Criminal Appeal No. 2 of 2003, High Court, Dar es Salaam Registry (Unreported).

Mohamed Ramadhani v. R. (1970) HCD 50

Musambi v. R. (1983) LLR 147 (CAK)

Ndirangu v. R. (1983) LLR 147 (CAK)

Nuhu Selemani v. R. (1984) TLR 93 (CA)

Omari Ahmed v. R. (1983) TLR 52 (CA)

Patrick s/o Isango v. R. (1967) HCD 442

Public Prosecutor v. Wilson (SCM) 1988

Protas John Kitogile and Another v. R. (1992) TLR 51 (CA)

R. v. Braithwaite (1983) All E.R. vol. 2

List of Statutes

Anti-Corruption Act, 1997 (Act 575 of the Laws of Malaysia)

Commission for Human Rights and Good Governance Act, 2001 [Cap. 391 R.E.]

Constitution of the United Republic of Tanzania, 1977 (Cap. 2)

Criminal Procedure Act, 1985 [Cap. 20 R.E. 2002]

Economic and Organised Crime Control Act, 1984 [Cap. 200 R.E. 2002]

Evidence Act, 1967 [Cap. 6 R.E. 2002]

Interpretation of Laws Act, 1996 [Cap. 1 R.E. 2002]

Investment in Tanganyika Government Securities Act, 1961

Judicature and Application of Laws Ordinance, 1920 [R.L. Cap. 2 R.E. 2002]

Laws Revision Act, 1994, [Cap. 4 R.E. 2002]

National Elections Act, 1985 [Cap. 343 R.E. 2002]

Penal Code, 1945 [Cap. 16 R.E. 2002]

Prevention and Combating of Corruption Act, Act No. 11 of 2007

Prevention of Bribery Ordinance, Cap. 201 (Hong Kong)

Prevention of Corruption (Amendment) Act, No. 2 of 1974

Prevention of Corruption Act, 1971 [Cap. 329 R.E. 2002]

Written Laws (Miscellaneous Amendments) [No. 3] Act,
No. 27 of 1991

Written Laws (Miscellaneous Amendments) Act, No. 15 of 2007

INTERNATIONAL DOCUMENTS

ADB–OECD Anti-Corruption Action Plan, 2001

African Union Convention on Preventing
and Combating Corruption, 2003

Civil Law Convention on Corruption, 2003

Criminal Law Convention on Corruption, 2003

OECD Convention, 1997

SADC Protocol Against Corruption, 2001

United Nations Convention against Corruption, 2003

United Nations Convention of Transnational Organised Crime, 2000

Vienna Convention on the Law of Treaties, 1969

Preface

Grappling With the Epitome of Corruption: The Case for Circumstantial Evidence in Tanzania. The choice for the topic of my book is a result or culmination of my experiences in the field of anticorruption, where I work and continue to witness in a bulk of corruption cases a lack of recognition of 'circumstantial evidence' during investigation and, subsequently, submission of evidence to the Director of Public Prosecutions (DPP) and, eventually, to courts of law.

In this book, I make a strong case for the utility of circumstantial evidence because it is an area that has not been given the prominence it deserves. This is so, for the traditional common law had seen and continues to see the reliability of evidence through the prisms of the 'direct evidence paradigm'.

Had it been given the prominence it deserves, we could see more corruption cases in courts of law, and the courts would expound and articulate the efficacy of circumstantial evidence in the dispensation of corruption cases.

Acknowledgments

I would like to express my profound gratitude to all who provided assistance and inspiration in various ways in the course of researching and writing this book. First and foremost, I wish to acknowledge support and assistance received from Prof. Leonard P. Shaidi and Prof. Ibrahim Juma. These two have given me immeasurable academic guidance and inspiration. They assisted me in clarifying the theoretical framework within which I could sensibly seek answers to questions that prompted me to wish to undertake the study. They were instrumental in my successfully resolving the many research methodology challenges I had to face. They offered friendly but firm criticism of my presentation of the study findings that are presented in this book. In the same vein, I wish to acknowledge my profound gratitude for the encouragement and academic support I received from Prof. Ronald Allen of the Law School, Northwestern University, Chicago, Illinois, whose writings I have found illuminating and insightful.

I would be less than just if I did not also acknowledge the indirect support and inspiration I received from all who have written on some aspect of the elusive subject of legal evidence, as well as those in the legal and law enforcement professions who have had to deal with the subject on a practical level, day in and day out, throughout their careers.

I also need to express gratitude to the Faculty of Law at the University of Dar es Salaam and the University of Dar es Salaam. Sincere gratitude must also be extended to my employer, the Prevention and Combating of Corruption Bureau (PCCB), in the President's Office, for giving me permission to undertake my studies and research.

In addition, let me put on record my appreciation of the great moral and related support received from my beloved wife, Sarah, and my three beloved children, Mhinde Evelyn, Shoma Carolyn, and Magembe Michael. I thank them for providing me with the space and inner strength to undertake the relevant research and write book.

Finally, I am indebted to the entire staff of Cambria Press for their patience, creativity, and great support. They made the entire book publishing experience a great joy.

All the same, all those whose assistance and inspiration has been acknowledged are absolved from responsibility for any residual inadequacies this book may still contain.

Abbreviations

ACS	Anti-Corruption Squad
AgJ	Acting Judge
All ER	All England Reports
AU	African Union
AUCAC	African Union Convention on Preventing and Combating Corruption
BSC	Belgium Shipbuilding Company
CA	Court of Appeal
CAG	Controller and Auditor General
Cap.	chapter
CB	A British Military Honorary Class
CJ	Chief Justice
CPI	Corruption Perception Index
DBS	Direct Budget Support
DFID	Department for International Development
DNA	deoxyribonucleic acid
DPP	Director of Public Prosecutions

EA	East Africa
EACA	East African Court of Appeal
EOCCA	Economic and Organized Crime Control Act, No. 13 of 1984
EU	European Union
FBI	Federal Bureau of Investigation
FCPA	Foreign Corrupt Practices Act
FIU	Financial Intelligence Unit
FSR	Financial Sector Reform
GDP	gross domestic product
HC	High Court
HIPC	Highly Indebted Poor Countries
HM	Her Majesty
ICAC	Independent Commission Against Corruption
ICB	international competitive bidding
JA	Justice of Appeal
JJ	Justices
LAAC	Local Authorities Accounts Committee
LGRP	Local Government Reform Programme
LJ	Lord Judge
LSRP	Legal Sector Reform Programme
MCA	Millennium Challenge Account
MDAs	ministries, departments, and agencies
MDG	Millennium Development Goals
MPs	Members of Parliament
NACSAP	National Anti-Corruption Strategy and Action Plan
NCB	national competitive bidding
ODA	overseas development assistance
OECD	Organization for Economic Cooperation and Development
PAC	Parliamentary Accounts Committee
PCA	Prevention of Corruption Act
PCB	Prevention of Corruption Bureau
PCCA	Prevention and Combating of Corruption Act
PCCB	Prevention and Combating of Corruption Bureau

PCO	Prevention of Corruption Ordinance
PFMRP	Public Financial Management Reform Programme
PPAC	Parliamentary Public Accounts Committee
PRS	Public Sector Reform (MKUKUTA)
PRSP	*Poverty Reduction Strategy Paper*
PSRP	Public Sector Reform Programme
U.K.	United Kingdom
UN	United Nations
UNCAC	United Nations Convention Against Corruption
UNDP	United Nations Development Programme
UNODC	United Nations Office on Drugs and Crime
USA/U.S.	United States of America
USAID	United States Agency for International Development
R	Republic, Regina, or Rex
R.E.	revised edition
RICO	Racketeer Influenced and Corrupt Organization law
SADC	Southern Africa Development Community
TI	Transparency International
TRA	Tanzania Revenue Authority
VFM	value for money
VP	Vice President

Corruption in Tanzania

Chapter 1

Corruption and Circumstantial Evidence

1.1. Background to the Study

The book deals primarily with the law of evidence in the context of circumstantial evidence as it applies to anticorruption efforts in Tanzania. Corruption is recognised throughout the world as a detrimental force that thwarts democracy and represses individuals. Corruption is to be found everywhere; countries only differ in their respective levels of commitment to reduce its viral and deleterious effects. Corruption is a more perverse and devastating problem in countries that are in the process of democratisation and development. The prevalence of international conventions and regional protocols against corruption is a clear testimony that corruption concerns all communities in the global village.

The common-law tradition of the law of evidence since medieval times depended on direct evidence that helps to establish essential elements of crime because the 'eyewitness paradigm' was seen as a more reliable form of evidence than circumstantial evidence. The law of evidence in medieval times did not contemplate corruption as understood today. Therefore, the law of evidence emphasised direct evidence as opposed to circumstantial evidence. Today the same contextual understanding—to give preference to direct evidence or the 'eyewitness paradigm'—has not changed. And yet practice has shown that there has been limited successful prosecution of corruption cases to conviction through the use of that traditional common-law paradigm. It is therefore in this context that this book advocates for the utility of circumstantial evidence in corruption cases. This is a necessary departure from the status quo—the common-law tradition of law of evidence, which overemphasises the reliability of direct evidence. If corruption cases are to be prosecuted successfully and the verdict of guilt entered, the paradigm shift to circumstantial evidence is the immediate alternative.

Production of evidence in court, whether in criminal or civil proceedings, employs both direct and circumstantial evidence depending on the nature of the case itself. The law of evidence does not discriminate the application of these two types of evidence in criminal and civil proceedings. Notwithstanding this fact, the standard of proof in criminal proceedings is higher than in civil proceedings; in the former, it must be beyond reasonable doubt, while in the latter, it is on the balance of probability.

This book addresses the issue of the effectiveness of the existing legal framework (legislative and interpretative) that is used in detecting, investigating, and prosecuting those alleged to have committed acts of corruption in Tanzania. It specifically examines the fundamental problem of overreliance on 'direct evidence' approaches distinct from 'circumstantial evidence' approaches in gathering evidence and prosecuting and securing convictions in corruption cases. The book provides what is considered to be strong support for the view that there is indeed a powerful case for Tanzania's legal framework to be oriented in favour of circumstantial evidence approaches in order to improve the effectiveness of the contribution of the legal system to the fight against corruption.

The book discusses the results of a study designed to show that the taking of a legal initiative in the form of the adoption of circumstantial evidence approaches, particularly in corruption cases in Tanzania, will advance the deterrence effect of legal anticorruption measures, particularly with a view to increasing the success with which prosecuted corruption cases are brought to the courts of law for judicial dispensation.

The role of circumstantial evidence is not an isolated alternative in a myriad or plethora of issues in the prevention and combating of corruption in any society. The narrow focus and choice of *the utility of circumstantial evidence* preferred in this book is built on such other existing initiatives against corruption as preventive measures, the capacity building and operational independence of the anticorruption institutions and strategies, the role of the media and civil society, the oversight role played by the legislature, giving voice to the voiceless, political will, ethics infrastructure, whistle-blowers' protection, risk management, and community education. Just as crime has symbolic meaning, so does the punishment. It is contended that if circumstantial evidence is properly understood, applied, and utilised by law enforcement agencies[1] and the judiciary, the results would immensely improve the quality of cases filed and the effectiveness of the legal system in contributing to the fight against corruption.

It is self-evident from both experience and practice that curbing corruption in any particular and meaningful setting should require both deterrent and preventive measures, and that no one measure should be sacrificed or overemphasised at the expense of the other.

Our findings partly make it apparent that corruption engenders wrong choices and distorts economic and social development nowhere with greater damage than in developing countries.[2] If corruption is left unabated, it will grow and become institutionalised, engendering a culture of illegality that in turn breeds inefficiency in public institutions and causes the economy to be destroyed, social values weakened, and the foundation of a nation shaken.

The government of Tanzania's policy against corruption is zero tolerance.[3] However, corruption depends on three factors, which must be understood if the government measures are to be effective. These factors are the overall level of public benefits available, the risk inherent in corrupt deals, and the relative bargaining power of the briber and the person being bribed.[4]

Corruption takes place where there is a meeting of opportunity and inclination.[5] Therefore, the strategies to contain it should address both elements. Opportunities can be minimised through systematic reforms, and inclinations can be reduced through effective enforcement and deterrent mechanisms. It is necessary that a legal framework be put in place that sends out a clear signal to the effect that, while it is difficult to stop people from revering neighbours with more money and wealth, people who have such money and wealth must be prepared to explain how they got them. For, as one Tanzanian legal scholar—Professor Leonard Shaidi—once pointed out, 'Corruption is largely the result of a competitive economy which reveres success based almost exclusively on money and accumulation of wealth'.[6] This being the case, Tanzania needs to have a legal framework in place that provides for effective legal mechanisms that hold such suspects accountable for ill-gotten wealth. One such mechanism is the efficacy of circumstantial evidence as a viable paradigm.

This book focuses on the examination and analysis of circumstantial evidence and makes a case for the view that Tanzania should move away from the traditional school of thought, with its emphasis on 'direct evidence' in prosecuting corruption, towards one that favours and accords more weight to 'indirect evidence' or 'circumstantial evidence'.[7]

1.2. Diversity in Corruption Theories

The theories and practice of corruption are based on the causes and effects of corruption. Most scholars and anticorruption reformers have examined the concept of corruption with a view to linking it with its causes and effects.[8] The general pattern of these theories seems to tilt the balance of emphasis one way or the other based on the background of the scholar or anticorruption reformer.

If the scholar is a political scientist, the analysis of corruption is likely to address the question of the legitimacy of the state. For a banker, the emphasis will be on the effects corruption has on investment. An economist would tie corruption to the downside of economic inefficiency. For an administrator, the emphasis will be on rules and regulations, while a lawyer's focus will be on the legal framework. Similarly, a sociologist will focus on the social context of corruption, and so on.

1.2.1. A Survey of the Problem in Tanzania

The Warioba Report[9] mapped the problem and magnitude of corruption in Tanzania and drew the conclusion that corruption has permeated all sectors and is therefore a serious issue that deserves special attention for its crippling effects on the economy, social fabric, and political legitimacy. The Warioba Report resulted in the formulation of the National Anti-Corruption Strategy and Action Plan (NACSAP). Anticorruption measures are also addressed in and linked to the Poverty Reduction Strategy of Tanzania, and corruption is identified as one of the impoverishing factors in Tanzania; thus, good governance constitutes the third of the three clusters of outcomes in the Poverty Reduction Strategy (MKUKUTA). (The Tanzanian government Poverty Reduction Strategy (MKUKUTA), has three clusters: Cluster 1 focuses on macroeconomic growth and stability, Cluster 2 seeks to institute sustainable reforms that addresses the Millennium Development Goals (MDGs), and Cluster 3 encompasses good governance and the fight against corruption.) Several researchers and scholars have emphasised that the structural characteristic of political markets in which there is little incentive for control by the voters and strong incentives for self-serving politicians to cater to interest groups is the principal factor in corruption.[10]

Surveys show that corruption is pervasive in areas that lack economic freedom; overexpanded and overregulatory governmental structures create incentives for corruption by encouraging the seeking of privileges. On the one hand, corruption is the cost of obtaining privileges that only the state can legally grant. Such privileges would include favouritism in taxation, tariffs, subsidies, loans, government contracting, and regulation.[11] On the other hand, corruption is the result of attempts to avoid the restrictions that accompany the use of privileges, taxes, and barriers to free trade.[12]

Edmond Mndolwa has highlighted the role played by the Controller and Auditor General (CAG) in containing the menace of corruption. He contended that, though CAG has reported and will continue to report to parliament, his reports will continue to be read and quietly filed away in the normal manner. More action beyond filing of these reports is warranted to ensure that checks and balances among the organs of the state are maintained.[13]

Mndolwa has observed the failure of Tanzanian public corporations to deliver the expected goods and services, creating a favourable breeding ground for corrupt practices. He pointed out several reasons why these public corporations failed to deliver. The method of making the appointments of the chief executive officers (CEOs) of these corporations invariably involves intense lobbying and undue influence.[14] CEOs appointed under such an environment will most likely succumb to corruption and undue jostling for favours.

1.2.2. Good Governance

Many social and economic scientists have attempted to define the term *good governance* from their perspectives without necessarily seeking to observe the concept from legal point of view. However, Kenneth K. Mwenda contended that a succinct legal definition of *good governance* remains elusive. Most of the definitions given are simply the restatement of existing concepts pertaining to constitutionalism, rule of law, accountability, transparency, and the doctrine of separation of powers.[15] The meaning assigned by the World Bank to the term *governance* is the exercise of political power to manage a nation's affairs.[16] It implies predictable, open policy making; a bureaucracy with a professional ethos; an executive arm of government accountable for its actions; and a strong civil society participating in public affairs—all operating under the rule of law. The Tanzanian government defines *good governance* as the exercise of official powers in the management of the country's resources for the betterment of life.[17]

Governance and accountability form the third cluster under the Poverty Reduction Stratergy (MKUKUTA) that provides the foundation for the government's intervention to reduce poverty in Tanzania. Governance and democracy overlap to a significant degree. They both emphasise structures, processes, and values that heighten legitimacy, accountability, and responsiveness in public affairs. However, governance and democracy are conceptually distinct.

Governance is conceived of as the effective management of public affairs through the generation of a regime (set of rules) accepted as legitimate, in the promotion and enhancement of societal values sought by individuals and groups. Good governance is the ability of public institutions to deliver quality goods and services to their clients or citizens with optimal consistency and satisfaction. This is manifested in the effective utilisation of taxes into equitable social and economic services and maintenance of law and order in the context of the rule of law.

Social decay and weakness of state institutions call for institutional renewal in the form of good governance to address economic achievement and growth. Governance became the agenda after the collapse of communism and of the central planning model in the former Soviet Union, which has been replaced by a capitalist model at a global level.[18] Governance is now a global concern and agenda. It is a rallying point at all global fora and international organisations such as the UN, the World Bank, the European Union, the Commonwealth, and certainly bilateral donors in sub-Saharan African.

The World Bank in particular began to use the term *good governance* in the early 1990s when it focused primarily on improving public administration. In a 1992 report on 'Governance and Development', the World Bank expanded the definition to include 'the manner in which power is exercised in the management of a country's economic and social resources for development'.[19] The International Monetary Fund (IMF) contributes to promoting good governance in member countries through its policy advice and, where relevant, technical assistance in the following two spheres:

- Improving the management of public resources through reforms covering public sector institutions; and
- Supporting the development and maintenance of a stable economic and regulatory environment conducive to efficient private sector activities.[20]

For the United Nations Development Programme (UNDP), governance and human development are indivisible entities: human development cannot be sustained without good governance, and governance cannot be sound unless it sustains human development. UNDP defines governance as the exercise of political, economic, and administrative authority in the management of a country's affairs at all levels. Governance comprises the complex mechanisms, processes, and institutions through which citizens and groups articulate their interests, mediate their differences, and exercise their legal rights and obligations. Good governance has many attributes; it is participatory, transparent, and accountable. It is effective in making the best use of resources and is equitable. In addition, it promotes the rule of law.[21]

Governance is participatory in the sense that it includes the state but transcends it by taking in the private sector and civil society. The three together create a favourable political and legal environment. The private sector generates jobs and income. The civil society facilitates political and social interaction—mobilising groups to participate in economic, social, and political activities. Because each has weaknesses and strengths, a major objective of our support for good governance is to promote constructive interaction amongst the three.[22]

Mwenda is of the strong view that such definitions do not constitute, jurisprudentially, well-set-out legal definitions of good governance.[23] He made a case that if, indeed, the term *good governance* is a legal concept, then it is not enough to state simply that good governance is epitomised by predictable, open, and enlightened public policy; a bureaucracy imbued with a professional ethos acting in furtherance of the public good; the rule of law; transparency processes; and a strong civil society participating in public affairs.[24] Good governance, according to Mwenda, 'refers simply to a collection of legal concepts that have been known to several lawyers time immemorial. There is nothing jurisprudentially new about the term *good governance*, although this term has attracted much intellectual curiosity and excitement'.[25]

Apart from the superficial treatment of the term *good governance* by many scholars and multilateral institutions such as the World Bank, IMF, African Development Bank, Asian Development Bank, and UNDP—as Mwenda postulated—a consensus on the definition of the concept of good governance is yet to be found.

Nonetheless, fighting corruption is about committed political culture that does not render lip service to anticorruption and good governance initiatives, but ensures that governance is improved and corruption is dealt with accordingly. Bad governance, however, is a failure of public institutions to supply society with a framework for a competitive process and sustainable development. Good governance is essential for developing an environment that promotes economic growth and minimises poverty. Sustainable development requires sound institutions as well as synergy between the economic and political spheres. For circumstantial evidence to be effective in the dispensation of justice against corruption, all legal institutions—including the judiciary, the police, the office of the DPP and the attorney general, the legal practitioners, and the Prevention and Combating of Corruption Bureau (PCCB)—must be strengthened in terms of capacities, training, and commitment to uproot corruption in society. Most importantly, the understanding of the utility of circumstantial evidence in corruption cases as *the common-law tradition* has not been able to effectively deal with the new trends of corruption and its predicates.

Research findings have demonstrated that corruption leads to lower capital inflows and lower productivity. Corruption may deter foreign investors because it is often associated with a lack of secure property rights as well as bureaucratic red tape and mismanagement.[26] The deleterious effects of corruption are devastating because of its pervasive, viral nature, and it is corrosive to the political and socioeconomic existence of our nation.[27]

One the one hand, corruption is an extra cost and a waste to taxpayers because, while it is true that governments should impose taxes for revenue collection—which, in turn, runs the activities of the government and enables the government to deliver its essential services to the citizens—taxes and tariffs become an opportunity for bribery. On the other hand, corruption creates uncertainties for the taxpayers, who invariably do not know quite how much they have to pay. It reduces the revenue accruing to the government.[28]

In its effort to curb corruption, the government of Tanzania introduced the national anticorruption initiative,[29] which proposed both preventive and deterrence measures to curb corruption in the country. However, these domestic initiatives target the demand side of corruption and naively ask corrupt leaders to judge themselves by collaborating with other stakeholders such as the private sector and civil society without focusing adequately on making corruption a high-risk undertaking.

Similarly, the report on the state of corruption in Tanzania implored that the long history of fighting corruption in Tanzania has revealed that there is a need to continue to update instruments and approaches for fighting corruption to cope with the changing nature and avenues of corruption as circumstances change.[30]

The *Tanzania Development Vision 2025* has three major foci: achieving high-quality livelihood for Tanzanians, attaining good governance through the rule of law, and developing a strong and competitive economy.[31] Corruption is a serious hindrance to the attainment of the national vision in Tanzania. Corruption is in addition a worldwide concern that calls for collective interventions through concrete, clear, concise, and comprehensive strategic action plans.

1.2.3. Corruption and Delivery of Social Services

The Warioba Report revealed that social service delivery by public institutions is crippled by corrupt transactions through public servants. It is observed that corruption downgrades the quality of social service delivery in Tanzania to a level below the expectations of the general public.[32] The National Afro Barometer Survey[33] also showed that Tanzanians see petty corruption by public officials as pervasive. The most common form is that which involves government officials at the local authority level, namely, the traffic police, court clerks, and magistrates. It is commonly held that corruption is rarely a victimless crime. However, Justice Heath held a different view: the state is also a victim of crime, including corruption, because it suffers financial losses as a result of nondelivery of goods for which payment should be made. Loss can occur as a result of simple theft and fraud; vehicles, equipment, and other goods are lost as a result of various schemes of corruption, fraud, theft, and negligent conduct or lack of control.[34]

Corruption can cause death as featured in a marine disaster of May 1996, involving a passenger liner *MV Bukoba*. This vessel capsized in shallow waters in Lake Victoria with the loss of an estimated seven hundred lives. A judicial commission report published in September 1996 blamed the Tanzania Railways Marine Division for operating the vessel without due care. The division was said to have been characterised by gross negligence, inefficiency, and corruption.[35] The government was also blamed for buying a defective ship, and the Belgian Shipbuilders (BSC) for supplying a vessel that did not correspond to the specifications and for not giving users adequate guidelines on how to handle the ship.[36]

1.2.4. Economic Growth and Sustenance

With a population of 33,671,453 people,[37] Tanzania remains one of the poorest countries of the world, although it is endowed with abundant natural resources. Tanzania heavily depends on international assistance revenue—this accounted for 10 percent of the gross domestic product (GDP) and 33 percent of the government budget in 2000. The revenue from overseas development assistance stands at US$1 billion per year, which makes Tanzania one of the most donor-dependent countries in sub-Saharan Africa. The Poverty Reduction Strategy adopted in 1997 has resulted in the Highly Indebted Poor Countries (HIPC) debt relief of 45 percent (US$7.6 billion) that allows the country to channel its resources to other priority areas.[38]

To capture the magnitude of corruption in economic terms, Alan Bacarese revealed that corruption represents 25 percent of the world's costs on government procurement. The Corruption Perception Index (CPI) for 2006 for Transparency International (TI) reflected that, of the US$4 trillion spent on government procurement annually, approximately US$400 billion will be siphoned off in corruption, classically in the form of bribes. Corruption is the cause of building unnecessary infrastructure that is of dangerously poor quality.[39] In 2004 the World Bank announced that over US$1 trillion were paid in bribes in one year alone.[40] In 2007 Bacarese contended that the figure was then five to six years out of date and did not represent the cost of large-scale fraud or embezzlement of public funds. From the African angle, the Economic and Financial Crimes Commission in Nigeria put the country's own corruption and theft at approximately £210 billion, or US$420 billion.[41]

The Poverty Reduction Strategy, together with the *Tanzania Development Vision 2025*, sets out the strategy and objectives for poverty eradication by 2010. To realise these objectives, the government came up with the medium-term strategy for poverty reduction (PSRP) that was developed in 2000 and seeks to reduce the incidence of absolute poverty from 48 percent to 42 percent by 2005, and down to 24 percent by 2010. The current GDP growth increased from 4.1 percent in 1998 to 7.1 percent in 2007. Agriculture, the backbone of the economy, is targeted to grow at 5+ percent per year. The government has also prioritised basic education, primary health care, water, roads, the judiciary, agriculture, and HIV/AIDS in its *Poverty Reduction Strategy Paper* (PRSP).[42]

These economic growth endeavours by the government can only be successful if corruption is tackled comprehensively and in a multifaceted approach, because it makes serious inroads into any meaningful economic, political, and social development in a country—more so in a poor country. This book is another attempt to demonstrate that corruption can be tackled from many fronts, including through the utility of circumstantial evidence in corruption cases to complement other prongs against the malaise.

1.3. The Policy Response to Corruption

Given the spread of corruption in the country as documented in the Warioba Report, it became evidently clear that the government had to come up with a clear policy and a multifaceted strategy to combat the scourge of corruption in a holistic fashion.

In response to the Warioba Report, the government came up with NACSAP, which is a policy and strategy document that was conceived on 29–31 March 1999 at the Momela Lodge, Arusha. Its aim is to address the challenges posed by corruption holistically and to find the means to deal with it strategically, involving all stakeholders. The government brought together members of the private sector, the public sector, civil society, and the media, as well as professionals, academics, and development partners or donors,[43] to discuss and agree on policy considerations and coalition building in developing a national vision that would guide the fight against corruption in Tanzania. In November 1999, NACSAP received cabinet approval and was brought into operation in 2000.[44]

NACSAP has identified four guiding principles for its implementation: (a) prevention, (b) enforcement and rule of law, (c) public awareness, and (d) institution building. The central theme of the present study is pegged on the enforcement and rule of law; therefore, we examine the efficacy and utility of circumstantial evidence. This theme is an important part of both the Poverty Reduction Strategy and NACSAP, as it is designed to concretise and support the efforts of the PCCB and the courts in order to reduce the levels of corruption in Tanzania and ensure that perpetrators realise that any indulgence in corruption is a high-risk undertaking; the utility of circumstantial evidence will be an effective tool to deter corruption, particularly the cooperation of the courts and law enforcement agencies.

The central theme of this study is in total agreement with Deepa Narayan's[45] elaboration on the role of institutions in the lives of the poor by either responding to or repressing their needs, concerns, and voices. When the poor and rich compete for services, the rich will always get the upper hand and priority. The fight against corruption becomes effective where the community is involved through public education, sensitisation, and outreach programmes at the community level. In addition, this cause can also be fought for through interactions found in development and social assistance involving the civil society, private sector organisations, and the media. They are found along a continuum, from the micro or local level to the macro or national and international levels.

The intent of combating corruption in Tanzania was translated into an institutional framework in the form of the NACSAP infrastructure. NACSAP is meant to correct the negative effects of corruption by strengthening systems of integrity, transparency, and accountability in public institutions. NACSAP focuses on causes and effects of corruption, plugging up loopholes in systems, procedures, rules, regulations, and laws, and changing the mind-sets of all players—particularly the citizens, through their civil society organisations, the media, and the private sector. Our theme is one area that NACSAP has to address, particularly the law against corruption (cap. 329), which is weak and has been overtaken by the demands of time that require an overhaul of that law in order to incorporate the best practices, such as the utility of circumstantial evidence in corruption cases, by examining the best practices in other jurisdictions and domesticating regional and international instruments against corruption, which Tanzania has ratified.[46]

NACSAP is national in its outlook, sectoral in its focus, and action oriented since it aims to strengthen systems that are transparent and accountable. The objectives of NACSAP are as follows:

- Comprehensive anticorruption law to be put in place (by repealing and replacing the current law—the Prevention of Corruption Act [PCA] of 1971);

- Identification of areas in government activities most prone to corruption and redressing them through a sectoral approach (Ministries, Departments and Agencies [MDAs] action plan);
- Identification of legal and administrative corruption remedies that provide adequate deterrence; and
- Triangular partnership (government, civil society, and private sector)—coalition building.

Principles of NACSAP are founded on *prevention* through simplification, demystification, and depersonalisation of the government and its programmes. The first principle—simplification of procedures—is aimed at reducing rent-seeking opportunities for corruption.

The second principle of NACSAP is enforcement, that is, to provide operational independence and effective discharge of the functions of the law enforcement agencies that are enjoined by law to curb the scourge—in this case the PCCB. In addition, the judiciary has to expeditiously dispose of corruption cases fairly and firmly to strengthen the objectives of the criminal justice system.

The third principle is public awareness, where the capacity to disseminate the rights and duties of the citizenry is emphasised. An informed citizenry is essential towards holding government accountable because that is where the role of the civil society and media becomes effective, as they play an important role in holding the state actors accountable for their action or omissions, or both. The fourth principle is institution building, where the oversight bodies are empowered adequately to discharge their functions effectively. In the case of the PCCB, the capacity to detect, investigate, and prosecute corruption cases must be strengthened and must translate the utility of circumstantial evidence to foster its capability to bring more and serious cases that can stand the evidential scrutiny of the courts of law.

These oversight bodies include parliamentary committees responsible for anticorruption and proethics measures,[47] the PCCB,[48] the Ethics Secretariat,[49] the Commission on Human Rights and Good Governance,[50] and the CAG.[51] And the fifth principle is the political will that must be demonstrable by political actors to attack both perceived causes and effects of corruption at a systemic level.

The seven priority areas of NACSAP are as follows:

- *The rule of law and legal framework* is to provide will facilitate sectoral law review and the creation of an enabling environment that restores confidence in the judiciary and law enforcement agencies.
- *Financial discipline and management* is intended to reduce and eradicate the siphoning of public funds by unfaithful and deceitful public officials who collude with a third party outside public institutions, on the one hand, and to increase revenue collection to finance the provision of social services and goods to the general public, as well as a recipe for economic growth, on the other.
- *Procurement* requires strict compliance with transparent administration procedures for the tendering for and the procurement of goods and services.
- *Public education* includes the creating of awareness in and the sensitisation of the citizens regarding their rights and responsibilities; this would involve the creation of innovative educational programmes that would further the awareness among the citizenry of the harm caused by corruption and inflicted on the economy, the ultimate purpose of which is to transform the fabric and values of the society.
- *Public service reforms* (i.e., capacity building) would help citizens and civil servants, likewise, understand that public officers are not 'masters' but 'servants' of the people, to whom they are accountable for their actions; public servants deserve a fair remuneration package.
- *Whistle-blowers and witness protection* call for cognisance of the fact that informers and citizens who come forward to the law enforcement agencies and report on corruption incidents are not protected. A legal framework has to be put in place to provide adequate protection and give confidence to players in anticorruption programmes.

- *The media* has the responsibility to report on corruption and corrupt elements without fear or favour and to publicise the harm that corruption can cause to the innocent, the poor, and the weak segment of the population.

Apart from MDAs, action plans and implementation of the identified activities, local government reforms have mainstreamed NACSAP, and a guide is now in use to facilitate all 116 local government councils of Mainland Tanzania to implement their individual action plans.

Attention is being emphasised so that, in the preparation of action plans, all sectors should ensure that participation and monitoring by the councils themselves is effectual. Each council is guided by its own peculiar circumstances in addressing corruption as a specific component. There is also the Good Governance Coordination Unit, which was established administratively by the chief secretary in 2001 to coordinate all good governance functions under the minister of state for good governance.[52]

The Good Governance Coordination Unit collects and processes all data from the different sectors (public, private, civil society, and media), and undertakes the evaluation and monitoring of the NACSAP process on a quarterly basis. All MDAs submit their reports on the implementation of their anticorruption activities to allow political actors to understand and give the required impetus to overcome the scourge. Publicity of the NACSAP findings is disseminated through quarterly reports, and recently the *State of Corruption in Tanzania Annual Report 2002* was released for public debate, monitoring, and participation of all stakeholders.[53]

1.3.1. Analysis of the Magnitude of the Reported Cases

Table 1 and chart 1 conveniently summarise the current data on the recorded scope of the problem nationally, at the level of complaints received on corruption, and action so far taken by the government of Tanzania for the period of January 1995 through May 2007. The practical application of circumstantial evidence is a process and has

TABLE 1. Prevention and combating of Corruption Bureau statistics of cases (numbers).

Year	Cases Reported	Cases Investigated	Cases Completed	Cases Transferred	Cases Prosecuted	Convictions Recorded	Acquittals Recorded	Admin. Action Taken
1995	261	261	145	–	8	1	7	–
1996	513	513	245	–	21	2	9	–
1997	510	510	289	–	9	1	4	–
1998	545	545	200	95	15	2	6	–
1999	1,116	1,116	304	209	62	9	25	–
2000	1,244	1,244	276	234	–	6	3	–
2001	1,354	1,354	285	154	57	–	–	1
2002	1,383	1,383	732	222	52	12	26	42
2003	2,285	1,796	540	36	60	9	28	21
2004	2,223	1,149	458	25	60	6	8	126
2005	3,121	677	540	2	50	6	10	111
2006	6,320	1,528	1,688	496	71	18	28	209
May 2007	3,424	619	781	254	63	19	13	43
Total	24,299	12,695	6,483	1,727	528	91	167	553

Source. The PCCB-HQ, May 2007.

stages. The study has taken the following practical stages into account: (a) complaints received, (b) cases investigated, (c) DPP consent, and (d) court consideration of circumstantial evidence (see table 1). The table also indicates 'cases transferred'; this means that, upon preliminary investigation or detection by the PCCB, no clues of evidence relating to corruption were found and thus the matter was transferred to the relevant authorities—including the police, the Tanzania Review Authority (TRA), TISS, the Ethics Secretariat, the Human Rights Commission, the Attorney General's Chambers (or the DPP's office), and the judiciary.

Other factors that explain why corruption cases fail to secure convictions include rushing cases to court without thorough prior investigation, the absence of a checklist to guide investigators and prosecutors in corruption cases, the lack of in-depth knowledge regarding circumstantial evidence by judicial officers, and a paucity of academic literature on and articulation of circumstantial evidence.

The number of cases reported to the PCCB per year has multiplied from 261 in 1995 to 3,424 by May 2007, which is a thirteenfold increase

CHART 1. Corruption of cases reported, investigated, and completed.

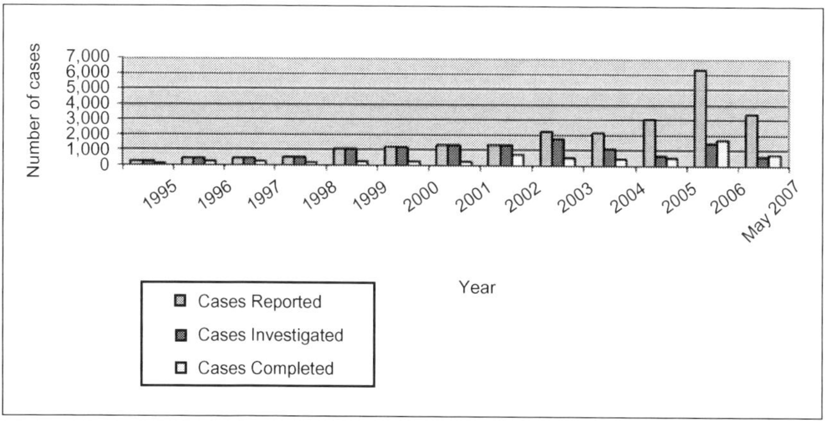

Source. Research data.

over the period. The efficiencies recorded are attributed to the expansion of the bureau into the regions and districts, as well as to the increased community awareness on the evils of corruption. The past five years have seen the PCCB receiving increased funding from the government, UNDP, the European Union (EU), and United States Agency for International Development (USAID) under the Millennium Challenge Account (MCA) for capacity building in community education, administration, and investigation components.

Until 2002 all cases that were reported to the bureau were investigated. However, this efficiency has been falling ever since, largely due to the magnitude and complexity of the recent cases that involve large amounts of money and high ranking officials, and since tracing the paper trail involves a lot of background checks, accounts tracking, international cooperation, mutual legal assistance, and extradition matters in relation to corruption offences that have been included in the Prevention and Combating of Corruption Act (PCCA). However, when dealing with these matters, the PCCB has to consult the Attorney General or Interpol, or both, through the Inspector General of Police—with the exception of Tanzanian embassies abroad to process such requests to obtain evidence beyond the country's borders.

The continued decrease of investigated cases is, most importantly, attributed largely to the nonuse of circumstantial evidence. For example, table 2 shows that in 2004 half of the cases (52 percent) were investigated, whereas only 18 percent of the cases received up to May 2007 have been actioned.

The number of cases whose investigation was completed is below two-thirds per year during this period. It takes a long time to conclude these investigations given the complexity and secrecy of the perpetration involved. From 2003 until May 2007, the percentage has fallen from 24 to 23 percent. This is a criterion on which to judge the bureau's performance and needs to be addressed seriously through the use of circumstantial evidence to contain the scourge. This is why the current study focuses on the use of circumstantial evidence to increase the number and quality of corruption cases that reach the courts of law.

TABLE 2. Prevention and combating of Corruption Bureau statistics of cases (percentage).

Year	Cases Investigated	Cases Completed	Cases Transferred	Cases Prosecuted	Convictions Recorded	Acquittals Recorded	Admin. Action Taken
1995	100%	56%	0%	3%	0%	3%	0%
1996	100%	48%	0%	4%	0%	2%	0%
1997	100%	57%	0%	2%	0%	1%	0%
1998	100%	37%	17%	3%	0%	1%	0%
1999	100%	27%	19%	6%	1%	2%	0%
2000	100%	22%	19%	0%	0%	0%	0%
2001	100%	21%	11%	4%	0%	0%	0%
2002	100%	53%	16%	4%	1%	2%	3%
2003	79%	24%	2%	3%	0%	1%	1%
2004	52%	21%	1%	3%	0%	0%	6%
2005	22%	17%	0%	2%	0%	0%	4%
2006	24%	27%	8%	1%	0%	0%	3%
May 2007	18%	23%	7%	2%	1%	0%	1%
Average	77%	33%	8%	3%	0%	1%	1%

Source. Research data.

1.4. Background to the Problem

Corruption cases that are administered and taken to courts of law by the PCCB fail to recognise and internalise the importance of circumstantial evidence, which contains the bulk of the collected evidence during the investigation of allegations received. Such lack of recognition of this important type of evidence makes cases brought before the courts of law too weak to pass the required threshold of prima facie evidence. This diminishes public confidence and expectations regarding the few prosecuted cases.

1.4.1. Statement of the Problem

There is no doubt that corruption is a crosscutting problem in our society that has permeated all segments of society and is a serious cause for concern in addressing problems of poverty and economic, social, and political matters in Tanzania. Through NACSAP, Tanzania gives a very high priority to the rule of law and legal framework.[54]

It is against this policy and background that the case for circumstantial evidence is here explored and examined to find out whether, in the larger picture of the rule of law, corruption can be effectively contained and minimised—albeit up to a degree possible. This book makes a strong case for the use of a 'circumstantial evidence test' to fight corruption in Tanzania. The study recognises that fighting corruption requires a multidimensional approach and needs the participation of all stakeholders.

We advocate for the theory of circumstantial evidence to be applied in corruption cases for the purpose of retooling the current practice to ensure that success in corruption cases is registered in courts of law, contrary to the current outcome, as demonstrated in the collected data that reflect the extent of the problem being addressed.

The reexamination of circumstantial evidence in this study is an attempt to employ it, together with existing judicial processes, in order to reverse the endemic trend. The study highlights the importance of a circumstantial evidence test in the judicial process as part of the holistic approach in the fight against corruption.

The main objectives of this study are to sharpen the deterrence measure by carrying an examination and analysis of circumstantial evidence and to identify the degree of probative value required to foster the admissibility of such evidence in corruption cases through the judicial process of adjudication.

Experience and practice in the area of combating corruption has with consistency and certainty shown that most of the corruption cases that are admitted to the court arena or jurisdiction are invariably based on circumstantial evidence, and the Tanzanian courts are weary of relying on such evidence unless 'the chain of circumstantial evidence is unbroken and leads to no other conclusion but the guilt of the accused persons'.[55] As we show in chapters 3 and 4 of the study, there is only one corruption case that reached the High Court (HC), and one of the appeal grounds was the reliability of circumstantial evidence in corruption cases.[56]

The choice of this circumstantial evidence tool or unit of analysis is deliberate because, in the rule of law and legal framework context, more often than not, corruption is an offence committed on the run: it is committed through conspiracy, in secrecy, and in the dark. It is therefore very difficult to prove a corruption case through direct evidence because it is reported after the event. By its very nature and essence, corruption is illusive and concealed in its operation. Therefore, to uncover it, the method of detection precedes the investigation; hence, in chapter 5, attention is devoted to the use of intelligence and undercover investigation in corruption and sophisticated economic crimes.

We examine the concept and practice of the circumstantial evidence test to be applied through the judicial process in corruption cases. This examination is linked to the way corruption has become so endemic in our society, and the tools that are available to reverse the trend have to be analysed and reexamined. Amongst these tools is the circumstantial evidence test in the judicial process.

It is important to focus on this tool because both deterrent and preventive measures are important and complement each other in thwarting the viral and corrosive effects of corruption on our society.

Several studies have been conducted on the theme of corruption in Tanzania. Nonetheless, there is no study at all that associates corruption and circumstantial evidence, advocating for the use of the latter.

It is against this background that the study seeks to examine the law of evidence and to bring to the fore the notion of circumstantial evidence and its application in corruption cases that are stuck in the law enforcement agencies—all because of the traditional common-law approach of distinguishing between 'direct' and 'circumstantial' evidence—so that they can reach court precincts.

1.4.2. Hypothesis

The study whose findings are reported in this book is guided by the following hypotheses:

- The Tanzanian government has not effectively sharpened the tools for the investigation and prosecution of corruption cases because the existing legal framework (legislative and interpretative) for the detection and prosecution of corruption cases is weak and inadequate, and is further weakened by the existing law. The traditional approach of common law to distinguish 'direct' and 'circumstantial' evidence has undermined the effectiveness of the law enforcement machinery to deal with corrupt elements in the society.
- The emerging approach of the case for circumstantial evidence is geared towards serving and curing the existing weakness of prosecuting corruption cases in court on the basis of the 'direct evidence paradigm'.
- The seemingly traditional approach of distinguishing between 'direct' and 'circumstantial' evidence has contributed to the weakness of the current legal framework for combating corruption.

1.4.3. Objectives and Relevance of the Study

The general objectives of the study are as follows:

- To critically examine and analyse the potential for circumstantial evidence in Tanzania and elsewhere (the U.S. and Commonwealth) and the extent to which this potential provides a viable and reliable tool to address failures of law enforcement agencies in Tanzania to prosecute corruption cases in courts of law; and
- To explore the theories, causes, and effects of corruption and their attendant linkages to circumstantial evidence with a view to curbing the vice.

1.4.4. Specific Objectives

Specifically, the study seeks to achieve the following objectives:

- To investigate the extent of the difficulties of establishing proof in corruption cases;
- To explore the means used by law enforcement agencies to collect evidence on corruption cases and covert operations; and
- To establish the weaknesses of the 'direct evidence paradigm' and to shift the focus to circumstantial evidence, which is a potential tool for the prosecution of corruption cases.

1.4.5. Relevance of Study

The study is based on the following assumptions:

- The study provides the relevance and utility of circumstantial evidence in corruption cases and other criminal cases.
- The study provides a new way of thinking about and approaching corruption cases through the utility of circumstantial evidence and its reliability in courts.
- The study provides a new legal framework to supplement the existing one in handling corruption cases.

1.4.6. Methodology and Sources

The following methods and sources were used to collect data and information relevant to the study:

- *Document review* (i.e., library research). Review of both primary and secondary sources relevant to the study of corruption and circumstantial evidence was conducted at various libraries in both Tanzania and the U.S. These include the University of Dar es Salaam main library; the Law School library of Northwestern University, Chicago, Illinois; the HC of Tanzania library; and LexisNexis and West law resources. The purpose of the review of the two sources was to find pertinent provisions, statutes, regulations, and cases that address the discrete factual issue of circumstantial evidence that this work is addressing; the use of the LexisNexis and West law databases, where all published and unpublished cases are available, afforded this work computer-assisted research that was comprehensive enough to inform the legal issue that this study is addressing.
- *Selected interviews.* The collection of data and relevant information required that discussions and interviews are conducted with selected law enforcement officers, prosecutors, and academics, on the one hand, and the general public and the private sector, on the other. The idea is to get their sense of the prosecution of corruption cases in Tanzania. Data collected by law enforcement agencies dealing with corruption is used to analyse the magnitude and scope of the problem under study.

1.4.7. Research Areas

Apart from Dar es Salaam, five other regions—Mtwara, Lindi, Shinyanga, Tanga, and Mwanza—were visited to obtain a fair view of the people's perception on the prosecution of corruption cases, particularly their views on circumstantial evidence, which is at the hub of this research process. The criteria for this selection were that they constitute a simple random sample of the country and that the researcher had preferred to have a fair view of the problem. It was intended that the theory of circumstantial evidence would be used, then tested by formulating expectations about the relationship postulated but not actually observed, and then checking to see whether there is a correlation between what is found on the ground and what was anticipated. The findings corroborated our hypothesis that circumstantial evidence is a viable and solid tool to rely upon in the prosecution of corruption cases.

The interviews took the form of a sampling technique for a few relatively compact geographical clusters, maximising the number of interviews undertaken with resources available. They were conducted with a selected cross section of stakeholders (judicial officials, prosecutors, professionals, and members of the civil society, the private sector, and religious bodies), enlisting their general perception on the issue of circumstantial evidence—the centrepiece of our research.

The sampling frame was a necessary instrument that this researcher had to use in order to draw the random sample, which is representative of the Mainland Tanzania population. Participatory interviews with focus groups, as previously stated, were conducted, along with an examination of different literature, on the one hand, and documents such as court records and judgments, on the other. The perception survey through which the summary of the interviews was compiled is used in this work to articulate the thrust of this study.

This work sought to underscore the lessons that had been obtained from both literature and the sampling methodology of the research. The rationale was to test the theory of circumstantial evidence in practice, to bring out that practice for the purposes of retooling the said theory, and to explore its potential in corruption cases in particular. It emerged from the interviews that 90 percent of the interviewees concurred with the traditional common-law view that direct evidence is more reliable than circumstantial evidence. In addition, less than 5 percent were of the view that circumstantial evidence is as reliable as direct evidence.

The study sought to show that there would be a profound effect of retooling circumstantial evidence to be applied in corruption cases because it would yield an increase in turnover of cases investigated through the application of circumstantial evidence, thus bolstering confidence in the PCCB and its capacity to increase the outcomes of cases taken to DPP; (a) to increase the number of cases taken to courts of law; to improve judicial jurisprudence in corruption cases, particularly the efficacy of circumstantial evidence; (b) to increase access to the criminal justice system; (c) to increase and sharpen the deterrent effect that in turn becomes a preventive tool; (d) to increase compliance and integrity in the public sector; (e) to restore public confidence in law enforcement; and (f) to reduce poverty by increasing productivity.

1.4.8. Context of This Research

Several studies have been conducted on the theme of corruption in Tanzania. Nonetheless, there is not a single study that has been conducted that links corruption and the case for circumstantial evidence. It is against this background that this study examined the law of evidence on circumstantial evidence and how circumstantial evidence could improve the quality of corruption cases that are stuck in the law enforcement agencies—due to the traditional common-law approach of making a distinction between 'direct' and 'circumstantial' evidence—to reach court precincts.

There is no single, universally accepted definition of corruption. However, corruption is commonly defined as the misuse of public office for private gain. Sevensson saw corruption as an outcome, a reflection of a country's legal, economic, cultural, and political institutions. He saw corruption as benefitting a few who bend the rules for their personal gain.[57] Conversely, corruption also is a reflection of bad policies or inefficient and ineffective institutions that are in place but collect bribes from individuals seeking preferential treatment although the rules prohibit doing so.

Bribes involve higher transaction costs than taxes because of the uncertainty to project the outcome and secrecy that necessarily accompany bribe payments. Bribery is also seen in political processes: lobbying or influence buying through a variety of means, such as political campaign contributions, gifts that are close to illegal payments and that constitute bribery, or postretirement jobs in private sector firms to officials and politicians assigned to regulate them.[58]

There is, however, a general consensus among practitioners in the field of anticorruption that the causes of corruption are greed, poverty, and opportunity with inclination.[59] It involves greed because those who are well positioned in society still extort money through bribery to amass more wealth than what they already possess. It is poverty driven because the needy would use every opportunity possible to demand a bribe using public power to ensure that they are able to survive and feed their extended families, given the small remuneration package they are given from their employment. All these are possible in a corrupt transaction where there is an opportunity to conceal the transaction and an inclination to indulge, especially where there are no high risks of detection or discovery. On the effects of corruption, there is a clear confluence of ideas that they are of social, economic, political, and cultural dimensions.[60]

The definition of the term *corruption* has raised a number of different connotations and interpretations depending on the objective sought. Nonetheless, the emerging trend seems to be unanimously in agreement that corruption is wrong and intolerable in any civilised society.[61]

The discussion on the effects or consequences of corruption begs the question, how do we measure the level of corruption in a country as a whole? The current measures proposed by several researchers, including TI, are based on perceptions of observers and participants. These studies on the perception index of corruption are correlated to ensure that a reasonable measure of fair assessment is generated.[62]

The studies conducted indicate that corruption places high costs on development in developing countries, including Tanzania. Most importantly, the heaviest cost is typically not the bribes themselves but rather the underlying economic distortions that they trigger. Langseth et al.[63] argued that corrupt leaders unquestionably deepen the poverty of their people. Public expenditure decisions are fuelled by private gain and subsidised by bribes with scant regard for the good of the country or its people. In the poorest countries—often those with corrupt elites—there is a manifest failure by government to pay a living wage to public servants. In most developing countries, the state is unable to afford to do so. Thus, inadequate remuneration of public officials is widely regarded as being a contributing cause of corruption at least at the petty corruption level, if not throughout the system.[64]

Charles Onyango-Obbo has described corruption as having devastating effects on the poor persons that the most corrupt nations have, which include large populations of illiterate peasants and urban riff raff. The majority of the corrupt persons have only recently come from villages. As a result, the village has not left the elite. This is one reason why, when leaders and officials steal, they are welcome home in the countryside with their loot as heroes. It would seem that the villagers still equate their children who get big jobs in towns to the hunters and warriors of old who used to plunder other communities' food, livestock, and women and return home with the booty.[65]

In their research, Chaligha et al. concluded that corruption breeds bad governance, which undermines democracy as it eliminates accountability, transparency, and equity in society. Corrupt officials have a tendency of being arrogant and are often prone to using their ill-gained wealth to trounce on the rights of the downtrodden citizens. Levels of perceived corruption differ among public agencies and officials. Tanzanian respondents (80 percent) perceived the police to be the most corrupt public institution in the country.[66]

This situation has seriously undermined the integrity and efficiency of the police force, tarnishing the image of the government among citizens. Good governance suffers under such circumstances. However, there is hope in the fight against this vice, for there has been a drop in perceived corruption among the police from 90 percent in 2001 to the current 80 percent.[67] Nicholas Goodling contended that major corruption scandals have crippled Nigeria over the past several decades. Between 1983 and 1999, the Nigerian government lost more than US$1 billion annually to smuggling and corruption, many with the collusion of the top elites of the nation. The situation in Nigeria provides a glimpse of how corruption can destroy an entire economy in a developing nation.[68]

The term *corruption* has not received a homogeneous or a unanimous global definition because one community would see a particular act or omission as corrupt while another may not see things that way. For example, gift giving in African traditions may be interpreted as corrupt by another society. It was common in traditional Africa before the advent of colonialism to carry a chicken or goat to a chief as a mouth opener for the chief, if you wanted your case to be heard, and that was not seen as bribery. Today, if the same is practised, it would be considered bribery. The same would be interpreted differently by different communities—for example, when you are supposed to give a tip to a porter in the hotel industry (particularly in the West) for carrying your luggage to your room or after taking your supper in a hotel the attendant would expect a tip.

Corruption is sometimes perceived as a 'developing south' phenomenon. The conventional view is that corruption is the abuse of public office for private gain.[69] Corruption and bribery have been used interchangeably, and the private sector has always been omitted or ignored in the definition of corruption. Corruption is prevalent both in the north and south. The Lesotho Highland Case[70] is clear testimony to the effect that big multinational corporations are capable of being found guilty of corruption. Abuse of political power by elites at the expense of the majority is another form of corruption. Shareholders in the corporate world have abused corporate trust, as in the Enron case.[71]

Public morality has been defiled at the altar of profit. Repositioning the definition of corruption should also address the interfaces between (a) politics and the economy, and (b) the public and private sector—a crosscutting phenomenon that involves theft, fraud, embezzlement, and money laundering, and is not restricted to purely commercial transactions, but also extends to social service delivery where such services are obtained at a fee. These crosscutting issues are important in the definition of corruption.

In defining corruption, one inevitably encounters legal, criminological, political, and cultural issues. One society perceives giving a gift to a public official as an act of corruption. Another society may consider it a duty to offer a chief or an elder a goat or a chicken as a mouth opener, and this may be regarded as a gesture of respect. However, Amaah et al. saw corruption as manifested in many forms.[72] They saw corruption and corrupt practices as varying from country to country. Nonetheless, corruption relates to conduct or behaviour of individuals in an organised society that affects morals through perversion or destruction of integrity.[73] There is no society in this planet, whether rich or poor, that can claim to be corruption free.

On the one hand, corruption involves rent seeking and receiving gifts and other advantages by public officials from, or in place of amounts due or payable to, government coffers.[74] Corruption may be found in political contributions or donations made to political parties and politicians so that, upon their assumption of power, favourable decisions and actions may be taken for the benefit of the contributors. Goodling, on the other hand, defined corruption as misuse of public authority for private gain, leading to the violation of the civic responsibility inherent in such authority. Any violations of common interest for special personal advantage are corrupt.[75] Philip M. Nichols defined bribery as a transaction in which an official misuses his or her office because of consideration of personal gain, which need not be monetary.[76] Longino, in his master's thesis,[77] examined five criminological theories of crime in locating corruption—namely, rational choice, strain, differential association, control, and historical. The rational choice theory emphasises free will in choosing to engage in a criminal act, while the strain theory explains that crime is a result of tension between the 'have-nots' and the 'haves'. The differential association theory maintains that a person acquires negative behaviour in the course of association with other people, and the control theory associates criminal acts with weak regulations, rules, and laws of a given society.

The historical theory examines the society at different times and looks at the way crime originated and has since changed with economic and social development.[78] The historical antecedents and cultural attitudes towards corruption in China, for example, were aptly put by Hilary Joseph as follows: from early Confucianism to contemporary communist ideology, the ideal of leadership has been the person of superior virtue who places the welfare of others above his own self-interest or self-gratification.[79]

The persisting image of an honest official is that of one concerned about the suffering of the masses who is willing even to commit suicide as the ultimate act of moral protest. Thus, the personal morality of a leader and his ability to discharge his public responsibilities are inseparable. Since a leader sets an example for all of society, corruption at the top spreads and eventually results in the downfall of the regime. It is unimaginable that a leader would publicly admit to moral failure and yet still claim competence to govern.[80]

In China, dereliction of duty is defined as a conduct that causes heavy losses to public property, the state, or people's interest. The rule applies to both acts and omissions by state personnel. It includes the misuse of official authority for private gain; however, unlike bribery, dereliction of duty does not require the solicitation or receipt of illegal consideration. Securing a job in government or a place in an institution of higher learning for unqualified applicants constitutes 'dereliction of duty'. Receipt of illegal consideration for doing so converts the offence to bribery.[81]

The previous examples from China are relevant to this study because cultural attitudes towards corruption are very important factors to consider, as we shall see when we address it in chapter 2.

This analysis poses a critical understanding of corruption and its manifestations, and we can link it with the main pillar of this study—circumstantial evidence. The question that we ask throughout is whether the claimed conclusion in a corruption case is a probable inference from the set of facts offered. This is the fundamental inquiry of inferential evidence that this book focuses on in chapter 4.

Experience and practice in the arena of combating corruption has shown with consistency and certainty that most of the corruption cases that are admitted to the court jurisdiction are invariably based on circumstantial evidence, and the Tanzanian courts are weary of relying on such evidence unless 'the chain of circumstantial evidence is unbroken and leads to no other conclusion but the guilt of the accused persons'.[82] The case of *Mohamed Rafiq al Baghdad and 6 Others*[83] is the only HC corruption case in Tanzania that focused its decision on the utility of circumstantial evidence, a matter that will be given an analytical view in chapters 3 and 4.

On the prosecution of corruption cases, it is relevant to examine what takes place in both China and the U.S. for purposes of analogy. Hilary Joseph observed that, in both those countries, prosecutors' decisions are influenced by 'political' factors—for example, whether a suspect has powerful supporters in high echelons of the government. Prosecutorial decisions are also influenced by political party affiliation, with greater readiness on the part of prosecutors to target someone from a rival political party or, in the Chinese case, someone who has fallen out of favour with the controlling faction of the Chinese Communist Party. In both countries, the prosecutions of corruption cases are frustrated by difficulties of proof—for example, the payments of bribes in cash and goods that are hard to trace, the issuance of bogus receipts, disguising bribes as service charges and processing fees, overinvoicing, and money laundering schemes using bank accounts of shell corporations. Thus, without direct evidence or testimony from a knowledgeable insider, corruption cases are extremely difficult to prove.[84]

On judicial corruption, the U.S. example provides an analogy to Tanzania as well, where law enforcement agencies fail to trace evidence, particularly where shell corporations are fronted to disguise corruptly acquired money or wealth because of the disguised scheme and operations of the perpetrators.

Hilary Joseph stated that the ultimate predicament of a corrupt judicial officer may be impeachment, removal from office, or criminal prosecution. Federal Judge Alcee Hastings was impeached and removed from office after being found not guilty of bribery. Federal Judge Walter Nixon was acquitted of bribery, convicted of perjury, and then impeached. Other judges have been impeached, even though no criminal misconduct was alleged.[85]

It is important that our judiciary in Tanzania should remain free of corruption because, since it is a custodian of our liberty and freedom, it would undermine the rule of law and the integrity of the judiciary as an independent branch of government if corruption reigns supreme in this important institution. The corrupt would find refuge and protection if the Tanzanian bar and judiciary are not clean of corruption.

Takrima, legalised bribery, which is addressed in chapters 2 and 3, is discussed here in the context of the U.S. case of *Rick Homans v. City of Albuquerque*,[86] which has bearing on political corruption in Tanzania for analogous purposes. The U.S. Supreme Court has developed a jurisprudential distinction between restrictions on political campaign expenditures and restrictions on campaign contributions. The Court has concluded that expenditure limits impose significantly more severe restrictions on protected freedoms than limits on contributions. That is, a restriction on the amount of money a person or group can spend on political communication during campaigns necessarily reduces the quality of expression by restricting the number of issues discussed, the depth of their expression, and the size of the audience reached. For these reasons, expenditure limits raise graver constitutional concerns and are invalidated more frequently by the courts.

As part of an overall restructuring of its city government in 1974, the city of Albuquerque, NM, amended its city charter and implemented an election code imposing disclosure requirements and limiting expenditure and contributions for municipal elections. More than 90 percent of voters approved these reform measures.[87]

The *Election Code*[88] provides as follows:

> No candidate shall allow or accept contributions or make expenditures in excess of the following for any election:
>
> 1. To a candidate for the office of councillor, contributions or expenditures equal to twice the amount of the annual salary

paid by the city of Albuquerque to councillors as of the date of filing of the Declaration of Candidacy.

2. To a candidate for the office of Mayor, contributions or expenditures equal to twice the amount of the annual salary paid by the City of Albuquerque to the Mayor as of the date of filing of the Declaration of Candidacy.

For the 2001 elections, the mayoral campaign expenditure limit was US$174,720. City council candidates were limited to spending a maximum of US$17,056. Violation of these limits carried a fine of up to US$500 per violation, removal from office, or a public reprimand.[89]

The rationale behind this limiting was threefold: (a) to deter corruption and appearance of corruption, (b) to equalise candidates' resources, and (c) to contain the skyrocketing costs of political campaigns.

To satisfy strict scrutiny review, Albuquerque must establish that its candidate expenditure restrictions are necessary to further a compelling state interest. The justifications for the limit are (a) the deterrence of corruption and enhancement of public confidence in the electoral process, and (b) the preservation of officeholders' ability to perform their duties without devoting excessive time to fundraising and to the encouragement of electoral competition.[90]

On public confidence and corruption, Justice Frankfurter, in the case, assessing the situation and competing interests, argued that one of the greatest political evils of our time is the apparent hold on political parties, which business interest and certain organisations seek and sometimes obtain by reason of liberal campaign contributions. Many believe that when an individual or association of individuals makes a large contribution for the purpose of aiding candidates of political parties in winning elections, they expect and sometimes demand—and occasionally at least receive—consideration by the beneficiaries of their contributions, which will frequently be harmful to the general public interest.[91]

In another case, *United States v. United Autoworkers*,[92] the U.S. Supreme Court deliberated over the issue of corruption in elections, and this decision has relevance to Tanzania as political funding and election campaign financing are matters that have bearing in regulating political corruption in Tanzania. The Court observed that corruption encourages the perception of impropriety within the electorate when large donors call the tune, which undermines the willingness of the voters to take part in democratic governance. Democracy works only if the people have faith in those who govern, and that faith is bound to be diminished when high officials and their appointees engage in corruption, which undermines good governance.[93]

The deterrence of corruption constitutes a compelling state interest. The question remains whether Albuquerque's expenditure limits are necessary to serve this end. The conclusion by the Court was that the record in that case did not aggregate to such 'convincing evidence' and, consequently, the court rejected the contention that the city's expenditure limits are necessary to prevent corruption.[94]

It is fair to conclude that electoral competition is another central component of democratic governance. In many respects, the ultimate weapon of public accountability in a democratic system is the ability of citizens to remove political actors through elections. Moreover, electoral competition is the mechanism that keeps accountability viable. High levels of campaign spending pose a threat to such competition because large incumbent war chests tend to discourage serious challengers.

Other jurisdictions have attempted alternative measures to minimise corruption: limiting the size of political campaign contributions, improvement of electoral competitions, enhancement of voter participation, and preservation of candidates' scarce time resources—all done within constitutional bounds.[95] These observations are relevant in reviewing political corruption in the relevant legislations that regulate it.

The U.S. Supreme Court likens 'corruption' to the 'subversion of the political process'. Elected officials are influenced to act contrary to their obligations of office by the prospect of financial gain for themselves or of the infusion of money into their campaigns. The hallmark of corruption is the financial quid pro quo: dollars for political favours. To contain bribery, multilateral efforts have been put in place. A number of international organisations have coordinated among their members to criminalise specific types of bribery—transnational bribery.[96]

Transnational bribery occurs when persons from one country bribe public officials of another country. The extraterritorial nature of the criminalisation of transnational bribery therefore operates in two directions: the courts of the businesspersons' home country reach conduct that occurs outside of the home country's physical borders, and the laws of the bribed official's country are given effects in courts outside of the borders of the host country. In Tanzania, PCCA has criminalised transnational bribery and corruption.[97]

Bribery as a phenomenon is as old as the bureaucratic system itself. While quantifiable data are impossible to obtain, reliable observations indicate that transnational bribery is widespread and that the incidence of transnational bribery is probably increasing. The offer of bribes and export of corruption by investors from western countries is one of the reasons.

To be able to curb this trend, the case for circumstantial evidence in corruption cases is pursued with a view to supplementing and retooling the deterrence effect against corruption. Corruption distorts national goals and vision.

In Tanzania, the country has adopted the *Tanzania Development Vision 2025*,[98] which has three major areas of concern: achieving a high-quality livelihood for Tanzanians, attaining good governance through the rule of law, and developing a strong and competitive economy.[99] Corruption is a serious problem to attain the said national vision in Tanzania. In addition, corruption is a worldwide concern that calls for all sorts of interventions through strategic action plans that are concrete, clear, concise, and comprehensive.

1.5. The Case for Circumstantial Evidence

Evidence is whatever comes before the court to establish or to challenge the facts, which are alleged. It may take the form of a witness testimony, documentary evidence, or exhibited objects. Circumstantial evidence is the major focus of this study, because it has not been fully explored and correctly understood as statistics gathered from the field indicate.[100] The problem of any misunderstanding springs from the common law itself, which distinguishes between two types of relevant evidence: direct and circumstantial.

Direct evidence is the presentation of evidence that, if believed, establishes an essential element.[101] It is the presentation of *the thing* itself for which persuasion is desired.[102] In this type of evidence, no inferences other than those pertaining to the credibility of the eyewitness mediate between the evidentiary facts, the facts of consequences, and the essential element that is required.[103]

In circumstantial evidence, however, the connection between an evidentiary fact and an essential element to an offence requires inferences that are controlled by legal rules based on objective criteria—what would a reasonable person, in the shoes of the defendant, be taken to intend or have in his or her mind, in performing a particular act or omission.[104]

Circumstantial evidence is proven by means, motive, and opportunity in ascertaining the commission of a crime, particularly corruption. Professor Allot clearly explained this by saying that there is often an absurd prejudice against circumstantial evidence, as if it were by its nature inferior to direct evidence given by a witness who actually observed the act in question. Direct evidence is also susceptible to all the weaknesses of observation and recollection; evidence of a circumstantial kind may well be less contestable and more easily relied on. To show that a defendant had the means, motive, and opportunity may go some way towards convincing us of his guilt. It may raise a prima facie case against him, which he is called upon to answer.[105]

It is legitimate to have regard to what was done or said—before, during, and after an incident—in order to decipher what was the apparent state of mind of the defendant in regard to the alleged offence. In English law, proof of possession of drugs is taken to raise a strong presumption of guilt intent, which the defendant must rebut, while all the time paying due regard to the principle that he is not required to demonstrate his innocence. It is sufficient for the prosecution to prove possession of any substance, which the defendant thought might be illegal, even if he did not know exactly what substance it was.[106]

Chief Justice (CJ) Gibson, in the English case of *Commonwealth v. Harman*,[107] representing the common-law understanding of circumstantial evidence, reasoned that no witness had been produced who saw the act committed, and hence it was argued for the prisoner that the evidence was only circumstantial and, consequently, entitled to a very inferior degree of credit, if any at all.

The Gibson's view is incorrect because the consequences of circumstantial evidence are the same as in direct evidence. Circumstantial evidence is sometimes as strong as positive evidence; in the concrete, it may infinitely be stronger. This study agrees with Professor Wigmore that a fact positively sworn to by a single eye witness of blemished character is not so satisfactorily proven, as is a fact that is the necessary consequence of a chain of other facts sworn to by many witnesses of undoubted credibility.[108]

CJ Shaw, in another old English case of *Commonwealth v. Webster*,[109] drew a clear understanding between direct and circumstantial evidence, namely, that each of these modes of proof has its advantages and disadvantages; it is not easy to compare their relative value. The advantage of positive evidence is strong where, for example, there is direct testimony to the fact to be proved by a witness who—if he or she is speaking the truth—saw it done, in which case the only question is whether he or she is trustworthy. The disadvantage, however, is that the witness may be false and corrupt, and that the case may not afford the means of detecting his or her falsehood.

However, in the case of circumstantial evidence, no witness can testify directly to the fact to be proved; instead, it is arrived at by a series of other facts, which by experience have been found associated with the fact in question to the extent that they lead to a satisfactory and certain conclusion. When footprints are discovered after a recent snow, it is certain that some animated being has passed over the snow since it fell, and, from the form and the number of footprints, it can be determined with equal certainty whether they are those of a man, bird, or a quadruped. Circumstantial evidence is therefore founded on experience and observed facts in relation to the fact sought.[110]

The advantage of circumstantial evidence is that the evidence comes from several witnesses and several sources; a chain of circumstances is less likely to be falsely prepared and arranged, and falsehood and perjury are more likely to be detected and fail in their purpose. In the investigation and prosecution of corruption cases, more evidence is circumstantial than direct because of the nature and essence of corrupt circumstances, hence the importance of understanding the potential that is likely to result from resort to circumstantial evidence to overcoming the necessity of direct evidence in the struggle against the corrupt elements in our society.

The disadvantages are that a jury or the court has not only to weigh the evidence of facts, but also to draw just conclusions from them; in doing so, they may be led by prejudice and partiality, or by want of deliberations and sobriety of judgment, to make hasty and false deductions—a source of error not existing in the consideration of positive evidence.[111]

Allen et al., in their analyses of the two types of evidence, concluded that, analytically, there is no difference between direct and circumstantial evidence because both require the jury to use inferential reasoning. Whereas in direct evidence, it has to be established as an essential element only if the court or the jury believes the eyewitness—and this requires inferential reasoning above the eyewitness' ability to observe the event correctly, to remember it, and to describe it accurately.[112]

These standard issues of credibility must be resolved by the fact finder in order to evaluate any testimonial evidence, and they are the kinds of issues about which people use natural reasoning constantly in their everyday lives. Generally speaking, then, what distinguishes circumstantial from direct evidence is the length of the inferential chain. It is important to note that the labels 'direct' and 'circumstantial' do not reflect the probative force of evidence.

Circumstantial evidence can often be more reliable than direct evidence. A fingerprint or blood spot found on a murder weapon, identified as the defendant's by fingerprint analysis or DNA testing, are examples of very accurate circumstantial evidence and are probably more reliable than many eyewitnesses are.[113]

DNA is the name for a chemical that is found in virtually every cell in the human body and that carries genetic information in the form of a code or language that, when translated, determines human physical characteristics and directs all the chemical processes in the body. The U.K. Forensic Science Services has established that half of the DNA is inherited from a person's mother, and the other half from his or her father. Siblings inherit different combinations of DNA from the same parents and are therefore different from each other. Each generation of people is a new and different combination of genetic material from the previous one.[114]

Except for identical twins, each person's DNA is unique and varies widely between people. The technique of DNA profiling is based on analysing and measuring these differences in lengths to establish the identity of an individual concerned in the commission of a crime, including corruption.[115]

Given the nature of corruption—and how it, as an offence, is committed in secrecy—the use of forensic science, especially DNA profiling, will enhance the quality of investigation techniques employed by the PCCB, particularly on the reliability and admission of circumstantial evidence in court—the central theme of this study.

Sir Rupert Cross came to the same conclusion that, if the only evidence that could be adduced were directly of facts in issue, or direct evidence, many claims would fail for lack adequate proof. At some stage, resort almost always has to be had to 'circumstantial evidence', which may be defined as any fact (sometimes called an 'evidentiary fact', 'factum probans' or 'factum probandum'). A typical instance is afforded by the statement of a witness at a trial for murder that he saw the accused carrying a bloodstained knife at the door of the house in which the deceased was found mortally wounded.[116]

It is in this context that this study advances the case for circumstantial evidence in corruption cases in Tanzanian courts because, as previously observed, the traditional view[117] of distinguishing between 'direct' and 'circumstantial' evidence diminishes the chances of corruption cases being tried and tested in courts of law, especially where their foundation is based on circumstantial evidence. Detailed treatment of the subject is found and connected to the only corruption case decided at the HC based on circumstantial evidence, which is discussed in chapter 4.[118]

1.5.1. Limitation of the Study

The study is not concerned with the broader issues of corruption as such. The scope of the study is limited to the examination and analysis of the traditional approach (common law) of distinguishing between direct and circumstantial evidence and how the use of circumstantial evidence can foster and improve the effectiveness of deterrent measures to minimise the viral effects of corruption in Tanzania.

Combating corruption requires both preventive and deterrent measures. There is good cause and reason to believe that deterrent measures have an immediate impact that would send a clear and loud message to both public servants and the general public that corruption is a high-risk undertaking. This study complements the existing works on the subject of corruption and law and the importance of refining the means within which prosecution of corruption cases can be improved and can bear the expected results.

ENDNOTES

1. Prevention of Corruption Bureau, established under the PCA, no. 16, of 1971 (Cap. 329 R.E. 2002), is the law enforcement agency charged with the responsibility of taking necessary measures for the prevention of corruption in public, parastatal, and private sectors.
2. P. Langseth and R. Stapenhurst, *National Integrity System Country Studies*, EDI Working papers (Washington, DC: Economic Development Institute of the World Bank, 1997).
3. Government of the United Republic of Tanzania, *National Anti-Corruption Strategy and Action Plans for Tanzania* (Dar es Salaam: Government Printer, 1999).
4. S. Rose-Ackerman, *Corruption and Government: Causes, Consequences and Reform* (London: Cambridge University Press, 1999).
5. Corrupt transactions are effected only if there is an opportunity by both the corruptor and 'corruptee' to agree on trade-offs. The opportunity is made available if there are loopholes and weaknesses in the respective system of social service delivery. A public official is willing to compromise his/her integrity for exchange of bribes from the private person given the weighing of risks available. By inclination a motivation, such an official allows himself with an opportunity to take the risk of soliciting or inducing another person to exchange something of value at the expense of the public good. See also Leonard P. Shaidi, *The Problems of Corruption in Tanzania* (master's thesis, University of Dar es Salaam, 1975)—the author gives a historical development of the PCA of 1971 with analytical emphasis on social classes and modes of production. The author also finds difficulties inherent in section 9 of the PCA.
6. Shaidi, *The Problems of Corruption in Tanzania.*
7. S. M. Phillips, *Famous Cases of Circumstantial Evidence* (Boston: Estes & Lauriat, 1874). Phillips, circumstantial evidence is only supplemental, and is only resorted to from want of original and direct proof. It can never be said that what is secondary is equal to that which is original—the thing substituted equal to that which is to supply.
8. Rose-Ackerman, *Corruption and Government.* Also see Omar Afzar, Youn Lee, and Arnold Swamy, 'The Causes and Consequences of Corruption', *Annals of the American Academy of Political and Social Science* 573 (2001): 42–56.

9. Government of the United Republic of Tanzania, *Presidential Commission of Inquiry Against Corruption in Tanzania* (Washington, DC: WB/ODA, 1996).
10. Sahr J. Kpundeh, Irene Hors, UNDP, and OECD, eds., *Corruption and Integrity Improvement Initiatives in Developing Countries* (New York: UNDP, 1998), 47.
11. The UN Convention Against Corruption adopted by the UN General Assembly signing ceremony took place on 9 December 2003 in Merida, Mexico; the OECD Convention Against Bribery, ratified by thirty-five countries around the world, UN Convention on Transnational Organised Crime, signed in Palermo, Italy, 12–15 December 2000; African Union on Preventing and Combating Corruption, adopted by heads of state and government in Maputo, Mozambique, July 2003; SADC Protocol Against Corruption was adopted by SADC heads of state and government at their August 2001 summit held in Blantyre, Malawi, making the first anticorruption treaty in Africa and has been ratified and became operational in 2005; ADB-OECD Anti-corruption Action Plan for Asia Pacific, endorsed in Tokyo on 30 November 2001; The twenty Guiding Principles for the Fight Against Corruption (1997)—the multidisciplinary principles cover the use of criminal and civil law measures, civil prevention, administrative reforms, transparency measures, and research. They are directed at encouraging individual countries to network among the rest and coordinate national measures as a further precaution against transnational corruption problems; the Criminal Law Convention on Corruption—with fourteen countries ratifying this legally binding instrument so far, this treaty contains provisions criminalising a list of specific forms of corruption, as well as private and public sector cases; the Civil law Convention on Corruption—entered in force on 11 November 2003. In its scope on forms of corruption to which it applies, it is narrower than the criminal law. The treaty covers only bribery and similar acts in both private and public sector circumstances; joint action to fight corruption in the private sector—the obligation of this action is to criminalise both active and passive corruption conducted in the course of any business activity; Organisation of American States have the Inter-American Convention Against Corruption, which is the first ever international convention adopted by a number of states in that region. The instrument has been ratified by twenty-two OAS states since it came into force in March 1997.
12. J. Edgardo Campos and Sanjay Pradhan, *The Many Faces of Corruption: Tracking Vulnerabilities at the Sector Level* (Washington, DC: The World Bank, 2007), 335–367.

13 Edmond B. Mndolwa, *Auditors Role in the Fight Against Corruption and Enhanced Good Governance*, Open lecture to Accounting Association, Faculty of Commerce and Management, University of Dar es Salaam, 22 February 2003.
14. Ibid.
15. Kenneth K. Mwenda, *Legal Aspects of Combating Corruption: The Case of Zambia* (Youngstown, NY: Cambria Press), 11.
16. UN Department of Economic and Social Affairs and UN Development Programme, *The Challenges of Restoring Governance in Crisis and Post-Conflict Countries*, 7th Global Forum on Reinventing Government Building Trust in Government, 26–29 June 2007, Vienna, Austria (New York: United Nations, 2007), 7–10.
17. Planning Commission, *National Framework on Good Governance: The Steering Committee Good Governance*, President's Office, December 1999 (Unpublished).
18. See www.worldbank.org; UN Department of Economic and Social Affairs, *The Challenges of Restoring Governance in Crisis and Post-Conflict Countries*.
19. UN Department of Economic and Social Affairs, *The Challenges of Restoring Governance in Crisis and Post-Conflict Countries*, 8.
20. International Monetary Fund, *Good Governance: The IMF's Role* (Washington, DC: IMF, 1997). IMF's traditional purview is on issues such as reform of the treasury, budget preparation and approval procedures, tax administration, accounting and audit mechanisms, central bank operations, and official statistics function. Similarly, there are reforms of market mechanisms that focus on the exchange rate, trade, and price and financial systems.
21. UNDP, *Governance for Sustainable Human Development*, A UNDP Policy Document (New York: UNDP, 1997).
22. Ibid.
23. Mwenda, 21.
24. Ibid.
25. Ibid., 22.
26. Transparency International, *Global Corruption Report 2004* (London: Pluto Press, 2004), 4.
27. See Edward G. Hoseah, *Essays on Combating Corruption in Tanzania and the Basic Legal Principals* (Dar es Salaam: Ecoprint, 1999).
28. Azfar, Lee, and Swamy, 'The Causes and Consequences of Corruption'.

29. Government of the United Republic of Tanzania, *National Anti-Corruption Strategy and Action Plan* (Dar es Salaam: Government Printer, 1999).
30. *State of Corruption in Tanzania Annual Report 2002*, ESRF/FACEIT (October 2002), 152.
31. Government of the United Republic of Tanzania, *Development Vision 2025: Tanzania at the Turn of the Century*, a World Bank Country Study (Washington, DC: The World Bank, 2001).
32. See Government of the United Republic of Tanzania, *The Presidential Commission of Inquiry Against Corruption.*
33. Amon Chaligha, Bob Mattes, and Annie Dzenga, *Public Perceptions on Democracy and Governance in Tanzania*, May 2004 (Unpublished).
34. Louis De Koker, B. A. K. Rider, and J. J. Henning, eds., *Victims of Economic Crime*, Transactions of the Centre for Business Law, 31 (Bloemfontein, South Africa: UOVS/UOFS, 1999), 2–3; see also Ellen S. Podgor, *Understanding International Criminal Law* (Newark, NJ: LexisNexis, 2004).
35. *Tanzanian Affairs* 79 (September 2004).
36. Ibid.
37. Tanzania Central Census Office, National Bureau of Statistics, Ministry of Planning and Privatization, Government Printer, January 2003, 2.
38. Interviewed Nyamtare Mukome, the National Authorising Officer, Tanzania Treasury for EU Support in the Country, 2005.
39. Alan Bacarese, Senior Anti Corruption specialist, International Centre for Asset Recovery, Basel, Switzerland, 'Asset Recovery and the United Nations Convention Against Corruption', Corruption Hunters' Network, 19–22 June 2007, Oslo, Norway (Unpublished).
40. Ibid.
41. Ibid.
42. *Poverty Reduction Strategy Paper* (PRSP) MKUKUTA, Tanzania Government (Treasury), 2005.
43. Government of the United Republic of Tanzania, *The National Anti-Corruption Strategy and Action Plans for Tanzania.*
44. Ibid.
45. Deepa Narayan et al., *Can Anyone Hear Us? Voices of the Poor* (Oxford: Oxford University Press for the World Bank, 2000), 9.
46. The enactment of the new law against corruption, the PCCA no. 11 of 2007, is clear testimony of the government's resolves to address the scourge comprehensively and holistically.

47. The Parliamentary Committee on the Constitutional and Legal Affairs is established under article 93 (1) of the Parliamentary Standing Orders pursuant to article 89 (1) of the United Republic Constitution 1977, issue of 2004, Office of the Parliament, Dodoma.
48. Prevention and Combating of Corruption Act, no. 11 of 2007.
49. The Public Leadership Code of Ethics Act, no. 13 of 1995.
50. The Commission for Human Rights and Good Governance Act, no. 7 of 2001, cap. 391 [R.E. 2002].
51. Article 143 (1) of the Constitution of the United Republic of Tanzania, 1977, cap. 2 [R.E. 2002].
52. Chief Secretary's Circular (2001) on the establishment of MDAs integrity committees.
53. NASCAP Quarterly Reports, GGCU, State House, Government Printer, 2002.
54. See Government of the United Republic of Tanzania, *The National Anti-Corruption Strategy and Action Plans for Tanzania.*
55. See the analogy in murder cases of the same principle in *August Mahiyo v. R.* (1993) TLR 117 (CA), *Hamdu Mussa Thimotheo and Majid Mussa Thimotheo v. R.* (1993) TLR 125 (CA), *Magendo Paul and Another* (1993) TLR 220 (CA), *Ally Bakari and Pili Bakari v. R.* (1992) TLR 10 (CA), *Protas John Kitogile and Another v. R.* (1992) TLR 51 (CA).
56. See analysis of Baghdad's case in chapter 3.
57. See Daniel Kaufman, *Empirical Frontiers and the Case for Collective Action, The Role of Bilateral Donors in Fighting Corruption, Improving Governance and Controlling Corruption* (Maastricht, the Netherlands: World Bank Institute, 25–27 April 2000).
58. Ibid.
59. See Vincent Green, 'An Approach to Investigating Corruption in Government', in *Government Ethics and Law Enforcement*, ed. Yassin El-Ayouty, Kevin J. Ford, and Mark Davies, 161–187 (New York: Praeger Publishers, 2002).
60. Ibid.
61. Jakob Svensson, 'Eight Questions About Corruption', *Journal of Economic Perspectives* 19, no. 3 (Summer 2005), 19–42. See also Robert Klitgaard, *Controlling Corruption* (Berkeley, CA: University of California Press, 1998). His understanding of corruption is simplified: Corruption (C) = Monopoly (M) + Discretion (D) – Accountability (A) and, I will add, – Transparency (T). If you apply this simplified formula to any potential case study for corruption, you will definitely arrive at a more probable than not conclusions.

I recommend this formula particularly when developing an anticorruption matrix that is intended as a preventive tool in any organisation.

62. See data generated by Business International, Economic Intelligence Unit, and Transparency International—P. Mauro, 'Corruption and Growth', *Quarterly Journal of Economics* 110 (1995), 681–712. Mauro relied on Business International that evaluated countries in terms of the degree to which business transaction involve corruption or questionable payments, bureaucracy and red tape—that is, the regulatory framework and environment that foreign investors must face when seeking approvals and permits—and efficiency and integrity—that is, countries are ranked on a scale of zero to ten for each index, with a higher number indicating better performance. There is a correlation between GDP growth and corruption. See World Bank's World Development Reports.
63. Langseth and Stapenhurst, *National Integrity System Country Studies*.
64. Ibid.
65. Charles Onyango-Obbo, *The East African*, no. 409, September, 2002.
66. Chaligha et al., *Public Perceptions on Democracy and Governance in Tanzania*.
67. Ibid.
68. Nicholas A. Goodling, 'Nigeria's Crises of Corruption—Can UN Global Programme Hope to Resolves the Dilemma?' *Vanderbilt Journal Transnational Law* 36 (May 2003): 997.
69. Phil Matsheza, *Corruption: Concepts and Definitions*, Mimeograph, presented on 5–9 March at Specialised Training workshop for Investigators and Prosecutors, Mombasa, Kenya.
70. See www.ipocafrica.org/Cases/highlands/anticorrupt/proj. In 1986 the Lesotho Highlands Water Project (LHWP) was set up between the governments of Lesotho and South Africa as a multibillion rand infrastructure project designed to control the flow of the Senqu/Orange river and, in doing so, to provide water for the people of Gauteng province, and electricity and money for the people of Lesotho. In 1993 the audit revealed substantial administrative irregularities within the Lesotho Highlands Development Authority (LHDA). After an audit of its CEO, Masupha Ephraim Sole, Sole was then subjected to a disciplinary enquiry, and subsequently he was dismissed. The investigations further had revealed that Sole was clearly living far beyond his means: his housing, cars, holiday arrangements, and instances of nepotism were the obvious indicators. Civil proceedings were instituted to recoup the funds that had been misappropriated by Sole. Civil proceedings began in 1996 and produced evidence of bank accounts that included

accounts with the Union Bank of Switzerland. The bank records obtained from Switzerland indicated that throughout the lifetime of the project, Sole, using 'middlemen' or intermediaries, had indirectly received vast sums of money from certain companies and consortia who had been awarded contracts in the project. The patterns, size, and timing of the payments gave rise to the notion that bribery had taken place on a massive scale. Sole was prosecuted as well as many of the corporations and members of consortia who had made secret payments into various Swiss bank accounts, together with the intermediaries who acted as conduits. In December 1999, nineteen defendants were charged with bribery. Sole also faced charges of fraud and perjury. In a comprehensive judgment, finding Sole guilty as charged, Acting Judge Cullinan, a former CJ of Lesotho, observed that the patterns of payments that had emerged during the trial had arisen from transactions which 'inextricably bound together' the defendant consultants/contractors, the intermediaries, and Sole himself. Sole was subsequently imprisoned for eighteen years, reduced on appeal to fifteen years. The trial of Acres International, the Canadian engineering company, now followed. Prior to the criminal proceedings, the World Bank had begun debarment proceedings against Acres and Lahmeyer, a German engineering consulting firm, both of which had received funding from the bank for the contracts. It is worth noting that the evidence of secret payments into numbered Swiss accounts was not deemed to amount to sufficient grounds for the debarment of the companies at that stage. Acres continued to apply for, and receive, funding for projects from the bank. However, the bank reserved its position, saying that it would reopen debarment proceedings if new evidence against Acres were to emerge from the criminal proceedings. The case is significant to the study because corruption is practised by multinationals that affect the economies of developing world. With the armoury of circumstantial evidence the corrupt company and individuals will find no refuge. From the perspective of the international community, these trials pose challenges to parties to the OECD Convention on Combating Bribery about the ways in which corruption is detected and punished in different parts of the world. Canadian lawyers have expressed doubt as to whether Acres would have been prosecuted in Canada. The high moral tone taken throughout by Acres, which has, throughout, been disinclined publicly to express remorse for its actions, might have deterred a decision to prosecute. Lhmeyer could not be prosecuted under the provision of German criminal law in any event, since corporate offenses are dealt with under administrative law only, punishable by means of fines; Fiona Darroch, Barrister at Law, Hailsham Chambers, London, August 8, 2004.

71. http://en.wikipedia.og/wiki/ENRON. Enron Corporation was an American energy company based in Houston, Texas. Before its bankruptcy in later 2001, Enron was one of the world's leading electricity, natural gas, pulp and paper, and communications companies, with claimed revenues of US$111 billion in 2000. It was discovered that Enron's recorded assets and profits were inflated, or even wholly fraudulent and nonexistent, by putting debts and losses into entities formed 'offshore' that were not consolidated in the company's financial statements and, in addition, by the use of other sophisticated and arcane financial transactions between Enron and related companies formed to take unprofitable entities off the company's books.
72. W. Paatii Ofuso-Amaah, Raj Soopramanien, and Kishor Uprety, *Combating Corruption: A Comparative Review of Selected Legal Aspects of State Practice and Manor International Initiatives* (Washington, DC: International Bank for Reconstruction, 1999), 2–3.
73. Ibid.
74. Ibid.
75. Goodling, 'Nigeria's Crises of Corruption'. See also J. G. Lambsdorff, 'The Economics of Corruption Handout', in *The Institutional Economics of Corruption and Reform: Theory, Evidence, and Policy*, ed. J. G. Lambsdorff (New York: Cambridge University Press, 2007), and N. Leff, 'Economic Development Through Bureau Corruption', *American Behavioural Scientist* 8 (1964): 8–14.
76. Philip M. Nichols, 'Colloquy: Regulating Transnational Bribery in Times of Globalization and Fragmentation', *Yale Journal of International Law* 24 (Winter 1999): 257.
77. Frederick Longino, *Understanding and Preventing Corruption in Tanzania* (master's thesis, University of Cambridge, 2001).
78. Ibid.
79. Hilary K. Joseph, 'The Upright and the Low-Down: An Examination of Official Corruption in the United States and the People's Republic of China', *Syracuse Journal of International Law and Commerce* 27 (Summer 2000): 455–466.
80. Ibid.
81. Ibid.
82. *Augustino Mahiyo v. R.* (1993), *Hamdu Mussa Thimotheo and Majid Mussa Thimotheo v. R.* (1993), *Magendo Paul and Another* (1993), *Ally Bakari*

and Pili Bakari v. R. (1992), *Protas John Kitogile and Another v. R.* (1992), *Protas John Kitogile and Another v. R.* (1992).

83. The HC Economic Criminal Appeal, no. 2 of 2003 (Unreported), Dar es Salaam Registry.
84. Joseph, 'The Upright and the Low-Down'.
85. Ibid.
86. U.S. App. LexisNexis 8317, 2004.
87. Ibid.
88. Ibid.
89. Ibid.
90. Ibid.
91. Ibid.
92. Ibid.
93. 382 U.S. 567, 576, IL. ED. 2d, 563, 77 S. Ct 529 (1957).
94. Ibid.
95. Ibid.
96. Ibid.
97. See A. Mitchell Polinsky, Steven Shavell, 'Corruption and Optimal Law Enforcement', *Journal of Public Economics* 81 (2001): 1–24, who underscore the fact that corruption is socially undesirable because it dilutes deterrence. Erick L. Richards, 'Federal Election Commission v. Colorado Republican Federal Campaign Committee', *American Business Law Journal* 40 (2002): 83.
98. Section 2 (2) and 21 of the PCCA, no. 11 of 2007.
99. See Government of the United Republic of Tanzania, *National Vision 2025*.
100. See tables 3 and 4 of this book.
101. A. N. Allot, 'The Chain of Evidence in Criminal Trials' in *The Magistrate in the Commonwealth Basic Principles and Practice*, ed. Margaret Rogers and Jane Kellock, 31 (London: Commonwealth Magistrates' and Judges' Association, 1979).
102. Ibid.
103. Ibid.
104. Ibid.
105. Ibid.
106. Ibid.
107. 4 pas. St 269, 271–273 (1846).
108. See Pranab Bardhan, 'Corruption and Development: A Review of Issues', *Journal of Economic Literature* 35, no. 3 (September 1997): 1320–1346.

109. 59 Mass. (5 cush.) 295, 311 (1850).
110. J. H. Wigmore and P. Tillers, *Evidence on Trial at Common Law*, vol. 1A (Boston: Little Brown and Company, 1983).
111. Ibid.
112. R. J. Allen, R. B. Kuhns, and E. Swift, *Evidence: Text, Problems and Cases*, 3rd ed. (New York: Aspen Law & Business, 2002), 147.
113. Ibid.
114. The UK Forensic Science Service, 'DNA—Present and Correct: A Guide to DNA Profiling', Priory House, Birmingham, United Kingdom. Also visit their Web site at www.fss.org.uk.
115. Ibid.
116. Sir Rupert Cross and Collin Tapper, *Cross on Evidence*, 7th ed. (London: Butterworths, 1990).
117. See the HC Economic Criminal Appeal, no. 2 of 2003 (Unreported), Dar es Salaam Registry.

Chapter 2

Corruption-Busting Policy Framework: Historical Background and Instruments

2.1. The Perspective of Corruption and the Tanzanian Environment

The preceding chapter dealt with the introduction and major highlights of the study. This chapter sets out a thorough discussion of the Tanzanian scenario in tackling the issue of corruption from policy orientation, legal framework, and government strategies as background material to the central thesis of this book: the case for circumstantial evidence.

The background is necessary to appreciate why in Tanzania circumstantial evidence—amongst other measures that are in place and or advocated for, such as preventive measures through research and community education on the evils and effects of corruption—is an important arsenal in confronting corruption.

2.2. Policy Orientation to Combating Corruption

The policy orientation to combating corruption in Tanzania can be discerned from the following four important documents: (a) Mwalimu Nyerere's speech on corruption,[1] (b) the proceedings in legislative council (Hansard) introducing the Prevention of Corruption Ordinance (PCO) of 1958,[2] (c) a government brief on achievements and challenges in the fight against corruption,[3] (d) President Jakaya Kikwete's statements on corruption,[4] and (e) the PRSP.[5]

In 1960 the late Mwalimu Julius Kambarage Nyerere, who later became the first president of the United Republic of Tanzania, said that corruption must be treated with ruthlessness because corruption and bribery are great enemies to the welfare of people. He was of the strong view that in a country, corruption should be treated in almost the same way as treason.[6]

Mwalimu Nyerere reiterated the same in 1978 when addressing the nation from Dodoma. He said that it is ridiculous that we are concerned with punishing petty thieves and ridiculing prostitutes who resort to shameful acts out of necessity while we condone people in high positions who take bribes.[7]

The judiciary, however, has on several occasions articulated its policy position on corruption. For example, the HC of Tanzania, through the CJ P. Georges in the case of *William Haining v. R*,[8] stated that the prevention and eradication of corruption in developing a society such as this are issues of the highest priority. The foundations of the nation are in the process of being laid and the national ethic formulated. Standards must of necessity be well and truly established. The proposed rule would impose no burden on the civil servant. He ought not in any event to accept gifts from people with whom he is likely to deal in the course of his official duties.[9]

Policy considerations were evident in the official statement when the then attorney general was introducing the anticorruption bill in the legislative council in 1958. The attorney general, D. Cole, remarked that it had never been found a practical possibility to make men honest by means of laws, and therefore all that the bill hoped to achieve was to make it more difficult for men to be dishonest and to make it easier for them to be detected and brought to justice if they were dishonest.[10]

On its part, the third government, led by President Benjamin William Mkapa, made its position on corruption clear in a statement echoed in the ruling party's 1995 election manifesto that identified corruption, *inter alia*, as one of the major social evils that pose big challenges to the country: corruption is a big problem in our society now and a threat to the security, tranquillity, and dignity of our nation. In the next five years, a Chama Cha Mapinduzi (CCM) government would intensify the battle against corruption.[11]

In his inaugural speech, ushering in his (fourth) government, President Jakaya Mrisho Kikwete disclosed that his government would accelerate the war against corruption in a more scientific way by addressing its root causes. He promised that there would be improvements in the remuneration for public officials in line with improved economic growth and enhanced government revenues. The intended goal was to reduce temptations for corrupt practices by some of these public officials as they attempted to make ends meet.[12]

President Kikwete also emphasised his determination to enhance transparency in government decision making and procurement, strengthening the resource and technical capacity of those organs at the forefront of the war on corruption, especially the PCCB, the police force, and the judiciary.[13]

Another important policy document is the *Poverty Reduction Strategy II*. This document clearly recognises governance and accountability to be critical components for poverty reduction in Tanzania. In the area of governance and accountability, PRSP aims at achieving four broad outcomes:

- Peace, political stability, national unity, and social cohesion nurtured and sustained;
- Democracy and political and social tolerance deepened;

- Good governance and the rule of law strengthened; and
- Accountability of leaders and public servants ensured.[14]

It is clear from the previously mentioned sources that in Tanzania there is a clear policy for combating corruption as summarised in the NACSAP that the government's policy on the fight against corruption is zero tolerance.[15]

The relevance of these policy orientations to this study is to show that, although the government has been clear on its policy for combating corruption from the early days of the country's independence, corruption still continues to make major inroads into the good governance, economic growth, and prosperity of the people of Tanzania.

Corruption cases that reach the court precincts are concluded with either a low rate of success or more acquittals for lack of direct evidence, on the one hand, and the society continues to get deeper into despair regarding the efforts that the government has pledged through its policies, on the other.

It is on these considerations that the study anchored itself on the circumstantial evidence paradigm that is advocated for in order to improve the content of cases that are submitted to court and for the trier of facts to make a decision based on a sound presentation of the collected evidence whose bulk is—as stated in the first chapter—in most cases, circumstantial in its nature and essence. Let us now turn to the political and economic environment of the country to provide the necessary background underlying this study.

2.3. Political and Economic Environment in Tanzania

According to the PRSP and the PSRP, at the turn of the century, Tanzania was seeking to move from reforms to sustainable growth and poverty reduction. Since its independence in 1961, Tanzania has been trying to rid the nation of the three archenemies: poverty, ignorance, and disease. For more than four decades now, the country has remained one of the poorest in the world. The nation is endowed with an abundance of a natural resource base, a suitable geographical location that is accessible to international markets, a stable political environment, and a cohesive national identity around a common language.[16]

Poverty, ignorance, diseases, and corruption are still the major challenges. The government of Tanzania, through the *Poverty Reduction Strategy*, intends to achieve faster, equitable, and sustainable growth by engaging all stakeholders and by exploiting intersector linkages and cross-sector collaboration in the pursuit of poverty reduction outcomes. Accountability in the use of resources, through monitoring and evaluation of the effectiveness of the strategy in reducing poverty, is key.

The *Poverty Reduction Strategy II* takes stock of the past three years from 2003 and records the following:

> Achievements have been recorded in the delivery of social services especially in primary education, basic health care and access to clear and safe water. GDP growth rate consistently rose in the past six years, reaching 6.2 percent in 2002. It declined to 5.6 percent in 2003 due to draught in the 2002/03 seasons. Inflation dropped to 4.4 percent in 2003 compared to 6 percent in 2000. In 2003 foreign reserves reached 8.9 'months of imports' compared to 6.3 'months of imports' in 2000. The nominal exchange rate is market-determined with the interventions limited to smoothing fluctuations. Also considerable increases in investments in infrastructure especially roads and communication systems have been recorded.[17]

Being cognisant of the enormous challenges that still lie ahead, the government takes note of the following:

> For poverty reduction, growth and macro-level achievements need to be adequately translated into micro-level welfare outcomes all the way to the household level. At the same time, there is a need to sustain the successes, further improve access and quality of social services and address concerns of vulnerable groups.[18]

Poverty Reduction Strategy II adopted an outcome-oriented approach, focusing on intersector linkages towards the achievement of results. Three broad outcomes of poverty reduction are identified, viz.,

- growth and reduction of income poverty;
- improved quality of life and social well-being; and
- governance and accountability.[19]

Poverty Reduction Strategy II contends that the focus of government centres on economic structures and processes such as public resources (financial and natural) management systems, personal security, tolerance and inclusion, and participation in decision making, such as through the local government reform process, and ensuring that the structures and systems of governance are representative and accountable. Human rights, a functioning and fair justice system, and war against corruption are key elements of this cluster.[20]

The government has initiated several reforms[21] aimed at contributing towards good governance outcomes, improved public service delivery, better economic management, positive cultural change, and democratic development.

In her assessment of the Tanzanian government's fiduciary risk through direct budgetary support from donors, Lettice Rutashobya stated that development partners provide direct budgetary support (DBS) to Tanzania. When financial aid is provided through budgetary support, development partners are not directly responsible for the use of these funds. However, they have to be satisfied that the resources are properly accounted for, that they are used for the intended purpose, and that the expenditure represents 'value for money' (VFM). The risk that funds will not be used in this way is referred to as a *fiduciary* risk.[22]

This risk may be viewed broadly as taking into account such factors as the nature of fiduciary contract between citizens and the state, the effectiveness of parliament as an oversight body, economic policy, sectoral policy, the effectiveness of government financial and legal systems and practices, and the degree of accountability—all of which may affect achievement of the desired purpose in a way that VFM is assessed.[23] According to Rutashobya's assessment, Tanzania's overall rating is a B- for these risk assessment criteria, especially on financial accountability and management. Nonetheless, the country's public procurement remains a high-risk area because, though most MDAs can use the threshold rules on procurement—such as international competitive bidding (ICB), national competitive bidding (NCB), restricted tendering, competitive quotations, single source procurement, and minor value procurement[24]—the overall problems, however, remain those of a weak fiduciary contract between citizens and the state, inadequate domestic revenue collection, limited delivery of public goods, inadequate monitoring, inefficient capacity, noncompliance, lack of enforcement, and inadequate oversight.[25]

On parliamentary oversight, Rutashobya reported that the Tanzanian parliament retains much of the legacy of the one-party era when it was essentially an extension of the Central Committee of the National Executive Committee of the Ruling Party, Chama Cha Mapinduzi. Members of Parliament (MPs) have no power to reorder government-spending priorities, although they do have the power through Parliamentary Public Accounts Committee (PPAC) and the Local Authorities Accounts Committee (LAAC), which are chaired by members of the opposition. There are generally no follow-ups on actions required to be taken by the executive branch of government.[26]

On revenue collection, Rutashobya found out that the tax-collection gap persists despite some major reforms of the tax system that led to the establishment of the Tanzania Revenue Authority (TRA), through the TRA Act No. 11 of 1995, as a government agency. Large leakages and noncompliance by individuals and legal entities are widespread. They are due to the transit trade and underinvoicing of imports. The capacity of the tax administration is still very weak. They exercise a lot of discretion, especially in relation to the complicated and ambiguous income tax act. There are large exemptions for investment promotion purposes; tax evasion and corruption are pervasive.[27] The weak areas just identified require strategic government interventions with a view to increasing efforts that will mobilise domestic resources through revenue collection, improve the investment climate, and increase the competitiveness and readiness of the economy to cope with the challenges of globalisation. All these initiatives can be meaningful only if corruption is minimised to a very low level—hence the importance of this study.

2.4. Globalisation and Corruption

After the end of the cold war, democratisation was given emphasis, and we witness great opportunities for rent seeking in transition economies and big scandals in high-income countries such as the U.S.,[28] Italy, and France, where VFM audits take place and the link with development is emphasised.

Michael Johnston argued that the same globalisation of markets and developmental inequalities that have helped draw renewed attention to problems of corruption in recent years also confront us with the dilemma of cross-border corruption. Cross-border corruption involving international interests, actors, capital, and economic processes (both licit and illicit) is a potentially serious problem in affluent and developing countries alike.[29]

The World Commission on the Social Dimension of Globalization[30] reported that one of the identified problems is the deficiency in governance due to the fact that global markets have grown rapidly without the parallel development of economic and social institutions necessary for their smooth and equitable functioning. The failure of the current international policies to respond adequately to the challenges posed by globalisation was also noted. Market-opening measures and financial and economic considerations predominate over social ones. Overseas development assistance (ODA) falls short of the minimum amounts required even for achieving the Millennium Development Goals (MDG) and tackling growing global problems.

The multilateral system responsible for designing and implementing international policies is also underperforming. It lacks policy coherence as a whole and is not sufficiently democratic, transparent, and accountable.

The rules and policies are the outcome of a system of global governance largely shaped by powerful countries and powerful players.[31]

It is from this background that one has to understand the impact of corruption globally and hence the need for international instruments against corruption—a subject matter that is canvassed in this chapter.

2.5. The Legal Framework for Combating Corruption

Strengthening the legal system is quite essential. The legal framework for combating corruption is examined with a view to identifying weaknesses or gaps that require fixing through the reenactment of a comprehensive anticorruption law that would meet the expectations of society at large, which is constrained by the negative impact of corruption in its efforts to build a strong economy and a prosperous nation.

The law against corruption in Tanzania was introduced through the Indian Penal Code during the British colonial dominion of the then Tanganyika in 1920, which contained a provision for public officials' bribery.[32] It came into force through cap. 16 of the laws of Tanganyika in September 1945, and, later in 1958, the same was promulgated by the legislative council as the Prevention of Corruption Ordinance.[33] After independence, the Tanzanian parliament enacted Act No. 16 of 1971 and the same was revised in 2002.[34]

The current law against corruption is contained in the PCCA, which replaced cap. 329, given that the time span of many subsequent technological advances, best practices, and evolving international and regional instruments against corruption at the global and local levels have overtaken the efficacy of the repealed law; these factors were a necessary recipe for the enactment of the PCCA to bring about conformity with comprehensive legislation that would stand the test of twenty-first-century expectations.

Looked at in retrospect, the law against corruption in Tanzania had its genesis in England. Tanganyika was under the British administration rule, and that had an obvious influence on the country. The English law against corruption was the Prevention of Corruption Act of 1906,[35] which had an influence on both cap. 400 and cap. 329, respectively, of the laws of Tanzania. To a certain extent, the PCCA has continued to retain the then four existing offences as part of the current twenty-four offences on corruption, which have also been influenced by regional and international instruments and best practices against corruption.

Among other legislative measures taken by the government was the establishment of a Permanent Commission of Inquiry (Ombudsman) in 1966.[36] The purpose of this was to check on the abuse of power by public officials. The Commission on Human Rights and Good Governance has since replaced the Ombudsman.[37] The establishment of the Ethics Secretariat headed by a commissioner in 1995[38] was another measure taken by the government. Other oversight institutions include parliament,[39] the CAG,[40] the office of the DPP.[41]

The Prevention of Corruption Ordinance, cap. 400,[42] was repealed and replaced by the PCA, which was later revised in 2000 as cap. 329.[43] Nonetheless, as already noted, it continued to retain most of the important features of the English Prevention of Corruption Act of 1906, as it is shown in the course of this study.[44]

The PCA came into force on 22 April 1971. The act created the ACS in its endeavour to execute its mandate to curb and control corruption in the country.

For a broader view and for comparison purposes, the British government had also an influence in Hong Kong, as it did in Uganda, Kenya, and Tanganyika. In Hong Kong, they enacted the Prevention of Bribery Ordinance[45] and the Independent Commission Against Corruption (ICAC) Ordinance, cap. 204, which created ICAC that had three mandates similar to the ACS, namely, prevention, investigation and prosecution, and advisory.[46]

In this chapter, highlights are given on other countries where anticorruption agencies that share similarities have also been established so that an inference may be drawn to show that even in other jurisdictions where anticorruption agencies are in place, certain features are worth comparing in the quest to understand the legal framework for combating corruption.

All of these are thus relevant to the theme of the study—circumstantial evidence in the context of legal framework against corruption.

In Zambia, a similar law was passed by parliament and the Anti-Corruption Commission was put in place to combat corruption[47] on similar lines as in Hong Kong and Tanzania. Botswana followed suit in 1994 by establishing a Directorate on Corruption and Economic Crime.[48] Malawi had to do the same in 1995 by creating a similar body, the Anti-Corruption Commission,[49] whose mandates were formulated along those of the Hong Kong ICAC and Tanzanian PCB then, now PCCB.[50]

Section 2A (3) of the Tanzania PCA spelled out the functions of the ACS as follows:

(a) To take necessary measures for the prevention of corruption in the public, parastatal, and private sectors;
(b) To investigate, subject to the directions of the DPP, and prosecute offences under this act and other offences involving corrupt transactions;
(c) To advise the government, the community, the corporations and institutions of the community, and other parastatal organizations on ways and means of preventing corruption.[51]

Likewise, Lesotho in 1999 established the Directorate on Corruption and Economic Offences, modelled along the Botswana Anti-Corruption Agency.[52]

The following functions of the directorate are stipulated in section 6 of the act:[53]

(a) To receive and investigate any complaints alleging corruption in any public body;
(b) To investigate any alleged or suspected offences under this act, or any other offence disclosed during such as investigation;
(c) To investigate any alleged or suspected contravention of any of the provisions of the fiscal and revenue laws of the country;

(d) To investigate any conduct of any person that, in the opinion of the director, may be connected with or conducive to corruption;
(e) To prosecute, subject to section 43, any offence committed under this act;
(f) To assist any law enforcement agency of the government in the investigation of offences involving dishonesty or cheating regarding the public revenue;
(g) To examine the practices and procedures of public bodies in order to facilitate the discovery of corruption practices and to secure the revision of methods of work or procedures that, in the opinion of the director, may be conducive to corrupt practices;
(h) To instruct, advise, and assist any person, on the latter's request, on ways in which corrupt practices may be eliminated by such person;
(i) To advise heads of public bodies on changes in practices or procedures compatible with the effective discharge of the duties of such public bodies that the director thinks necessary to reduce the likelihood of the occurrence of corruption practices;
(j) To educate the public against the evils of corruption;
(k) To enlist and foster public support in combating corruption;
(l) To undertake any other measures for the prevention of corruption and economic offences.

On her part, Mauritius has legislated two important pieces of legislation for combating corruption, fraud, and money laundering.[54] The functions of the ICAC in Mauritius are the following:

(a) Educate the public against corruption;
(b) Enlist and foster public support in combating corruption;
(c) Receive and consider any allegation that a corruption offence has been committed;
(d) Detect or investigate any act of corruption;
(e) Investigate the conduct of any public official that, in its opinion, is connected with or conductive to corruption;

(f) Monitor, in such manner as it considers appropriate, the implementation of any contract awarded by a public body, with a view to ensuring that no irregularity or impropriety is involved therein;
(g) Examine the practices and procedures of any public body in order to facilitate the discovery of acts of corruption and to secure the revision of methods of work or procedure that, in its opinion, may be conducive to corruption;
(h) Advise and assist any public body on ways and means by which acts of corruption may be eliminated;
(i) Undertake and assist in research projects in order to identify the causes of corruption and its consequences on, *inter alia*, the social and economic structure of Mauritius;
(j) Cooperate with all other statutory corporations that have as object the betterment of the social and economic life of Mauritius;
(k) Draft model codes of conduct and advise public bodies as to the adoption of such codes as may be suited to such bodies;
(l) Cooperate and collaborate with international institutions, agencies, or organisations in the fight against money laundering and corruption;
(m) Monitor current legislative and administrative practice;
(n) Advise the parliament committee on such legislative reform as it considers necessary to foster the elimination of acts of corruption;
(o) Detect and investigate any matter that may involve the laundering of money or suspicious transactions that are referred to it by the Financial Intelligence Unit (FIU);
(p) Execute any request for assistance referred to it by the FIU;
(q) Take such measures as may be necessary to counteract money laundering in consultation with the FIU;
(r) Cooperate and collaborate with the FIU in fulfilling common objectives.[55]

The Mauritius anticorruption law was proclaimed on 1 April 2002 and came into force on the same date. The same law ensures that the ICAC is answerable and independent in its functions. Section 20 (2) of the act[56] provides that the commission shall act independently, impartially, fairly, and in the public interest.

Section 20 (3) of the same act stipulates that the commission shall not be under the control or direction of any other person or authority. However, section 39 makes provisions for accountability mechanisms through the establishment of advisory committees; they are expected to act as checks and balances.[57]

Being aware of the link between corruption and money laundering promulgated financial crimes by passing the Financial Intelligence and Money Laundering Act in 2000. Therefore, the ICAC-Mauritius, has the mandate to detect and investigate any matter that may involve the laundering of money or any other suspicious transaction that is referred to it by the FIU.[58]

In its annual report, ICAC-Mauritius made the following statement:

> The legislator in its wisdom connected the two legal instruments for logical reason as very often the offences of corruption and money laundering are interlinked the rationale being to enable the Commission as the law enforcement agency to work in collaboration with the FIU and other regulatory bodies to fight corruption and money laundering.[59]

The Malaysian Anti-Corruption Act[60] prescribes the function of the Anti-Corruption Agency as to achieve the following goals:

(a) Receive and consider any report of the commission of an offence under this act and investigate such of the reports as the director general or officers consider practicable;

(b) Detect and investigate

  (i) Any suspected offence under this act;

  (ii) Any suspected attempt to commit any offence under this act; and

  (iii) Any suspected conspiracy to commit any offence under this act;

(c) Examine the practices, systems, and procedures of public bodies in order to facilitate the discovery of offences under this act and to secure the revision of such practices, systems, or procedures as in the opinion of the director general may be conducive to corruption;
(d) Instruct, advise, and assist any person, on the latter's request, on ways in which corruption may be eliminated by such person;
(e) Advise head of public bodies of any changes in practices, systems, or procedures compatible with the effective discharge of the duties of the public bodies as the director general thinks necessary to reduce the likelihood of the occurrence of corruption;
(f) Educate the public against corruption; and
(g) Enlist and foster public support in combating corruption.

The preceding comparisons and references are relevant to this study to show that the legal framework for curbing the vice is more or less the same except that Tanzania, by repealing the PCA with the PCCA, has achieved a more comprehensive approach and incorporation of the United Nations Convention Against Corruption (UNCAC) mandatory provisions against corruption.

At this juncture, it is also important to bring into focus the regional and international initiatives for combating corruption that have previously been alluded to, which have a direct impact on the Tanzania's legal framework against corruption, particularly the new law against corruption (PCCA) that was passed by the parliament in April 2007.[61]

Three important instruments are hereto examined, and their relevance and impact are related to Tanzania's efforts in preventing and combating the scourge. Implicitly, the instruments bring to the fore the utility of circumstantial evidence, particularly the new twenty offences in the PCCA.

Tanzania is part of the global village, and any reform that it initiates has to be linked to wider global efforts to curb the scourge that has been recognised the world over as one of the stumbling affronts to democracy, development, and the realisation of the rule of law, which is the heart of democracy and development in any modern state. The importance of democracy and development is founded on three major issues. Firstly, Tanzania signed and ratified the three regional and international instruments against corruption by the end of the year 2004. Secondly, Tanzania is bound by these international instruments, and, therefore, they are to be assimilated and integrated into domestic laws and jurisdiction. Thirdly, they set out best practices and areas considered mandatory to be adopted by States Parties adhering to the conventions and regional protocol.

The Vienna Convention on the Law of Treaties[62] regulates international conventional obligations, both multilateral and bilateral, that are regulated by the same general principles of international law.

The Vienna convention defines the term *treaty* as an international agreement concluded between states in written form and governed by international law, whether embodied in a single instrument or in two or more related instruments, regardless of its particular designation.[63] The term *treaty* is therefore generic, encompassing all international agreements, protocols, exchanges of notes, and declarations, regardless of designation.[64] The treaties derive their legal force from the principle *pacta sunt servanda*.[65]

We begin our examination with the Southern Africa Development Community (SADC) Protocol Against Corruption, followed by the African Union (AU) Convention on Preventing and Combating Corruption, and finally, the UNCAC, which Tanzania is signatory to and forms part of the States Parties adhering to the instruments.

2.5.1. SADC Protocol Against Corruption, 2001

SADC member states share a common vision to stamp out corruption. In carrying out this endeavour, this protocol was witnessed and signed in Blantyre, Malawi, on 14 August 2002 by all heads of state and governments of the SADC region.[66]

The protocol entered into force after the nine instruments of ratification of the protocol were deposited to the secretariat in Windhoek, Namibia, the head office of the SADC secretariat.[67] So far, nine member countries have ratified the protocol.[68]

The purposes of the protocol are spelled out in article 2 of the protocol:

(a) To promote and strengthen the development, by each of the State Parties, of mechanisms needed to prevent, detect, punish, and eradicate corruption in the public and private sectors;
(b) To promote, facilitate, and regulate cooperation among the State Parties to ensure the effectiveness of measures and actions to prevent, detect, punish, and eradicate corruption in the public and private sectors;
(c) To foster the development and harmonization of policies and domestic legislation of the State Parties relating to the prevention, detection, punishment, and eradication of corruption in the public and private sectors.

Article 3 provides for what constitutes acts of corruption:

(a) The solicitation or acceptance, directly or indirectly, by a public official of any article of monetary value or other benefit, such as a gift, favour, promise, or advantage for himself or herself or for another person or entity, in exchange for any act or omission in the performance of his or her public functions.
(b) The offering or granting, directly or indirectly, by a public official of any article of monetary value or other benefit, such as a gift, favour, promise, or advantage for himself or herself or for another person or entity, in exchange for any act or omission in the performance of his or her public functions;
(c) Any act or omission in the discharge of his or her duties by a public official for the purpose of illicitly obtaining benefits for himself or herself or for a third party;
(d) The diversion by a public official, for purposes unrelated to those for which they were intended, for his or her own benefit or that or a third party, of any movable or immovable property, monies, or securities belonging to the state, to an independent agency, or

to an individual, that such official received by virtue of his or her position for purposes of administration, custody, or for other reasons;

(e) The offering or giving, promising, solicitation, or acceptance, directly or indirectly, of any undue advantage to or by any person who directs or works for, in any capacity, a private sector entity, for himself or herself or for anyone else, for him or her to act, or refrain from acting, in breach of his or her duties.

The protocol deals with both public and private sector corruption. Preventative measures are provided for in article 4. Jurisdiction of the protocol is in article 5. Article 6 deals with acts of corruption relating to a foreign state official. Article 7 calls for the harmonisation of policies and domestic legislations. Confiscation and seizure are provided for under article 8. Extradition is dealt with in article 9. Mutual legal assistance is provided for in article 10. Regarding the relationship with other treaties, it is stated in article 14 that, '[s]ubject to the provisions of Article 3, paragraph 2, this Protocol shall in respect of those countries to which it applies, supersede the provisions of any treaty or bilateral agreement governing corruption between any two state parties'.

It is important to note that since Tanzania is a signatory and ratified this treaty in 2003, the PCCA has domesticated some of the salient features of the SADC Protocol Against Corruption.

2.5.2. African Union Convention on Preventing and Combating Corruption (AU Convention), 2003

The AU, like the SADC countries, has resolved to approach corruption in a holistic fashion, and hence the creation of the African Union Convention on Preventing and Combating Corruption (AUCAC). This convention was adopted in Maputo, Mozambique, on 11 July 2003 by thirty-two out of fifty-three of the heads of state and governments.[69] It symbolises regional consensus on criminalisation, international cooperation, and asset recovery. So far, fifteen instruments of ratification have been deposited at the AU secretariat in Addis Ababa. The convention came into force on 5 August 2006, thirty days after the deposit of the fifteenth instrument of ratification.

The general structure of the convention can be summarised as follows. Overall, there are twenty-eight articles. Articles 1, 2, 3, 4, and 13 provide for definitions, objectives, principles, scope of application, and jurisdiction. Article 6 provides for laundering of the proceeds of corruption. Article 7 relates to the fight against corruption and related offences in the public service. Article 8 deals with illicit enrichment. Article 9 provides for access to information.

Article 10 focuses on the funding of political parties. Articles 11 and 12 incorporate private sector, civil society, and media. Articles 15, 18, 19, and 20 deal with extradition, cooperation and mutual legal assistance, and international cooperation and national authorities.[70] Articles 16 and 17 focus on the confiscation and seizure of the proceeds and instrumentalities of corruption and bank secrecy. Article 22 is for follow-up mechanisms, and articles 5, 21, 23, and 24 provide for the relationship with other agreements and final clauses on issues such as signature, ratification, accession, entry into force, reservations, amendment, denunciation, depository, and authentic texts.

The AU Convention, as a regional instrument addressing corruption with a comprehensive framework and setting common standards for the region, has benefits for the people of Africa: the convention covers both the supply and demand sides of corruption in public and private sectors. The convention provides for a broad range of criminal offences focused on the public sector, internal accounting, and auditing systems.[71]

The convention also provides for prevention mechanisms required in the public sector, such as the declaration of assets by designated public officials, the creation of a code of conduct and monitoring body, and ensuring proper management of tendering and hiring procedures. Additionally, restrictions on immunity for public officials are provided.

The convention also demands transparency in political funding[72]—it is unique convention in this respect because there is no other convention that clearly addresses this delicate issue. It makes it a mandatory provision on this subject.

The convention recognises the role of the private sector in addressing the problem of corruption and, particularly, private-to-private corruption.[73] Education and raising awareness, as part of preventive measures, as well as access to information for the media and the involvement of the civil society and the private sector in preventive measures, are thoroughly addressed in the convention. The PCCA has domesticated the salient features of the convention and is thus relevant to this study because the legal framework for curbing corruption has a direct impact on the theme of the study—the utility of circumstantial evidence in corruption cases.

Highlights of the major weaknesses of the convention, however, are as follows:

- No provision on statutes of limitation is provided;
- No requirement of liability of companies is articulated;
- No provision for sanctions is stated; and
- No peer review process is disclosed.

2.5.3. The United Nations Convention Against Corruption (UNCAC), 2003

Corruption, as a global problem, has to be confronted globally since no single state, rich or poor, is not afflicted by the malaise. The developing world is even deeply dented by the viral effect of corruption. All nations of the world have agreed to have a legal framework to guide states on how best to deal with corruption and coordinate them through United Nations Office on Drugs and Crime (UNODC).

The UNCAC has a total of seventy-one articles. Articles 1–4 are general provisions for purpose of the convention, definitions, scope, and protection of sovereignty. Articles 5–14 deal with preventive measures. These include the establishment of independent anticorruption bodies, anticorruption policies and practices, public procurement and management, public reporting, prevention in judiciaries and prosecution services, codes of conduct for public officials, prevention of money laundering, participation of civil society, and measures to prevent corruption in the private sector.

Article 15–42 provide for criminalisation and law enforcement. Article 2 of the convention does not define the term *corruption* because of three major considerations:

(a) The convention covers various existing forms of corruption: offences of bribery, embezzlement, laundering of proceeds of crime, concealment, obstruction of justice, knowledge, and intent;
(b) Corruption is a fluid and evolving concept: it covers whistle-blowers (Articles 32–35), compensation for damage, cooperation, bank secrecy, and jurisdiction (Article 42) are well articulated therein so that that there is no longer safe haven for such offenders. Articles 43–50 cover international cooperation, mutual legal assistance, and extradition;
(c) It enables states to deal with other forms that may emerge in the future.

Articles 51–59 deal with asset recovery, and return and disposal of assets through confiscation. Articles 60–62 provide for technical assistance and information. Articles 63–64 set out mechanisms for implementation. Articles 65 and 67 handle implementation of the convention and settlement of disputes. Signature, ratification entry into force, and depository are provided for in articles 67–71.

States Parties adopted the UNCAC on 31 October 2003. One hundred and forty signatories to the convention were recorded by 9 December 2005. Sixty-one States Parties ratified the convention as of 31 July 2006. The convention entered into force on 14 December 2005, ninety days after deposit of thirtieth ratification. The convention is designed to meet multidimensional challenges.[74]

There are mandatory offences that States Parties to the UNCAC have to legislate and harmonise into their domestic law. These are bribery of national public officials (art. 15); active bribery of foreign public officials (art. 16); embezzlement, misappropriation, and other diversion of property by a public official (art. 17); money laundering (art. 23); and obstruction of justice (art. 25). The PCCA has incorporated these mandatory provisions to confront corruption holistically, and they are thus relevant to the cutting theme of this study—circumstantial evidence.

Other criminal offences the convention has prescribed to be included in the domestic legislation are passive bribery of foreign public officials (art. 16), trading in influence (art. 18), abuse of functions (art. 19), illicit enrichment (art. 20), bribery in the private sector (art. 21), and embezzlement in the private sector (art. 22). The UNCAC is important to this study because Tanzania has domesticated some of the important and mandatory provisions in the PCCA, as is highlighted in chapter 3 of the study, which have bearing to the cutting theme of circumstantial evidence, particularly on the collection of evidence and courts' consideration.

2.5.4. Common Elements to the Three Regional and International Instruments Against Corruption

The three instruments previously listed have one common purpose, namely, to promote and strengthen measures to prevent and combat corruption.[75] The PCCA has adopted this approach of prevention and combating corruption. The scope of these instruments covers actions ranging from the prevention, investigation, and prosecution of corruption, to the freezing, seizure, confiscation, and return of the proceeds derived from offences established in the conventions and protocol.[76] Codes of conduct for public officials are reflected and echoed in the three instruments.[77] Whereas the three instruments also cover public procurement,[78] access to information and public reporting as a preventive measure is listed thereof to bring about transparency and accountability in the public sector.[79]

The three instruments also cover private sector corruption;[80] participation of civil society in the engagement to curb the scourge is also well covered by the instruments.[81] Measures to prevent money laundering, along with the freezing and confiscation of proceeds of crime, are well covered by the three instruments;[82] embezzlement, misappropriation, or diversion of property by a public official; trading in influence[83] and the abuse of office[84] are prescribed in the instruments.[85]

Specialised bodies that are independent to combat corruption[86] are to be established in the respective States Parties to the instruments and should overcome obstacles created by bank secrecy.[87] The international cooperation central to curbing corruption,[88] extradition,[89] and mutual legal assistance[90] is well covered in all three instruments, as is the law enforcement cooperation[91] and exchange of intelligence and information on corruption.[92]

The preceding highlight is relevant to the cutting theme of this study—circumstantial evidence—because it provides a broader understanding of the current legal framework of curbing corruption and the PCCA in Tanzania. The international and regional instruments against corruption that have just been discussed provide the relevant material and set the stage for best practices that will inform the operationalisation of the PCCA, which has introduced a comprehensive legal framework to prevent and combat the scourge. The new law will take into account circumstances of twenty-first century, unlike the repealed cap. 329 enacted in 1971, where certain realities and the sophistication of committing crimes—particularly corruption—were nonexistence or not understood at the time in Tanzania.

Its relevancy to circumstantial evidence includes the introduction of new provisions relating to corruption in the private sector, corruption in procurement, corruption in auctions, sexual corruption, and corruption in employment. The inclusion of embezzlement, money laundering, and freezing of assets into new law are important provisions that would in most cases depend on circumstantial evidence to be able to stand and be tested in courts of law.

ENDNOTES

1. Hansard, 35th Session, Debate on the Budget, 17 May 1960, 'Corruption as an Enemy of the People', in Nyerere, *Freedom and Unity* (Dar es Salaam: Oxford University Press, 1966), 81.
2. Hansard, 23rd Session, vol. 4 (1958), 1125. See www.parliament.go.tz.
3. Government of the United Republic of Tanzania, *Tanzania's Third Phase Government Fight Against Corruption: A Brief on Achievements and Challenges, 1995–1999* (Dar es Salaam: Government Printer, 1999).
4. J. M. Kikwete, *Speech by President of the United Republic of Tanzania*, on inaugurating the Fourth Phase Parliament, Parliament Buildings, Dodoma, Government Printer, 30 December 2005.
5. Government of the United Republic of Tanzania, *Poverty Reduction Strategy II* (Dar es Salaam: Vice President's Office, 2004).
6. Nyerere, *Freedom and Unity*, 81.
7. *Daily News*, 6 February 1978.
8. (1970) EA 620.
9. Ibid.
10. See Hansard, 35th Session.
11. See Government of the United Republic of Tanzania, *Tanzania's Third Phase Government Fight Against Corruption.*
12. See Kikwete, *Speech by President.*
13. Ibid.
14. Ibid.
15. Ibid.
16. Government of the United Republic of Tanzania, *Poverty Reduction Strategy II.*
17. Government of the United Republic of Tanzania, *The National Anti-Corruption Strategy and Action Plans for Tanzania.*
18. Government of the United Republic of Tanzania, *Tanzania at the Turn of the Century*, viii.
19. Government of the United Republic of Tanzania, *Poverty Reduction Strategy II.*
20. Ibid.
21. Ibid.
22. Ibid.
23. Public Service Reforms Programme (PSRP), Local Government Reform Programme (LGRP), Public Financial Management Reform Programme

(PFMRP), the Legal Sector Reform Programme (LSRP), Financial Sector Reform (FSR), and Sector Specific Reforms (health, lands, water, etc.).

24. Prof. Lettice Rutashobya, *Fiduciary Risk assessment For the Provision of Direct Budgetary Support in Tanzania*, unpublished report submitted to the Department for International Development (DFID) Tanzania, May 2004.
25. Ibid.
26. Ibid.
27. Ibid.
28. Ibid.
29. Ibid.
30. See Robert Williams, *Political Scandals in the U.S.* (Edinburgh: Keele University Press, 1998).
31. Michael Johnston, 'Cross-Border Corruption: Points of Vulnerability and Challenges for Reform', in *Corruption and Integrity Improvement Initiatives in Developing Countries*, ed. Sahr J. Kpundeh, Irene Hors, UNDP, and OECD (New York, UNDP, 1998), 13.
32. See the Judicature and Application of Laws Ordinance, 1961.
33. Cap. 400 of the laws of Tanganyika.
34. Cap. 329 (R.E. 2002).
35. International Labour Organization, *A Fair Globalization: Creating Opportunities for All*, World Commission on the Social Dimension of Globalization (Geneva: International Labour Organization, 2004) xi.
36. The Republican Constitution of Tanganyika Act, 1962.
37. Ibid; see parts 2 and 3 of the commission's report for detailed discussions on impact of globalisation to governance.
38. See volume 8 of *Halsbury's Statutes of England and Wales*, 4th ed (London: Buttersworth, 1985), 236. Public Bodies Corruption practice Act, 1916.
39. See the Commission for Human Rights and Good Governance Act, cap. 391 (GN. no. 89 of 2001).
40. See article 132 (1) of the constitution, 1977, established the Public Leaders Ethics Secretariat (see act no. 12 of 1995).
41. Article 62 (1) of the Constitution of the United Republic of Tanzania, 1977, establishes parliament.
42. Article (1) of the Constitution of the United Republic of Tanzania, 1977, establishes the office of controller and auditor general.
43. See Sections 89 and 90 of the Criminal Procedure Act, 1985, cap. 20 (GN. no. 375 of 1995)—consent of the DPP to undertake prosecution of corruption cases. Section 3 (2) of the Economic and Organized Crime Control Act, 1984, cap. 200 (G.N. no. 191 of 1984)—consent of the DPP is required. Once consent to prosecute has been granted, section 27(3) (a)

of the Economic and Organized Crime Control Act, 1984 (GN no. 191 of 1984) provides that '[e]very legally qualified person working with the Prevention of Corruption Bureau is hereby appointed a prosecuting of Corruption Bureau is hereby appointed a prosecuting officer for the purpose of that Act'.

44. See the Tanganyika Penal Code—Section 91 contained public officials' bribery. It was borrowed from Indian Penal Code in 1920; see the 'reception clause' of Judicature and Application of Laws (Cap. 2).
45. Cap. 329 (R.E. 2002).
46. In *R. v. Newbould* (1962) All ER, vol.1: Judge Winn traces the laws on corruption in England, and that may be cited together as the Prevention of Corruption Acts, 1889–1916, of all the legislative provisions enacted to control corruption and to prevent corruption by the provisions in those three acts. The earliest of the three is that of 1889.
47. L.N. 58 of 1971 and came operational on 14 May 1971 (act no. 7 of 1974).
48. Botswana Prevention of Corruption and Economic Offences, act no. 13 of 1994.
49. See act no. 14 1980, later repealed by act no. 42 of 1996.
50. Act no. 13 of 1994.
51. PCA, cap. 329 (R.E. 2002).
52. PCCB stands for Prevention and Combating of Corruption Bureau, which replaced the Anti-Corruption Squad by virtue of act no. 27 of 1991. The PCA became operational on 15 January 1975 by virtue of GN no. 17 published on 10 January 1974 through the Prevention of Corruption (Amendment) Act no. 2 of 1974.
53. Cap. 329 (R.E. 2002).
54. Botswana Prevention of Corruption and Economic Offences Act no. 13 of 1994.
55. Ibid.
56. Mauritius Prevention of Corruption Act, 2002, and the Financial Intelli gence and Money Laundering Act, 2000.
57. Ibid.
58. Ibid.
59. See ICAC, *Independent Commission Against Corruption Annual Report 2002/2003* (Port Louis, Mauritius: ICAC, 2003), 16.
60. Malaysia Anti-Corruption Act, 1997 (act no. 575 of the Laws of Malaysia). The act came into force on 2 September 1997.
61. The PCCA, no. 11 of 2007.

62. Ibid.
63. Anti-Corruption Act, 1997 (act no. 575 of Laws of Malaysia). The act came into force on 25 September 1997.
64. (1969) 8 ILM 679.
65. See article 2 of the Vienna convention, 1969.
66. Robert M. MacLean, *Public International Law*, 4th ed. (London: HLT Publications, 1995), 151.
67. It is a fundamental norm embedded in article 26 of the convention that 'every treaty in force is binding upon the parties to it and must be performed by them in good faith'. The state cannot evade this international obligation by invoking its constitution or domestic legislation as justification for its failure to perform a treaty. See Permanent Court of International Justice, Advisory Opinion (PCI), Polish Nationals, in *Danzig Case* (1931) PCIJ Reports, Series A/B No. 44, 24.
68. Southern Africa Development Cooperation consist of Angola, Botswana, Democratic Republic of Congo, Kingdom of Lesotho, Malawi, Mauritius, Mozambique, Namibia, Seychelles, South Africa, Kingdom of Swaziland, United Republic of Tanzania, Zambia, and Zimbabwe.
69. See articles 18 and 20 of the SADC Protocol Against Corruption.
70. Botswana, Malawi, Mauritius, South Africa, Tanzania, Zambia, and Zimbabwe.
71. As of 10 August 2004.
72. AU Convention on Prevention and Combating Corruption, 2003. See the full text at www.unodc.org/pdf/southafrica/southafrica_corruption.pdfa and www.africa-union.org/root/au/Documents/Treaties/treaties.htm.
73. See article 15 of the African Union Convention on Preventing and Combating Corruption, 2003.
74. Article 10 of the convention.
75. Articles 4 and 11 of the convention.
76. Challenges on human rights, democracy, sustainable development, rule of law, stability, peace, and, above all, good governance. See www.unodc.org/unodc/en/crime_convention_corruption.html.
77. See UN Convention against Corruption, 2003, AU Convention on Preventing and Combating Corruption, 2003, and SADC Protocol against Corruption, 2001. See the texts at www.sadc.int/english/documents/legal/protocols/corruption.php and www.unodc.org/pdf/crime/convention_corruption/signing/convention.php and www.sadc.int.
78. Ibid.
79. Ibid.

80. ibid.
81. Article 10 of the UN Convention, article 9 of the AU Convention, and article 4 of the SADC Protocol.
82. Article 12 of the UN Convention, article 11 of the AU Convention, and article 4 (2) of the SADC Protocol.
83. Article 13 of the UN Convention, article 12 of the AU Convention, and article 4 of the SADC Protocol.
84. Articles 14 and 31 of the UN Convention, articles 6 and 16 of the AU Convention, and article 8 of the SADC Protocol.
85. Article 17 of the UN Convention, article 4 (d) of the AU Convention, and article 3 (d) of the SADC Protocol.
86. Article 18 of the UN Convention, article 4 (f) of the AU Convention, and article 3 (f) of the SADC Protocol.
87. Article 19 of the UN Convention, article 4 (c) of the AU Convention, and article (3) of the SADC Protocol.
88. Article 6 of the UN Convention, article 5 (3) of the AU Convention, and article 4 of the SADC Protocol.
89. Article 40 of the UN Convention, article 17 of the AU Convention, and article 8 of the SADC Protocol.
90. Article 43 of the UN Convention, article 19 of the AU Convention, and article 10 of the SADC Protocol.
91. Article 44 of the UN Convention, article 15 of the AU Convention, and article 9 of the SADC Protocol.
92. Article 46 of the UN Convention, article 18 of the AU Convention, and article 10 of the SADC Protocol.

Chapter 3

Examination of PCCA and Its Application

3.1. Anatomy of Corruption Offences

In the previous chapter, the focus was to provide the policy framework of anticorruption initiatives in Tanzania, the historical background to the legislative framework to preventing and combating of corruption, understanding regional and international instruments ratified by Tanzania and the mandatory requirements imposed by the instruments and domestication of those instruments through the PCCA.[1]

In this chapter, the focus is on the application of the PCCA and the court precedents on the four offences that have been in existence before the enactment of the PCCA, especially decisions of the Court of Appeal (CA)—which is the supreme court of the land whose decisions are binding—and on examining them in relation to the principal theme of this study, namely, circumstantial evidence.

Finally, an analysis of the PCCA supplies the necessary understanding as to why the study advocates for circumstantial evidence as a potentially more robust weapon against corruption, and the evidence to establish the commission of this criminal conduct is, by and large, dependent upon circumstantial evidence.

To prove corruption, one has to show the defendant's motive and the opportunity that the defendant had to seize the occasion to commit the crime—and here the understanding of circumstantial evidence is crucial, particularly the way courts have interpreted the law and applied a circumstantial evidence test.

The study has found only one, very recent HC case—that of *Mohamed Rafiq @ Baghdad and 6 Others*[2]—about which the author has pondered at great length and applied a circumstantial evidence test in a corruption case.

The following analysis highlights why circumstantial evidence has to be understood in the context of corruption offences—as distinct from its interpretations in the normal understanding in the penal code offences—and why a balance must be struck and the tension or dilemma as to what is more reliable and compelling—direct or circumstantial evidence—be resolved, given the perceptions as shown in the survey the study has conducted.[3] The theme of the study, therefore, is that circumstantial evidence is a more robust weapon to use in prosecuting corrupt elements in our society because, without that, the society will continue to distrust the government—and particularly the courts—reinforcing the current belief that only the small fish are caught and dealt with, while the bigger ones are left 'scot free' because there is no firm resolve by the government to deal with high-profile or grand corruption cases.[4]

3.2. Mohamed Rafiq al Baghdad and 6 Others

The facts of the case are as follows: Mohamed Rafiq al Baghdad, a Tanzanian of Asian origin, conducted businesses including speculation in land disposal, which was a lucrative business, especially in central and in prime areas in Dar es Salaam, the business capital city of Tanzania.

In order to facilitate his business, Baghdad created a network within the Ministry of Lands and Human Settlement (a registry within a registry) that would allow him to access title deeds and other relevant documents pertaining to land ownership and take advantage of the weak system of record management at the land registry within the ministry, as well as some land officials involved in that scam, who supplemented their low salaries through acceptance of bribes. To do so, the seven accused persons with whom he was charged were his facilitators while in public office within both the ministry and the city council of Dar es Salaam.

In order to be in control of the land speculation business, Baghdad had to have access to the relevant land documentations that were needed to access and control his business. The investigation that was conducted by the PCB revealed, upon searching his premises, that he was found in possession of many title deeds, including 120 letters of offer that belonged to other persons, and he was also found in possession of two notepads that he kept for his record. Entries in those notepads revealed the names and signatures of those who were in his payroll for different roles they had played to facilitate his business to acquire land through illegal means, including bribery.

The case was filed before the Resident Magistrate's Court at Kisutu in Dar es Salaam. The trial's principal resident magistrate was presented with various counts falling under the PCA, read together with the Economic and Organized Crime Control Act, no. 13, of 1984 (EOCCA).[5] Most notable was the offence of corrupt transaction with an agent contrary to section 3 (2) of the PCA, read together with the EOCCA. The prosecution, in the first count, alleged that the accused jointly gave a Peugeot 504 saloon car with registration no. MB 5220, valued at TSh (Tanzanian shillings) 1.8 million to Shaaban Malipula, an assistant lands officer, as an inducement to assist in the acquisition of plots of land by the two accused, or an enterprise managed by them—matters that are in relation to the affairs of the second accused's principal.

In the second, third, fourth, fifth, and sixth counts, Baghdad alone was charged with corrupt transaction with an agent—specifically, that on diverse dates, he corruptly offered TSh 100,000 to Ashura Lyema, the eighth accused; TSh 400,000 to Ramadhani Chambika, the fifth accused, TSh 500,000 to Niibogora Kileo, the fourth accused; TSh 810,000 to Theobald Msafiri, the third accused; and, lastly, TSh 20,000 to Clemence Chilumba, the sixth accused. The prosecution further alleged that all this money was offered to the officers as an inducement to facilitate the acquisition of plots of land by Baghdad or an enterprise managed by him, matters that were in relation to the affairs of the accused's principal. In the alternative counts, the second, third, fifth, sixth, and eighth accused persons were charged with obtaining advantage without lawful consideration, contrary to section 6 of the PCA. It was alleged by the prosecution that they received the aforementioned sums of money knowing or having reason to believe that the first accused was or was likely to be concerned in transactions with themselves as public officers.

Baghdad was also faced with the offence of leading an organised crime racket contrary to section 5 (1) (a) of the first schedule, too, and section 59 (2) of the EOCCA. The allegations were that, between 1982 and 1998, Baghdad intentionally managed and financed a criminal racket by organising and corruptly offering money to a group of officials in the Ministry of Lands and the city council of Dar es Salaam for purposes of obtaining preferential allocation of plots of land to him or to an enterprise managed by him. Several witnesses testified for the prosecution on the alleged counts, and, in response to the accusations against him, Baghdad testified that he dealt in the real estate business and that he purchased and sold the alleged plots. The letters of offer found with him were copies, because the originals were surrendered to the purchasers upon sale of the plots. Baghdad did not deny that his coaccused were known to him, and he specifically conceded to having offered money to the eighth accused to enable her to pay her house rent. On the vehicle offered to Malipula, Baghdad defended himself by claiming that he had offered the vehicle to the Al-Masjid Neemat'ullah mosque, where Malipula also was an affiliate, and that the mosque leaders were so old that Malipula had to drive the vehicle for them to ease the transport problems that the mosque was facing. He denied ownership of one hundred plots, but accepted ten of them. He admitted to have used his influence in the state house to push through his business. Regarding the notepads, he conceded that they were to keep an account of all payments and cash received for his record. He also testified that he gave money to the head of surveys and mapping at the ministry for purchase of cement and transport—and that, in his view, was not corruption at all. Baghdad also conceded to having offered rice and some kilos of sugar to the sixth accused as an Idd El-Fitry (i.e., Muslim day of celebration after the Ramadhan fast) donation. The trial's principal resident magistrate, in his judgment, found that 'it cannot be controverted that the first accused knew all the accused persons so it could not have been an accident that their names appeared in the diaries', or notepads, and that

> these diaries cannot be a madman's diaries and the first accused could not have been wasting his time making those entries. In view of this a mere denial of names appearing therein cannot be accepted when taken in conjunction with other pieces of evidence.

The magistrate also found that the public officers in the case compromised their integrity for little things that Baghdad offered them. In his own words, the principal resident magistrate deplored the culture of corruption in society, declaring that

> a government officer, however junior, goes to beg for two kilograms of sugar and goat meat from a businessman does not impress me as a philanthropist incident, because a businessman will normally never offer his money for free. On a more serious note, the first accused was a Real Estate Agent who would stop at nothing to get as many plots as possible. This is lucrative since it is in evidence that he sold a plot for 20 million shillings. This being the case, to know as many people as possible within the Lands Ministry was the most desired thing. He could therefore not be expected to be dishing out money just like that without expecting any returns. He must have known the returns. As it is, however, there is no direct evidence to lead us to conclude how his money was repaid but I have no doubt in my mind that the accused had established a syndicate.

In another important finding by the trial magistrate on the car offered to Malipula, the magistrate found that

> there were very big attempts to show that the vehicle was purchased for the Mosque upon request by the Mosque Committee. Minutes to that effect were tendered and marked as exhibit DI. I emphatically regret to say that the said minutes do not say so. What they say is that it was Malipula himself [second accused] who requested for it and nowhere is it said in those minutes that the Committee recommended having the motor vehicle registered in an individual's name to avoid a crisis. It therefore follows that evidence to this effect by the accused himself (Malipula), first accused, seventh accused and Aziz Dilunga (DW2) was their own invention. But even if the Committee had so resolved, that would have been a very strange and queer arrangement because as it agreed, the mosque stood to lose it if say, Malipula passed away. When the above is given due weight, it follows that the trio attempted to use the Mosques to make sure their dirty tricks were well covered. I find it established that the said vehicle was purchased for the second accused and it remains his property.

On the section 6 offence under the PCA, the principal resident magistrate's interpretation was that it left no doubt that the PCA absolutely prohibits public officials from receiving consideration from members of the public who have or are likely to have official affairs with them.

> Evidence in this case leaves no doubt that, by the nature of the first accused's business, employees of the lands Ministry or any Land Department had to avoid taking any favours from him. By not avoiding it, they certainly collided with the law. In sum total I entertain no doubt that the evidence placed before the court, though circumstantial, suffices to sustain conviction in respect of all the accused for the offences facing them.

The HC also had the opportunity to consider this case on an appeal filed by the appellants (accused persons), which was based on one important ground for appeal: the trial magistrate erred in law and, in fact, in holding that the evidence placed before the trial court, through circumstantial evidence, sufficed to sustain a conviction in respect of all accused (appellants) for the offences facing them.

Judge Mwaikugile recited cases[6] referred to by both the appellants and respondent—which basically say that for the court to convict an accused person based on circumstantial evidence, the following principle is to be borne in mind: that circumstantial evidence should be incapable of any other reasonable explanation other than the guilt of the accused person and incompatible with his innocence. Judge Mwaikugile set himself to answer the following question after examining the evidence: was this the position in the conviction of the appellants by the trial magistrate?

In response to his framed question, Judge Mwaikugile reasoned that the findings of the trial magistrate were vague and ambiguous due to his failure to mention whether the conviction was founded on principal counts or alternative counts, or both. He faulted the trial court that its findings were vague and ambiguous to sustain any conviction. On his analysis of the utility of circumstantial evidence, Judge Mwaikugile was of the view that the evidence on record could not link the appellants with such alleged acts as bribes that were offered with a corrupt motive.

The learned judge declared that 'the prosecution had failed beyond reasonable doubt to prove the existence of a corrupt motive on the part of the appellant's' without linking his declaration and the evidence on record. There is a gap between the evidence on record and the theories of circumstantial evidence, as shown in the previously cited cases, in which the judge found himself. This analysis seeks to bridge that gap and define what really amounts to circumstantial evidence.

In their book on the law of evidence, Rantanlal and Dhirajlal[7] explained more clearly that motive is the principle embedded in circumstantial evidence. That motive that induces a party to perform an act, or preparations that he or she makes in its commission, will be taken into account. Evidence of motive or preparations becomes important when a case depends upon circumstantial evidence. Motive, therefore, is that which moves a person to perform a particular act.[8]

There can be no action without a motive; a motive must exist for every voluntary act. The voluntary action of a sane person has an impelling emotion or motive. Motive is the emotion that is supposed to have led him to act, which is proven by the conduct of a person.[9] Though faulting the findings of the trial magistrate on the corrupt motive, the appeal judge himself failed to justify his decision, other than to cite the authorities referred to by parties to the appeal. What would have been more helpful for the judge to do is to relate his understanding of circumstantial evidence and the findings of the trial magistrate—this he failed to do.

What are the principles of circumstantial evidence? Simply explained, circumstantial evidence means that the prosecution is relying upon evidence of various circumstances relating to the crime and the defendant that, taken together, will lead to the sure conclusion that it was the defendant who committed the crime. For conviction on circumstantial evidence to stand in the instant case, the judge should consider whether it reveals any other circumstances, which are or may be of sufficient reliability and strength to weaken or destroy the prosecution case.[10]

Judge Mwaikugile ignored the findings of the trial magistrate that 'it cannot be controverted that the first accused knew all the accused persons so it could not have been an accident that their names appeared in the diaries'. Instead, he entertained speculation. Speculating in a case amounts to no more than guessing or making up good theories without good evidence to support them—and this should never be done.

The judge also ignored the trial magistrate's findings that

> the first accused was a Real Estate Agent who would stop at nothing to get as many plots as possible. This is lucrative since it is in evidence that he sold a plot at shs 20 million. This being the case to know as many people as possible within the Lands Ministry was the most desired thing. He could therefore not be expected to be dishing out money just like that without expecting any returns.

The adequacy of motive of the defendant can only be ascertained by inferences drawn from the facts of the case.

On the count relating to section 6 of the PCA, Judge Mwaikugile held that

> there was no concrete evidence to show that the sums of money paid and material if any had been so paid for the purposes of inducement to the relevant Appellants to assist the first Appellant in the acquisition of plots.

He further reasoned that

> the relevant Appellants in their defence on record either denied to have received the alleged sums of money from the first Appellant or where it was admitted reasonable explanations was given to show what it was intended for.

In justifying receipt of bribes by public officials from businessmen who have an interest in the public service—such as Baghdad, in this case—Judge Mwaikugile cited the case of *R v. Mtetewaunga*,[11] where Judge Mapigano held that

> public service does not entail public servants to be outcasts from the public. For a public servant to have a friend who is a member of the public for that matter or a businessman is not an offence and receiving gifts from such a friend without pointing out and proving the offence committed is not an offence.

With due respect to Judge Mwaikugile—who was relying on the reasoning by Judge Mapigano in relation to an entrapment set up by the ACS against Mtetewaunga, the defendant in that case—the facts of this case were not similar to Baghdad's case, as we now relate. In the Baghdad case, the issue was not entrapment but rather bribing public officials in the Ministry of Lands with a view to acquiring plots in prime land within the city of Dar Es Salaam. In the alternative to counts of corrupt transactions in relation to the second, third, fourth, and eighth defendants—namely, Shaaban Rashid Malipula, Theobald Msafiri, Niibogora Kileo, and Ashura Lyema—counts for obtaining advantage without lawful consideration, contrary to section 6 of the PCA, were preferred.

Had he looked closely at the evidence on record, as previously highlighted, he would have found that there was ample circumstantial evidence to connect each accused through inferences of facts presented in court, and that Baghdad masterminded the whole racket in real estate business. The fact that Baghdad had a real estate business, and thus that he needed to befriend lands officers to facilitate his acquisition of the said plots, is a clear and important fact that the judge ought to have considered in analyzing the evidence before him. The judge did not relate these facts to the notepads and circumstances in which Baghdad's network operated. It is by inference of these facts that the judge ought to have related, in his reasoning and evaluation, the evidence on record to either fault the decision of the lower court or otherwise in this case. Makame, JA, reasoning in *Mariam Siri v. R*,[12] is very helpful to appreciate and apply the circumstantial evidence test. In Justice Makame's own words,

> The doubt required to detract from the certitude necessary for conviction in criminal cases is only reasonable doubt, not fanciful doubt. Absolute certainty, almost impossibility, is not necessary in establishing criminal guilt. It is enough as in this case, that one feels certain that an accused person is guilty.[13]

In the case of *R v. Stephen Dominic Mtetewaunga*,[14] the facts of the case are simply summarised as follows. On 29 May 1986, one Exaud Swai lodged a complaint with the minister for lands, and the defendant was, *inter alia*, to give an opinion on the complaint brought to the minister by Swai. On 6 June 1986, the complainant and the defendant met for a drink at a club called Lango la Jiji People's Social Club, situated at Magomeni, in the hours of the evening. The two happened to know each other and were residents of the same locality, Magomeni. On several occasions, they had met in pubs and drank together in friendliness and at times bought drinks for each other. In the course of drinking that evening, the defendant happened to appraise Swai about the minister's displeasure with his letter of complaint and asked him to call at his office the following day to fetch the letter. On the same day, Swai laid information to ACS to the effect that the defendant was soliciting a bribe of TSh 3,000 from him so that he might let his appeal pass.

On the following day (7 June 1986), a trap was set up by the ACS against the defendant, and a sum of TSh 2,000 was given to Swai, being powdered and marked currency notes of the TSh 100 denomination. Swai then went to the office of the defendant and, after a brief conversation with him, handed over the money to the defendant. Swai then got up and left without collecting the letter. Soon thereafter, ACS officers, who were around to witness the transaction, stalked into the office of the defendant, apprehended and searched his person, and recovered the trap money. What is interesting in this case is that the day (7 June 1986) when Swai went to the defendant's office was a Saturday—not a work day for a public office.

In his defence testimony, the defendant recounted that Swai was a drinking pal and regarded him as a friend. He denied ever soliciting a bribe from Swai and claimed that he had directed his personal secretary to hand over to him the letter of reply to his complaint on the fateful day. When Swai entered his office, he had asked him whether the secretary had given him his letter of reply, and he said Mtetewaunga had been given the letter and that Swai had asked Mtetewaunga if he was going to drop in the club in the evening. He replied to say he had an appointment at Upanga, which he felt obliged to keep. Swai then produced the trap money and gave it to him, saying, 'Take this amount for your weekend'. He claimed that he received the money and pocketed it without counting it. He said he received the money in good conscience and that it never crossed his mind that there was anything wrong or sinister about the money. Judge Mapigano's findings in the case were based on the credibility of the witness rather than on the contents of what transpired on the material day. In his own observation, the judge stated, '[W]e think we are right in saying that the accused gave his evidence with simplicity, clarity and a measure of humility and that there is no way one could resist getting impressed by his evidence'. He had received the money in the context of a brotherly relationship that then existed between them. Swai's character became the court's basis for discounting the testimony of the prosecution's star witness in deciding the case. The judge stated his opinion of the witness' character in declaring him 'a rough man and of a boisterous cast of mind', and with regard to the letter of complaint that Swai relied on in his testimony, the court noted that 'the Minister directed the letter exhibit PL, be returned to him. On our part we have refrained from taking such a course and we have instead just filed the letter away'. The court further considered the ingredients of section 6 of the PCA, that is, that the prosecution bears the burden to prove the following matters: that the accused was a public officer at the time of the commission of the offence; that he obtained for himself an advantage, to wit, a sum of TSh 2,000 that he obtained for himself an advantage from a person whom he knew or had reason to believe to have been, to be, or likely or about to be concerned in a matter or transaction with himself as a public officer; and that he gave for the said advantage with no lawful consideration.

Judge Mapigano's findings in the case were that the defendant was a public officer at the material time; that it was not in dispute that he obtained for himself the pecuniary advantage of TSh 2,000 from Exaud Swai; that the defendant knew at the time that Swai had been concerned in a matter with himself as a public officer; and that the words 'to have been concerned' showed that the obtaining of an advantage would be an offence even if it was obtained after the proceeding or business is over.[15] As to whether the defendant obtained unlawful consideration, the judge ruled out that it was not the case in Mtetewaunga's case. Citing the decision in *DPP v. Jaffari M. Mfaume Kawawa*,[16] Judge Mapigano observed that love and affection does not constitute a consideration in that context. However, there are times when civil servants face the woeful circumstances where a public officer's house is struck by lightning, resulting in deaths of some members of his family and the destruction of his property. In such situations, receiving any valuable assistance that might be extended from neighbourhood, relatives, and friends would not amount to an advantage obtained or accepted by the public officer within the scope of section 6. The reason behind this is that 'under those circumstances the public officer has a moral or social right to get such aid and assistance'.

Again, the circumstances pertaining to Mtetewaunga's[17] and Jaffari Mfaume Kawawa's cases[18] are totally different from what Judge Mapigano was alluding to be a moral or social right. So, in Baghdad's case,[19] the circumstances do not amount to a moral or social right such that he should be allowed to bribe and give gifts to public servants while attending him in their official capacity in his quest to acquire land in prime areas within the city of Dar es Salaam.

We are not talking of a *tsunami catastrophe* situation here; rather, we are concerned with the public officers' integrity in discharging their public duties to the general public. In order for the public to trust public servants and their government, it is important that the law should be interpreted to achieve its intended objectives, so that the prohibition embedded in section 6 of the PCA against public servants receiving bribes, inadequate considerations, and even gifts from the people with whom they come into contact in the delivery of social and public goods that are free, and where a public servant acts to the contrary—the law has to punish such intolerable behaviour against public morality. If the court fails to see this important aspect of punishing wrong doers who commit corrupt transactions or corruption offences, the society will lose trust in the efficacy and validity of the rule of law, which the court has to jealously protect.

3.3. The Highlights of the PCCA

The PCCA has captured both the prevention and combating of corruption, as the title of the act itself demonstrates. There are seven chapters in the new act. The preamble to it underscores that corruption is an obstacle to the principles of democracy, good governance, and human rights, and poses a threat to peace, tranquillity, and security in our society. The preamble reaffirms the principles of freedom, equality, justice, brotherhood, peace, and the right to property ownership through lawful means. Cognisance of globalisation and technological advancement have made it necessary to reinstitute the PCCB—through the application of modern tactics and strategies of preventing and combating corruption—and to ensure that the bureau effectively contains corruption and corrupt practices, and that the bureau is operationally independent and effective in its performance.

Part 1 is about preliminary provisions, covered in sections 1–4, which include the title of the act and the application of the act in Mainland Tanzania and elsewhere.[20] Interpretation provisions[21] are followed by the objectives of the law, which are to promote and enhance good governance and the eradication of corruption.[22]

Part 2 covers the establishment of the PCCB[23] and reassures its independence.[24] The composition and functions of the bureau, which bring into effect both preventive and enforcement measures, are provided for.[25] Functions of the PCCB—and, particularly, prevention of corruption provisions—are given more prominence in the act, as reflected in section 7; clauses (a)–(d) deal with preventive mechanisms, while clauses (e) and (f) deal with enforcement.

The powers of the director general and the delegated powers thereof are also stated.[26] The powers of the officers of the bureau, along with safeguards against the abuse of powers, are stated in the act.[27] Section 14 of the act, which provides for reporting of activities of the bureau to the president on or before 31 March of each year, should be read together with section 48, which requires the Director General to submit the annual PCCB report[28] to the minister responsible, who will lay the same report before the national assembly.[29]

Part 3 provides for corruption and related offences most significantly, adding twenty offences to the existing four offences dealing with corruption in the country.[30] The Act has added more offences that have incorporated the mandatory offences under UNCAC, best practices considerations, and stakeholders' views. The offences include corrupt transactions in contracts,[31] corruption offences in procurement,[32] corrupt transactions in auctions,[33] application of the Public Procurement Act,[34] corruption in employment,[35] bribery of foreign public officials,[36] sexual favours,[37] possession of unexplained property,[38] embezzlement and misappropriation,[39] diversion,[40] aiding and abetting,[41] abuse of position,[42] conspiracy,[43] trading in influence,[44] transfer of proceeds of corruption,[45] presumption of corruption,[46] false pretence to be an officer of the bureau,[47] disclosing investigation conducted or being conducted by the bureau to the suspect or unauthorised persons,[48] and freezing of assets.[49]

Part 4 handles the forfeiture of proceeds of corruption and its legal applications.[50] Part 5 deals with institutional cooperation, such as law enforcement agency cooperation.[51] Part 6 deals with the finances of the bureau and mandates that the minister responsible is required to lay the PCCB report before the national assembly during the sessions immediately following the date of submission of the report.[52]

The valuation of corruptly acquired property is based on market prices at the time of purchase; in cases relating to construction materials and building, market valuation shall apply.[53] Immunity of PCCB officers in the course of execution of their official duties;[54] protection of whistle-blowers;[55] protection of witnesses, experts, and victims;[56] mutual legal assistance;[57] extradition;[58] the DPP's fiat;[59] powers of the minister to make regulations;[60] and repeal provision of cap. 329 are dealt with in this act.

There has been a debate and demand from stakeholders for there to be specific provisions on political corruption in the PCCA. The government position is that, instead of dealing with consequences in the PCCA, it is better to deal with the problem from its source, which is the Political Parties Act[61] and the Elections Act.[62] The government has suggested that there would be a national debate on political corruption by involving all political parties and other stakeholders to ensure that the source of funding for political parties and their political campaign funding are made transparent and regulated by law. Once this is done, the PCCA will be amended accordingly to ensure that political corruption is addressed holistically, taking best practices into account.[63]

On absolute discretionary powers given to the DPP, PCCA has put a time limitation of sixty days during which the DPP has to make a decision once the record with evidence has been submitted to him by the PCCB.[64]

3.4. Interpretation of Corruption Offences and the Import of Circumstantial Evidence in the PCCA

In the investigation of corruption cases, it is usually difficult to find direct evidence, given the nature of the offence itself. However, circumstantial evidence frequently becomes more readily available in such cases. Circumstantial evidence commonly comes from several witnesses and different sources. A chain of circumstances is less likely to be falsely prepared and arranged. It is through indirect evidence that inference is drawn and persuasion is produced. In corruption cases where, invariably, there are no eyewitnesses—given the nature of the crime itself (secrecy and conspiracy)—the most effective evidence to use is circumstantial evidence. It is the application and deduction of a fact logically and reasonably drawn from another fact or group of facts established by evidence. It is not necessary that facts should be proved by direct (eyewitness) evidence; they may be proved by circumstantial evidence or a combination of both direct and circumstantial evidence.

Given this context, we can now turn to a discussion of the relevant legislation that relates to corruption in Tanzania. The PCCA has enlarged and expanded the scope of 'corrupt transactions' offences, which were originally covered under section 4 of the repealed cap. 329. They are divided into two parts and continue to be retained in section 15 of the PCCA. Part one comprises 'corruptly soliciting' or 'accepting or obtaining' or 'agreeing to accept' or 'attempting to obtain any advantage as an inducement' or 'reward for doing' or 'forebearing to do' or 'having done' or 'forborne to do anything in relation to a principal's affairs' or 'business'. The second part involves 'corruptly giving', 'promising to give', or 'offering any advantage' to any person as an inducement to or reward for doing, or forebearing to do, anything in relation to a principal's affairs or business.

It must be borne in mind that all these transactions must be done corruptly and must involve some advantage. The legislation does not define the word 'corruption'. According to the UNCAC, the omission of a definition was made deliberately because what constitutes corruption today in this society may not be the same in another society. Langseth informed that, in the negotiations of the UNCAC, it was felt that it would not serve any useful purpose to attempt to provide a definition to the term; instead, the convention provided a list of specific types or acts of corruption for that purpose.[65] In that spirit, in the PCCA, 'advantage' is regarded as the 'gift of any property, movable or immovable, loan, fee, reward or favour and includes valuable consideration of any kind, discount, commission, rebate, bonus, deduction or percentage', as well as employment or rendering services in any capacity.[66]

For comparative purposes, the Nigerian government has also passed a law against corruption to include economic offences. The Corrupt Practices and Other Related Offences Act of the Federal Republic of Nigeria defined 'corruption' so as to include bribery, fraud, and other related offences.[67]

The Nigerian law against corruption uses the word 'gratification' instead of 'advantage', which is broader and includes:

(a) Money, donation, gift, loan, fee, reward, valuable security, property—being property of any description, whether movable or immovable—or any other similar advantage, given or promised to any person with intent to influence such a person in the performance or nonperformance of his or her duties;
(b) Any office, dignity, employment, contract of empowerment, or services, and any agreement to give employment or render services in any capacity;
(c) Any payment, release, discharge, or liquidation of any loan, obligation, or other liability, whether in whole or in part;
(d) Any valuable consideration of any kind, any discount, commission, rebate, bonus, deduction or percentage;
(e) Any forbearance to demand any money or money's worth or valuable thing;
(f) Any other service or favour of any description—such as protection from any penalty or disability incurred or apprehended, or from any action or proceedings of a disciplinary, civil, or criminal nature, whether or not already instituted, and including the exercise or the forbearance from the exercise of any rights or any official power or duty; and
(g) Any offer, undertaking or promise, whether conditional or unconditional, of any gratification with the meaning of any of the proceeding paragraphs (a)–(f).[68]

The Zambian legislation against corruption[69] defines 'corruptly', which is similar to the repealed Cap. 329, as '[i]n relation to the soliciting, accepting or obtaining or giving any of the aforementioned things by way of a bribe or other personal temptations or inducement'.[70]

The relevance of these comparisons from other jurisdictions to this study is that, in them, corruption is given a wider meaning, and that, in proving such an offence, it requires the understanding of circumstantial evidence, which is founded on the motive of the suspect, his inclination to gain advantage, and, above all, an opportunity to commit the offence, especially where deterrence is less effective.

3.5. Interpretation of Corrupt Transactions

Section 15 of the PCCA provides for corrupt transaction offences. Several cases illustrate the judicial interpretations of what amounts to 'corrupt transactions'. These judicial interpretations are analysed in context and linked to the cutting theme of this study—circumstantial evidence.

The case of *Attorney General v. Shamba Ali Kajembe*[71] was decided by the East African Court of Appeal (EACA), presided over by Sir Kenneth O'Connor, president, Briggs, VP, and Forbes, JA, on 21 July–11 August 1958. The appeal arose from the decision of Judge Harbord. The issue for consideration on appeal was, firstly, whether money paid to a policeman for compensating the complainant was received corruptly, and, secondly, whether corrupt motives in a giver and recipient in corruption are relevant.

Briefly, the facts of the case were as follows. Zena, the daughter of Mzee, had a brother, Jafferi, who stole a bicycle in August 1956 from one Simon, and sold it to Ali Juma. In Aril 1957, on being found in possession of the bicycle, Ali Juma was arrested. He told the police that Jafferi had sold it to him. The respondent was then a subinspector of police at Kigoma, where the case was being investigated. Hearing of the investigation, Zena telegraphed Jafferi at Mwanza, telling him that the cycle was in police hands and to send a receipt to price his title to it. Zena did not then know that Jafferi had stolen the bicycle. The police learnt about the telegram and the respondent sent for Zena, saying the matter was serious. Zena asked him how it could be put right and whether her brother could be fined. Simon later came to Zena's house and told her he would drop the case if compensated, whereupon Zena told him she was taking money to the respondent, who could buy Simon a new bicycle; if the money was insufficient, Simon could take back his cycle and some money as compensation for being deprived of it. When Zena arrived at the police station, the respondent was not there, but he came to Zena's house the next day, accompanied by a plainclothes constable, at which time Zena handed over TSh 340 to the respondent, who took it and left, assuring her she need not worry further. Simon did not get any of the money and, when Jafferi was convicted later at Mwanza and imprisoned, Zena demanded her money back, saying that since there had been no fine, the money was not needed. The respondent subsequently returned TSh 100 to Zena; however, before he had repaid the whole, an investigation into the respondent's conduct was begun by his superiors, and he was later charged with and convicted of official corruption, contrary to section 91 (1) of the penal code.

On appeal, it was contended for the respondent that the facts did not disclose the offence charged. The judge who heard the appeal held that Zena, an African, thought that the cycle owner would himself get the case against her brother withdrawn on receiving what was justly due to him, and that the case would then fall away of itself. The judge held that Zena's intention in giving the money to the respondent was innocent, as she wished to get the cycle owner to withdraw his complaint, and the respondent could not be guilty of corruptly receiving the money so tendered. He accordingly allowed the appeal and quashed the conviction. The attorney general appealed against this decision.

Upon hearing the appeal, the EACA held that in charges of corruption under section 91 (1) of the penal code, it is the mental attitude of the recipient that is crucial in determining whether or not an offence has been committed; if the recipient accepts a gift that he knows to be corruptly given, on account of some act or omission in the discharge of his duty, or with intent to influence him thereafter, so that he may do some act or may make some omission—the recipient is guilty of the offence, and it matters not that he may have no intention of showing a favour to the donor. A corrupt intention on the part of the giver, however, is not an essential ingredient of the offence. Secondly, the court concluded that since the money was not received by the respondent for himself, but for Simon, *per curiam* the court held that '[w]e do not think that a benefit obtained for another, in which the accused is entirely disinterested, could be said to have been obtained by him corruptly'. Thirdly, relevant to circumstantial evidence was the magistrate's inference that receipt of the money by the respondent was incompatible with a vigorous and honest prosecution of Jafferi, which was a possible but not an inevitable inference, and there was an element of doubt, of which the respondent should have been given the benefit. The appeal was, consequently, dismissed.

The importance of the *ratio decidendi* in this case is that, in corruption cases, more often than not, the prosecution would be required to show in evidence the motive of the defence to prove its case and the resultant advantage that the defendant has derived from the corrupt transaction.

The court's emphasis on motive is based on the fact that to prove corruption through direct evidence is a daunting task and, invariably, it is not possible to do so because of the nature and essence of corrupt transactions, which are committed in the dark, and parties are always reluctant to disclose the nature of corrupt transaction itself, even when they are arraigned by law enforcement agencies responsible for stumping out such crimes.

In the case of *R v. Hashim Jiwa*,[72] the EACA, presided by Sir Graham Paul, CJ (Tanganyika), Edwards, CJ (Uganda), and Judge Thacker (Kenya), considered the decision from HM supreme court of Kenya based on unlawfully selling intoxicating liquor to a native. The issue for consideration was whether a police trap and genuine police spies are not accomplices.

On 5 February 1948, the appellant was charged before the resident magistrate, Nyeri, sitting at Fort Hall, on five counts—setting out offences under the Liquor Ordinance (1934), the Defence (Control of Distribution and Rationing of Foodstuffs) Regulation (1944), and the Defence (Control of Prices) Regulations (1945)—to which he pleaded not guilty. The appellant was the proprietor of a shop at Fort Hall, where groceries and liquor were sold. The case for the prosecution was that on 20 December 1947, witness Simon Njeroge went to the appellant's shop and, in the course of conversation, the latter asked him, 'Can you get a man to buy some sugar and European liquor?' Njeroge replied that he could buy them himself.

The following day, Njeroge saw the appellant alone and asked him the price of a full bag of sugar. The appellant said he would want KSh (Kenyan schillings) 175. Njeroge thought this price too high and went to consult one Fernandes, the district commissioner's clerk. Fernandes reported to Mr. Cumber, the district officer, into whose presence Njeroge was later brought. It was quite frankly admitted by Mr. Cumber and Fernandes that they then hatched a plot. It was arranged that Njeroge should carry out the proposed purchase of sugar and liquor from the appellant with the objective of obtaining evidence of 'black market' practices against him. Njeroge set out with marked currency notes and purchased from the appellant 448 pounds of sugar and one bottle of Emu brandy for KSh 350 and KSh 23, respectively, whilst Fernandes and two police *askaris* (Walter and Ambrose) stood close by to watch. No evidence was led for the defence. The resident magistrate found that there was no case for the appellant to answer on the charge of selling one bottle of Emu brandy at an excess price, but convicted him on the four remaining counts, imposing fines totalling KSh 6,500, or thirteen months' imprisonment in default.

The appellant appealed to the supreme court of Kenya, sitting in its appellate jurisdiction. The appeal from conviction on the fourth count of selling sugar at an excess price was allowed, but as regards the three remaining counts, the appeal was dismissed. Then the appellant appealed to the EACA against convictions on counts one, three, and five (the details of which are set out in the following judgment)—the main argument being that the district officer, the clerk Fernandes, and the two police *askaris* (Walter and Ambrose) were all accomplices of the witness,

Simon Njeroge, and the appellant, and that their evidence required corroboration. The court held that the district officer, Fernandes, the two *askaris*, and Njeroge, in regard to the respective parts they played in the transactions, were genuine police spies, and therefore, not being accomplices, did not require corroboration.

As it is shown in chapter 5 of this study, entrapment in corruption cases is a common device used by law enforcement agencies to catch offenders, given the nature of corruption as an offence on the run and the difficulty that it imposes on detection by normal means—unless entrapment is deployed.

In another case, *Wanjir w/o Muriri v. R*,[73] in answering the question as to whether the use of entrapment was legitimate, the EACA found that what is at the heart of the question for consideration is the nature of the offence and the frame of mind of the accused, and not the provision of the means to commit the offence or its seriousness.

Commenting on this case, Alex Muganda opined that in all cases where the defence has raised the allegation that the defendant has been framed without his or her knowledge, the courts, rather than requiring the defendant to substantiate his allegations, have required the prosecution to prove its case beyond reasonable doubt that the evidence was not fabricated.[74] The principle that is advanced here is that the prosecution has a duty to prove its case beyond reasonable doubt.

However, in the landmark case of *William Haining v. R*,[75] the interpretation of section 3 of the Prevention of Corruption Ordinance[76]—which contains similar wording as section 15 of the PCCA—was expounded with clarity. Reading the decision of the EACAC, Law, the JA clarified by stating that, if this section stood alone, it would be for the prosecution to prove beyond all reasonable doubt that when the appellant accepted a gift of a car from Zahir Ahmed, he did so corruptly as a reward for having done, or foreborne to do, something in his capacity as regional engineer in relation to the affairs of his principal. But section 3 (1) does not stand alone. In the case of public servants, it has to be read together with section 8 of the ordinance, which deals with the proof of proceedings under section 3 of the ordinance.[77]

The circumstances that would assist the prosecution to prove such corrupt transactions are based on circumstantial evidence, because corrupt transactions are founded on circumstances that must show the motive of the accused, his inclination to commit the offence, and the opportunity to take advantage of the circumstances present at the material time. Other cases have dealt with 'corrupt transaction' of any person or agent, particularly the phrase 'for any other person'.[78]

One such case was that of *Patrick s/o Isango v. R*,[79] where the accused, a ten-cell leader, was convicted of a corrupt transaction. The principal evidence against him was that of the complainant, who testified that he paid the accused TSh 100 as a reward for forebearing to arrest the complaint for cattle theft. The court (Georges, CJ) held that at law, the presiding judge had no powers or duties in relation to arrest other than those possessed by all citizens. Therefore, this transaction was not in relation to his principal's affairs and did not come within the terms of section 3 (1).

R. v. Smith,[80] an English decision, was concerned with a 'gift' offered to an officer of a public body in respect of a transaction in which the public body was concerned, whether the gift was 'corruptly' offered or if the one offering had no intention of carrying out the transaction. The object of section 1 (2) of the Public Bodies Corrupt Practices Act (1889) was to prevent officers or servants of public bodies being put in a position where they are subject to temptation; a person acts 'corruptly' within the meaning of the subsection if he deliberately offers a fee or reward to an officer of a public body and with the intention that the person to whom the offer is made should enter into a corrupt bargain, even if the one offering has no intention of carrying out the transaction and accepting the favour that he sought.[81]

In *Mayagila s/o Sima v. R.*,[82] the complaining witness had been charged with cattle theft and had properly been released after the investigation of a police inspector.

Afterwards, the accused, who was a special constable, demanded payment of TSh 100 from the complainant, purportedly on behalf of the inspector. The complainant paid under threat of a new prosecution. There was no evidence that the inspector was involved. The court held that, although a crime was undoubtedly committed, the crime charged was not proven. At the time of the solicitation, nothing could be done—or be foreborne to be done—in relation to the principal's affairs. The accused was acting entirely for himself, and it was immaterial whether he could himself have caused the complainant to be rearrested.

In the case of *Korba s/o Farah v. R.*,[83] the accused was convicted for violating section 3 (2) of the Prevention of Corruption Ordinance, cap. 400. The evidence was that he had paid TSh 300 to an area commissioner in an attempt to obtain a permit to transport maize. Two constables who were in the vicinity immediately arrested him by arrangement. The accused's defence was that the area commissioner had no power to issue the permit. The court held that it was no defence that the area commissioner had no authority to issue the desired permit, since the accused intended for him to act as an intermediary and influence the members of the board empowered to issue such permits.[84]

A broader view was adopted in the case of the *DPP v. Mustapha Peter*[85] by Judge Mfalila (as he then was) that it is not even necessary to consider whether he had the power to do so or whether it was his concern—it is sufficient that he sought to use his position in government to obtain advantage.[86]

3.6. USE OF DOCUMENTS INTENDED TO MISLEAD THE PRINCIPAL

The offence of using of documents with the intention to mislead is provided for under section 22 of the PCCA. This section has never been well understood in the past or tested in the highest court of the land, especially in the repealed PCA, cap. 329. However, the history of section 22 of the PCCA and its application can be understood from this historical background, and the way forward can be predicted in the context and utility of circumstantial evidence.

The English Prevention of Corrupt Act (1906) embodies a similar provision to section 22 of the PCCA. The case of *Sage v. Eicholz*[87] speaks it all. In that case, the king's bench was faced with an appeal by the appellant, G. C. Sage, against the respondent, charging that he knowingly gave a form of claim for empty bottles in respect of water rates payable by owners to an agent of the Metropolitan Water Board, which was false in a particular material and was intended to mislead the water board, contrary to section 1 (1) of the Prevention of Corruption Act:

> If any person knowingly gives to any agent, or if any agent knowingly or with intent to deceive his principal, any receipt, account, or other document in respect of which the principal is intended and which contains any material particular, and which to his knowledge is intended to mislead the principal; he shall be guilty of a misdemeanour, and shall be liable on conviction to imprisonment, with or without labour for a term not exceeding two years, or to a fine not exceeding £500.

At the close of the case for the prosecution, the magistrate held that no case had been made out. He found that the person to whom the document was handed was an agent of the board, but that no attempt was made to corrupt him or any other servant of the board. He was of the opinion that the operation of the act was limited to the prevention of the corruption of agents, and in that opinion, he was guided by the title and general phraseology of the act.

On appeal, Judge Bray held that in his view, the words of the act are perfectly clear and unambiguous. The expression 'knowingly' is deliberately used in the third paragraph instead of the word 'corruptly', and 'knowingly' does not necessarily involve any element of corruption. The substitution of the word 'knowingly' was probably made because of the great difficulty of proving corruption. Under those circumstances, the court has no right to restrict the plain meaning of the words merely because the act is entitled 'An Act for Better Prevention of Corruption'. In his opinion, the magistrate's decision was wrong in law, and the case must go back to him to be heard.[88] Judge Lawrence concurred with Judge Bray and further added the following:

> I do not agree with him in thinking the words 'his' towards the end of the third paragraph of S.1, sub-s. (1) applies only to the

> agent. It applies to either the agent or the giver of the document according to circumstances. If it applied only to the agent, the position would be redundant, for the necessity of the agent doing the act 'knowingly' with intent to deceive his principal.[89]

The second English case, *Regina v. Tweedie*,[90] discussed a similar provision in section 5 of the Tanzania PCA. The employee in the case falsified the employer's document that was prepared for internal accounting purposes—was any offence committed under the Prevention of Corruption Act 1906?[91]

Section 1 (1) of the Prevention of Corruption Act (1906) dealt in the first paragraph with the acceptance of bribes;[92] in the second paragraph, it dealt with the giving of bribes;[93] and the third paragraph provided as follows:

> If any person knowingly gives to any agent, or if any agent knowingly uses with intent to deceive his principal, any receipt, account, or other document in respect of which the principal is interested, and which contains any statement which is false or erroneous or defective in any material particular, and which to his knowledge is intended to mislead the principal; he shall be guilty of an offence.[94]

The facts of this case were that an employee of a company dealing in precious metals was instructed by his employers to sell a quantity of silver and platinum as the market was likely to fall, but he failed to do so. The following day, the market fell; the employer handed to a member of the employer's accounting staff a trading sheet falsely showing the sale of a quantity of silver and platinum. From that trading sheet, the accounts department would make out invoices and the dealing accounts with customers. The employee was arraigned on an indictment, which, by count 2, charged him with corruption, contrary to section 1 (1) of the Prevention of Corruption Act. He was subsequently convicted. On allowing appeal against conviction, Lawton Drake, LJ, and Hob House, JJ, held that since the first two paragraphs of section 1 (1) of the Prevention of Corruption Act referred to dishonest conduct by an employee with a third party affecting the employer, and since the ordinary meaning of 'receipt' and 'account' in the third paragraph referred to interparties documents, the words 'or other documents' on their true construction also referred to documents passing between parties; accordingly, since the trading sheet on which the appellant had given false details of the sale of precious metals was an internal document of the company that did not pass to a third person, the appellant's deception of his employers did not amount to an offence under the section.[95]

The case of *Sage v. Eicholz*[96] was cited and applied with approval. Lawton, LJ, reading judgment on behalf of his brethren, made the following statement:

> As pointed in SAGE v EICHOLZ (1919) 2K.B. 171, the word 'corruptly' from the third branch of this subsection—is deliberately omitted from the third that omission is to my mind readily explained by the fact that it is frequently found impossible to prove that an agent has been corrupted; and in view of that difficulty it was thought sufficient, in order to establish an offence on the part of the giver, to prove that he knowingly gave to an agent a document which contained a statement that was false, erroneous, or defective, intending it to mislead the principal, to prove the agent, knowing that the document was false, used it with intent to deceive his principle. We accept and adopt what was said in that case.[97]

The court concluded further that the document relied upon by the prosecution was one that intended to go to a third party. It had none of the characteristics of an interparties document. It did not acquire these characteristics merely because its existence started the procedures by which interparties documents would come into existence. If the prosecution's contention were right, the third paragraph would apply to any false document knowingly used by an employee with the intent to deceive or mislead his employers. An employee who put a false entry on a time sheet would be guilty of an offence under the 1906 act. Parliament could not have intended that this should be so. The court adjudged that the third paragraph did not apply to the facts of this case.[98]

The repealed section 6 of PCA, cap. 329, which is now embodied in section 22 of the PCCA and was likened to the provisions of the penal code,[99] section 317, provides as follows: any person who, being a clerk or servant, or being employed or acting in the capacity or a clerk or servant, does any of the acts following with intent to defraud—that is,

(a) destroys, alters, mutilates, or falsifies any book, document, valuable security, or account that belongs to or is in the possession of the employer, or any entry in any such book, document, or account, or is privy to any such act; or
(b) makes, or is privy to making, any false entry in any such book, document, or account; or
(c) omits, or is privy to omitting, any material particular from any such book, document, or account—is guilty of a felony and is liable to imprisonment for fourteen years.

This penal code offence refers to 'fraudulent false accounting' and cannot be the same as section 22 of the PCCA; otherwise, parliament would have not enacted the provisions of section 22 of the PCCA.

The enactment of the PCCA has included specific provisions relating to embezzlement and misappropriation as a category of corruption offences,[100] which in the repealed cap. 329 were never envisioned.

Section 318 of the penal code provides that

> [a]ny person who, being an officer charged with the receipt, custody or management of any part of the public revenue or property, knowingly furnishes any false statement or return of any money or property received by him or entrusted to his care, or of any balance of money or property in his possession or under his control, is guilty of a misdemeanour and shall be and shall be liable to imprisonment for seven years.

This section covers 'false accounting by a public officer' and should not be likened to the provisions of section 22 of the PCCA, of which the latter intended to deal with the document that passes interparties;

the previous cases demonstrated the actual application of the provisions under section 22 of PCCA.

With this in mind, our law enforcement, the PCCB, and the office of the DPP should now be able to prosecute cases falling under this provision effectively and with certainty of the efficacy of the said provision, by applying circumstantial evidence, which has remained untested at the highest court of the land for the past thirty years or so.

3.7. Section 23: Public Officer Obtaining Advantage Without Lawful Consideration or Without Adequate Consideration

The section provides as follows:

> Any person who, being a public officer, solicits, accepts or obtains or agrees to accept or attempts to obtain for himself or for any other person, any advantage without lawful consideration or for a lawful consideration which knows or has reason to believe to be inadequate, from any person whom he knows or has reason to believe to have been or to be, or to be likely, or about to be, concerned in any matter, or transaction with himself as a public officer, or having any connection with the official functions of himself or of any public officer to whom he is subordinate, or from any person whom he knows or has reason to believe to be interested in or related to or acting for, or on behalf of the person concerned, or having such a connection, shall be guilty of an offence and shall be liable to an imprisonment for a term not exceeding seven years or to a fine not exceeding twenty thousand shillings or to both such imprisonment and such fine, and in addition, the court may order that the amount or value of any advantage received by him or any part thereof, be forfeited.

Inadequacy of consideration received judicial definition in the landmark case of *William Haining v. R.*[101] in a decision of the EACA. The court defined inadequate consideration to mean less than the market value of the thing accepted, and consideration includes a loan. A promise to repay a loan without interest is not an adequate consideration; the accused must prove on balance of probabilities that he or she did not accept the advantage corruptly as an inducement or reward.[102]

It is clear that section 8 of Cap. 400 of the repealed Cap. 329 is akin to section 35 of the PCCA, which transfers the evidential burden of proof to the accused so that the advantage shall be deemed to have been offered or obtained corruptly—and hence involving inducement—unless the contrary is proved. Section 3 of the PCCA defines advantage to include 'valuable consideration of any kind'.

Law, JA, further clarified that the deeming applied both to the consideration having been accepted corruptly, and as an inducement or reward, and the burden of proving the contrary in both these respects, on a balance of probabilities, lies with the accused person.[103]

The issue of evidential burden of proof is again well articulated in the case of *R. v. Girdham*,[104] which is important in corruption cases, particularly where circumstantial evidence is considered. Once it has been proved or admitted that the defendants had received the goods or services from the companies under a bargain or contract, the goods or services were presumed under section 2 of the 1916 act to have been received corruptly, and the burden of proof lay with the defendants to explain the receipt of the goods or services.

R. v. Manners[105] is also a relevant case of considerable importance relating to an agent receiving consideration in the discharge of his official function, where circumstantial evidence as an eyewitness would not normally be present to adduce the relevant evidence. The particulars of the offence were that on or about the seventeenth day of April, 1968, in the jurisdiction of the Central Criminal Court, being an agent of the North Thames Gas Board, the accused corruptly accepted for himself a gift or consideration, namely, the discharge of his debt of £541.5 in respect of the purchase of a Hillman Hunter motor car as an inducement to show favour to J. Murphy and Sons, Ltd., in relation to the business of the North Thames Gas Board.[106] The court held that where it is proved that any money, gift, or other consideration has been paid or given to or received by a person in the employment of His Majesty—or any government department or a public body—by or from a person, or agent of a person, holding or seeking to obtain a contact from His Majesty—or any government department or public body—the money, gift, or consideration shall be deemed to have been paid or given and received corruptly as such inducement or reward, as is mentioned in the act, unless the contrary is proved.[107]

The section was also well articulated in the case of *The DPP v. Jaffari Mfaume Kawawa*[108] that constituent ingredients of an offence of corruption under section 6 of the PCA are as follows: (a) the accused must be a public officer; and (b) solicits or accepts or obtains, or agrees to accept or attempt to obtain, for himself or for any other person, any advantage; and (c) there is no lawful consideration given by him or her, and he or she knows or has reason to believe that lawful consideration that he or she gives is inadequate; and (d) knows or has reason to believe that such advantage is from a person who has been, or is likely or about to be, concerned with him in any matter or transaction as a public officer, or having any connection with his official function or of any public officer to whom he is subordinate, or has reason to believe to be interested or to be related to, action for, or on behalf of the person so connected or having such a connection. 'Consideration' must be valuable and not good, meritorious, or moral consideration based on natural love and affection. 'Adequate consideration' means consideration that is not less than the value of the accepted thing.

The court reproduced the contents of section 7 of the PCA in its holding. There has never been any dissatisfaction by practitioners on this section, and the interpretation of the court on this provision has never raised any controversy if any at all. As we draw a conclusion on the application of section 7 of PCA, the English cases of *R. v. Braithwaite* and *R. v. Girdham*[109] are instructive. Lord Lane, CJ, held that since the word 'consideration' was defined in both the 1906 and 1916 acts as including valuable consideration, it was used in those acts in its legal sense, or connoting the existence of some kind of contract or bargain between the parties in contrast to the situation envisaged by the word 'gift', namely, where there was no such contract or bargain between the parties and therefore no consideration. It followed that, once it was proved or admitted that the defendants had received the goods or services from the companies under a bargain or contract, the goods or services were presumed under section 2 of the 1916 act to have been received corruptly, and the burden of proof then lay with the defendants to explain the receipt of goods or services.[110]

The previously cited cases are relevant to the study of circumstantial evidence because inadequate consideration can be proved in court by adducing evidence that shows the unbroken chain of evidence from several sources or witness.

These cases are also illustrative and lay the foundation of the importance and utility of circumstantial evidence, particularly in corruption cases where such potential utility has never been exploited to its maximum by law enforcement agencies, particularly the PCCB. It is the contention of this study that a witness may lie but circumstances cannot. As for evidence, there is no difference between circumstantial evidence and direct evidence. The only difference is in the proof; the latter directly establishes the commission of the offence, whereas the former does so by placing circumstances, which lead to irresistible inference of guilt, and further it must be such that within human probability, the act must have been done by the accused.

3.8. Requiring Public Officers to Account for Their Acquired Properties

Section 26 of the PCCA may require public officers to give, within such time and in such manner as may be specified in the notice, a full and true account of all or any class of properties that such public officers possess and may also, by the same or subsequent notice, require such public officer to give a true account of how he acquired such property. To ensure that the public officer provides a true account of the property, Section 26 (3) creates an offence for knowingly giving a false account in relation to any property.

The offence that is created by this section is in subsection (3), which states that any public officer who fails to comply with the notice issued to him or her, pursuant to this section, or who knowingly gives a false account in relation to any property, shall be guilty of an offence. This section is straightforward and has raised no complaints regarding its application.

3.9. Section 27: Possession of Unexplained Property

The PCCA has done away with the repealed section 10 of the PCA, which was one of the most difficult offences to investigate given the wording of the section itself, which this study found to be an unnecessary mouthful for the following reasons.

Firstly, it was one of the longest sections in the PCA, covering more than four pages. Secondly, it has been applied differently by different HC judges and has been the cause of confusion regarding the correct interpretation of what the law sought to achieve, as this study attempts to show Thirdly, PCB investigators were insisted upon to prove that the properties alleged to have been acquired by the suspected public officer must have been 'corruptly acquired', or that such benefit of services been 'corruptly received', and the suspected public officer must satisfy the court that he or she did not 'corruptly acquire' the property, or did not 'corruptly receive the benefit of services'.

The EACA, in the case of *DPP v. Felician Tibakweitira*,[111] was of the view that where an official is found to be in possession of property apparently disproportionate to his means, he or she may have acquired it by corruption or in some way that is illegal but not necessarily corrupt, or possibly in a way that, although not illegal, might be regarded as discreditable.[112] This sort of interpretation has rendered the PCCB work most onerous because that interpretation creates a loophole in favour of the defendant.

In another case, *John Kachuri v. R.*,[113] Lugakingira, AgJ (as he then was), held that before the burden shifts to the defence in offences involving being in possession of property corruptly acquired contrary to section 9 (1) of the PCA, the following two stages must be covered:

(a) There must be reasonable suspicion that the accused corruptly received the property found in his possession; and

(b) The prosecution must adduce evidence showing that the property was acquired in circumstances suspiciously like those of corruption.

Another case on the same issue is that of *Ben Zuberi Mwamba v. R.*,[114] D'souza, AgJ, held as follows:

(a) To prove corruption is not enough to simply show that the property was acquired illegally or through discreditable means, because such property may not necessarily be corruptly acquired;
(b) Failure by the accused to explain how he or she acquired the property will not in itself justify an inference that it was corruptly acquired;
(c) An official found in possession of property apparently disproportionate to his or her means of income may have acquired it by corruption, or in some way that is illegal or discreditable; and
(d) Before the burden of proof shifts to the defence in offences involving being in possession of property corruptly acquired, there must be reasonable suspicion of corruption or unlawful acquisition.

However, the CA of Tanzania took a different approach from that of the HC, as we observe in *Gaiden Nelson Mapunda v. R.*,[115] holding that where a public officer is found with property whose value is disproportionate to his or her own known sources of income, there is a prima facie case of corruption. The burden of proving that the property has not been corruptly acquired is upon the accused and the standard of proof is on a balance of probabilities.[116]

It is critical to elaborate at this point why there is a distinction between standard of proof and evidential burden of proof, because it has raised some concerns in other fora where human rights activists have perceived evidential of proof on the part of the accused as an encroachment to his or her fundamental rights as provided for under the constitution.

Section 112 of the Tanzania Evidence Act[117] clearly stipulates that the burden of proof as to any particular fact lies on that person who wished the court to believe in its existence, unless it is provided by any law, the proof of which shall be with any particular person.[118]

It should be said from the outset that, while the presumption of innocence is fundamental, it is not an absolute right immune from derogation; such exceptions are found in certain criminal offences such as corruption. The PCCA is clear on such exceptions.[119]

Alfred Rupert Neale Cross clarified further on the meaning of burden of proof, stating that the nature of the burden of proof is obscured by the use of the term in a number of different senses, which are distinguished. The key to clarity in this whole area lies in the precise definition and discrimination of the issues to be tried and of the facts upon whose determination they depend.[120]

According to Cross, the legal burden of proof is the obligation of a party to meet the requirements of a rule of law that a fact in issue be proved or disproved either by the preponderance of evidence or beyond reasonable doubt, as the case may be.[121]

This is what is known as the legal burden—that is, the obligation of a party to meet the legal requirements of proof. Lord Denning coined this phrase 'legal burden'.[122] Phipson referred to it as the burden of proof on the pleadings.[123]

Dickson, CJ of the Canadian Supreme Court, described this as chaos and brought order to bear in *R. v. Shwartz*,[124] where he stated that the party who has the persuasive burden is required to persuade the trier of fact that a certain set of facts existed. Failure to persuade means that the party loses. The party with an evidential burden is not required to convince the trier of fact of anything, only to point out evidence that suggests that certain facts existed. The phrase 'onus of proof' should be restricted to the persuasive burden, since an issue can be put into play without being proven. It is important not to identify the evidential burden solely with the accused. The crown has the evidential burden of leading evidence—which, if believed, would prove each element of the offence charged. If the crown does not even meet this evidential requirement, the case never goes to the trier of fact; the accused has a right to a directed verdict of acquittal.[125]

Nonetheless, the English leading and landmark case of *Woolmington v. Director of Public Prosecution*[126] is instructive. The facts of this case can be summarised as follows. Reginald Woolmington's wife, Violet, left him to live with her mother. The defendant visited his wife Violet to convince her to return. On 10 December 1934, the defendant cycled round to their house in an attempt to induce her to return home. The next-door neighbour, a Mrs. Smith, heard the sound of a gun at about 9:30 a.m., and as she looked around, she saw the defendant mount his bicycle and ride away. Mrs. Smith entered the neighbour's home and found the dead body of Violet. A note was later found in the defendant's coat pocket, which suggested that he intended to kill his wife and then himself. The CA of England, Lord Viscount Sankey, dismissing the accused's appeal, explained the meaning of burden of proof on the part of the defendant in the following terms.

> Where intent is an ingredient of a crime there is no onus on the defendant to prove that the act alleged was accidental. Throughout the web of the English criminal Law one golden thread is always to be seen, that it is the duty of the prosecution to prove the prisoner's guilt subject to what I have already said as to the defence of insanity and subject also to any statutory exception. If at the end of and on the whole of the case, there is reasonable doubt, created by the evidence given by either the prosecution or the prisoner, as to whether the prisoner killed the deceased with a malicious intention, the prosecution has not made out the case and the prisoner is entitled to an acquittal.[127]

Deducing from this cases, it is clear that there is no shifting of the standard of proof; rather, there is onus of evidential burden on the part of the accused. Nonetheless, where the offence demands 'intent' as a necessary ingredient of a crime, the prosecution must prove that there was intention, and the standard is the same—beyond reasonable doubt.

However, where there is statutory exception to the general common-law rule that dispenses intention in the commission of a crime, and then the evidential burden applies to the accused. Nonetheless, the legal burden or standard of proof does not change on the part of prosecution to prove its case beyond reasonable doubt, no matter what.

It is also a settled principle of law that, although the prosecution bears the burden of adducing sufficient evidence to raise the issue of its existence beyond reasonable doubt, the accused bears also the burden of adducing evidence on a reasonable possibility of the existence of the defence.[128]

It should be noted further that the offence under section 9 of the PCA was the result of the investigation conducted in compliance with sections 8, 12, or 13 of the PCA.[129] Finally, section 27 of the PCCA has taken into account the mandatory provisions of UNCAC and the best practices to replace the complicated section 10 offences under the PCA.

3.10. Whistle-Blower and Witness Protection

The importance of having whistle-blower protection has been echoed in many forums where citizens have questioned their safety against the powerful corrupt elements in our society, who resort to retaliatory measures to the extent of threatening or harming innocent citizens who volunteer to report corruption incidents within their precinct.

Section 51 of the PCCA provides protection to whistle-blowers, including informers: no information relating to commission of an offence in relation to corruption shall be admitted in evidence, whether under civil litigation or criminal prosecution. A whistle-blower can be defined as including an individual member of the public reporting, through her conscience, corrupt elements in society and their activities, to save and prevent the general public from harm that corruption inflicts upon.

A whistle-blower and a witness to corruption incidents are important partners in the fight against corruption because they send a warning alarm that a crime is being or likely to be committed, and they must be protected by law. Remedies must be availed to them, particularly when they are disposed to abuse by the corrupt and powerful suspects of corruption and other crimes, who in turn use their public office and or their money to turn the scales against these victims of crime. The need to protect these potential victims of corruption is founded on their dignity, and the best interest of our criminal justice system is to secure their cooperation in such a way that their dignity and humanity is respected.

Section 52 of the PCCA provides such protection to witnesses, experts, and victims of corruption-related matters. The law shields them from being treated as accomplices by reason of receiving, making payment, or delivering any advantage on behalf of an accused person.

By protection, we are concerned with their right to speech, life, and liberty so as to shield them from any form of hardship, abuse, neglect, or retaliation—including physical, psychological, mental, and emotional abuse of any form, as well as demotion. These victims of crime have the right of reparation, which includes achieving full redress, reintegration, and recovery from the suffering sustained. They are entitled to compensation programmes that the government should make clear in its policy and legislation.

3.11. Corrupt Electoral Practices

This is an area that has raised a lot of public concern, particularly on *takrima*—that is, voter buying, which has received parliamentary legitimacy in recent years. Section 115 of the Elections Act (1985)[130] created an offence of bribery, treating, or undue influence. Section 116 imposes a penalty for impersonating—or aiding, abetting, counselling, or procuring the commission of the offence of impersonation. Section 117 (1) of the Election Act disqualified any person who is convicted of a corrupt practice, during a period of five years from the date of conviction, from being registered as a voter or from voting at any election under the act or any other written law.

Section 118 created the offence of bribery before or during the campaign period where any person who directly or indirectly—or by any other person on his behalf—gives, lends, or agrees to give or to lend, or offers promises, or promises to procure—or to endeavour to procure—any money or valuable consideration to or for any voter, or to or for any other person, in order to induce any voter to vote or to refrain from voting, or who corruptly does any such act on account of such voter having voted or refrained from voting at any election.[131]

Treating was defined to mean every person who, before or during the campaign period—directly or indirectly—by himself, his agent, or by his political party on his behalf, gives or procures—or agrees to give or to procure, or to endeavour to procure—any office, place, or employment to or for any voter, or to or for any person on behalf of any voter—or to or for any other person—in order to induce such voter to vote or to refrain from voting, or who corruptly does any such act on account of such voter having voted or refrained from voting at any election.[132]

What are even more interesting are the provisions of subsection 2 of section 118, which stated, '[T]his section shall not extend to any money paid or agreed to be paid for or on account of any expenses lawfully and *bonafide* incurred at or concerning any election'.

Subsection 3 of section 118 further legalised bribery, as it provided as follows:

> Where it is alleged that the act constituting bribery was committed by an agent or any other person on behalf of the candidate, it shall be a defence for the candidate if he proves that it was committed without his knowledge, consent or approval or that of his agent.[133]

Subsection 4 of section 118 further blessed voter buying as follows:

> For the purposes of this section, an act or transaction shall not be deemed to constitute bribery if it is proved to have been designed to advance the interests of community fund raising, self-help, self-reliance, or social welfare projects within the constituency and to have been done before the campaign period.[134]

Section 119 (1) of the act created a treating offence where a person corruptly—by himself or by any other person—either before, during, or after an election, directly or indirectly gives or provides, or pays wholly or in part, the expense of giving or providing food, drink, entertainment, or provisions to or for any person for the purpose of corruptly influencing that person to vote or to refrain from voting at such election; the one who accepts or takes such food, drink, entertainment, or provision shall be guilty of the offence of 'treating'.

However, subsection 2 of section 119 legalised 'treating' in that anything done in good faith as an act of normal or traditional hospitality shall be deemed not to be treating.[135]

Section 120 covered undue influence in that, where use of threats, force, or violence—or restraint—inflicts, or threatens to inflict, any temporal or spiritual injury, damage, harm, or loss upon or against any voter in order to induce or to compel such voter to vote or refrain from voting at any election through abduction, duress, or any fraudulent contrivance shall be guilty of undue influence.[136]

Section 121 of the act created offences of bribery, treating, and undue influence in favour of members and officers of the electoral commission. It was submitted that, by enacting *takrima*—vote-buying provisions—parliament had legitimised bribery and corruption in the electoral process, and it is my further submission that parliament should amend such offending provisions and strike them out from the statute of elections.[137]

Gaudens P. Mpangala observed that corruption in the political process happens when established laws, rules, and procedures for a particular process are bent or violated for personal advantage or for the advantage of one's political party. Such political processes in the election include registration of voters, nomination of candidates, campaigns, voting, counting of votes, and announcement of results.[138]

The findings of the PCCB during the 2000 general elections concluded that traditional hospitality was granted in the form of cash, food, or other valuable goods. The givers concerned argued that the issuing of those items to voters in good faith was not regarded as corruption. However, it was not easy to distinguish between good faith and other types of treating. Normal hospitality granted in the electoral laws contributed greatly to increased corruption in various elections where candidates deceived people under the umbrella of hospitality. Most people seem to be forced to accept bribery in the form of hospitality to elect leaders who otherwise would not have been their choice.[139]

For the purposes of analogy, the U.S. Supreme Court, while confronted with a similar problem of political corruption in election in the case of *United States v. United Auto Workers*,[140] observed that corruption in elections leaves the perception of impropriety unanswered, and the cynical assumption that large donors call the tune could jeopardise the willingness of voters to take part in democratic governance. Democracy works only if the people have faith in those who govern, and that faith is bound to be shattered when high officials and their appointees engage in activities that arouse suspicion of malfeasance and corruption.[141]

The court concluded with the following words:

> Electoral competition is another central component of democratic governance. In many respects, the ultimate weapon of public accountability in a democratic system is the ability of citizens to remove political actors through elections. And, electoral competition is the mechanism that keeps accountability viable. High levels of campaign spending pose a threat to such competition because large incumbent war chests lend to discourage serious challengers.[142]

The same is true in Tanzania during elections. In the landmark petition to challenge as unconstitutional sections 98 (2) and 98 (3) of the Electoral Law (Miscellaneous Amendment) act no. 4 of 2000—The Legal and Human Rights Centre (LHRC) 1st Petitioner, Lawyers' Environmental Action Team (LEAT) 2nd Petitioner, National Organization For Legal Assistance (NOLA) 3rd Petitioner against The Attorney General, the Respondent[143]—the HC of Tanzania dealt at length with the issue of African hospitality during elections, which is commonly known as *takrima*.

In that case, the main issue for the court to decide was whether to annul that part of act no. 4 of 2000, which amended section 98 (2)—now section 119 (2) (R.E. 2002) of the Elections Act, cap. 343—by deleting and replacing it with a new subsection and adding a new subsection 3. According to the petitioners, the impugned provisions were volatile of articles 13 (1)–(2), 21 (1)–(2), and 29 (1) of the Constitution of the United Republic of Tanzania on the grounds that they encouraged corruption in elections and impinged on the right to equality before the law and the citizen's right to vote and be voted for in fair and free elections. Further, the provisions also infringed several international human rights instruments to which Tanzania is a party. The court was presided over by three judges—Kimaro, Massati, and Mihayo, JJ—who dealt at length with the controversial issue of vote buying, or *takrima*.

Judge Mihayo was of the opinion that *takrima* provisions in an election were discriminatory because they sought to legalise an action in relation to one group of the society, which would be illegal if done by another in the same society. The judge was of the firm view that African hospitality has been known for ages. It does not need codification. It is priceless, humble, and timeless. It does not resurface with the advent of elections. If this happens, it ceases to be African hospitality. It becomes business. In pure African hospitality, it is the host who entertains mostly relatives and friends—not the guest.[144]

The court struck out the *takrima* provisions in the Elections Act, on the basis that the said provisions were unnecessary and created classes on what should be a level playing field, thus favouring the financially well to do and thus offending the constitutional provisions of articles 13 (1)–(2) and 21 (1)–(2) of the Constitution of United Republic of Tanzania.[145] Judge Kimaro wrote the judgment on behalf of her brethren. The cases of *Rev. Christopher Mtikila v. Attorney General*[146] and *Julius Ishengoma Francis Ndyanabo v. Attorney General*[147] featured prominently as supporting authority for disposing the locus standing issue, as challenged by the attorney general, that corporations and corporate entities are not natural persons within the assigned and intended meaning in the Elections Law. The court held that the definition of the term *person* was given by the Interpretation of Laws Act[148] to include corporate bodies like petitioners in that instant case.

Judge Kimaro concluded that the *takrima* provisions were not necessary at all and there was no lawful object intended to be achieved by the *takrima* provisions apart from legalising corruption in election campaigns. It is not a societal interest that *takrima* be legalised because it is discriminatory between high-income earners and low-income earners, and it fosters selected classes of persons to have an advantage in the electoral process, thus negating the intended goal of free and fair elections. The majority of the poor are manipulated through *takrima* to cast their votes during elections. It was therefore hoped that the parliament in Tanzania would carry out the necessary amendments to the Electoral Law after the HC struck out the offending provisions of *takrima*.

3.12. Valuation of Property Corruptly Acquired

Section 49 of the PCCA set out the criteria for carrying out valuations of properties that are being investigated on corruption allegations. Where the subject matter involves a building, the method of valuation shall be market value of building materials at the time of construction or actual construction value. In case the building was purchased, the method of valuation shall be the actual price of purchase or market value of such building or property.

The CA has in the past dealt with such issues. Mwakasendo, JA (as he then was), in the case of *Edom Godfrey Mlinga v. R.*,[149] expounded the meaning of market value as follows: 'Market value is determined by the local conditions and market value of the properties in the area at the material time'.[150]

ENDNOTES

1. The PCCA, no. 11 of 2007, which came into force on 1 July 2007 through GN no. 153 of 22 June 2007.
2. HC of Tanzania Economic Criminal Appeal no. 2 of 2003 (Dar Es salaam registry) originating from Economic Case no. 77 of 1998 of the resident magistrates' court at Kisutu, Dar es Salaam (unreported). It is also sad to note that Judge Mwaikugile rendered his decision in this case in 2007 while he heard the appeal in 2003. Five years later, the decision was rendered while the defendants had already served their jail term of five years.
3. See table 3 and chart 2 in chapter 4 of this study.
4. See *Rai Newspaper* dated 5–11 July 2007, the article 'Mawaziri waache kuwalinda wabadhirifu' by Elias Msuya, which reinforces the widely held belief that the government has dealt with small fish only, and remain complacent to dealing with the big fish. Transparency and accountability on corruption and governance issues remains one of the serious concerns by the general public.
5. Economic and Organised Crime Control Act no. 13 of 1984.
6. *Abdul Muganyizi v. R.* (1980) TLR no. 263, *Mswahili Mulugala v. R.* (1977) LRT no. 25, *Sharmpal Singh v. R.* (1960) EA 762 (CA), *August Mahiyo v. R.* (1993) no. 117 (CA), *Hamdu Mussa Thimotheo and Majid Mussa Thimotheo v. R.* (1993) TLR no. 125, *Dhalay v. R.* (1997) LLP 514 (CAK), *Kipkering Arap Koske and Another v. R.* (1949) EACA Report 135.
7. Ratant Lal and Dhiraj Lal, *The Law of Evidence*, 21st ed. reprint (New Delhi, India: Wadwa and Company Nagpur Publishers, 2006), 75.
8. Ibid.
9. Ibid., 75–76.
10. UK Judicial Studies Board Web site at http://www.jsboard.co.uk/criminal_law/cbb/mf_04.htm.
11. *R. v. Stephen Dominic Mtetewaunga* (1986), HC Economic Crimes Case no. 5 of 1986, Dar es Salaam Registry (unreported).
12. The CAT, Criminal Appeal no. 3 of 1990, decided by Makame, Ramadhani, and Mnzavas, Justices of Appeal, Dar es Salaam Registry (unreported).
13. Ibid.
14. *Mtetewaunga*.
15. Judge Mapigano made reference to the case of *Ramadhan Masoud v. R.* (1974) LRT 31, 114.

16. (1981) TLR 149.
17. *Mtetewaunga.*
18. *Jaffari Mfaume Kawawa.*
19. *Baghdad.*
20. Section 2 of the act.
21. Section 3 of the act.
22. Section 4 of the act.
23. Section 5 of the act.
24. Section 5 (2) of the act.
25. Sections 6 and 7 of the act.
26. Sections 8 and 9 of the act.
27. Sections 10–13 of the act.
28. The report shall contain income and expenditure, and performance of the functions of the bureau for the year ending for scrutiny of the National Assembly.
29. Sections 47–48 of the act.
30. Cap. 329 (R.E. 2000). These offences include corrupt transaction (bribery) as provided under section 4, use of document to mislead the principal in section 6, public officers obtaining advantage without lawful consideration or without adequate consideration in section 7, and being in possession of property corruptly acquired as provided in section 10.
31. Section 16 of the act.
32. Section 17 of the act.
33. Section 18 of the act.
34. Section 19 of the act.
35. Section 20 of the act.
36. Section 21 of the act.
37. Section 25 of the act.
38. Section 27 of the act.
39. Section 28 of the act.
40. Section 29 of the act.
41. Section 30 of the act.
42. Section 31 of the act.
43. Section 32 of the act.
44. Section 33 of the act.
45. Section 34 of the act.
46. Section 35 of the act.
47. Section 36 of the act.
48. Section 37 of the act.

49. Section 38 of the act.
50. Sections 40–44 of the act.
51. Sections 45 and 46 of the act.
52. Sections 47 and 48 of the act.
53. Section 49 of the act.
54. Section 50 of the act.
55. Section 51 of the act.
56. Section 52 of the act.
57. Section 54 of the act.
58. Section 55 of the act.
59. Section 57 of the act.
60. Section 59 of the act.
61. Political Parties Act 1992, cap. 250 (R.E. 2002).
62. National Elections Act 1985, cap. 343 (R.E. 2002).
63. The winding speech to the National Assembly of the Hon. Prime Minister Edward Ngoyai Lowassa at 7th session of Parliamentary debate. See Hansard, Parliamentary Debate 7th sitting, 20 April 2007, Parliament Office, Dodoma.
64. Section 57 (2) of the act.
65. Peter Langseth, discussing the UN Convention against Corruption, UNCDO, Proceedings Document on the Strengthening Judicial Integrity and Capacity in Indonesia, Kendari, 7–8 October 2004.
66. Cap. 329 (R.E. 2002).
67. The Prevention of Corruption Bureau.
68. Section 2 of the PCA, no. 16 of 1971 (as amended), Cap. 329 (R.E. 2002).
69. Act of 2000, Cap. 359, LFN 69.
70. Ibid.
71. *Attorney General v. Shamba Ali Kajembe* (1958) EA 505.
72. *R. v. Hashim Jiwa* (1958) EA 505.
73. (1958) EA 505 Wanjiri m/o Mwiriri.
74. Alex Muganda, *The Prevention of Corruption Act: Its Weaknesses and Suggested Amendments* (1995, Unpublished, 1995).
75. (1970) EA 620.
76. Cap. 400 of the laws of Tanganyika.
77. Ibid.
78. Prevention of Corruption Ordinance, cap. 400. Section 3 (1) provides that 'any person who by himself or by or in conjunction with any other person, corruptly solicits, accepts or obtains, person for himself or for any other person, any advantage as an inducement to, or reward for, or otherwise on

account of, any agent (whether or not such agent is the same person as such first-mentioned person) doing, or forebearing to do, or having done or foreborne to do anything in relation to his principals affairs or business shall be guilty of an offence'.

79. (1967) HCD 442.
80. (1949) 2 All ELR.
81. Ibid.
82. (1967) HCD 62.
83. (1967) HCD 92.
84. Ibid.
85. (1980) TLR 193.
86. Ibid.
87. (1919) 2 KB 171.
88. Ibid.
89. Ibid.
90. The Weekly Law Reports, 13 April 1984.
91. Penal Code, [Cap. 16 R.E. 2002].
92. Ibid.
93. Ibid.
94. Ibid.
95. Ibid.
96. (1919) 2 KB 171.
97. The Weekly Law Reports.
98. A similar provision is section 4 (1) of the PCA, cap. 329 (R.E. 2002).
99. Section 28 of the PCCA.
100. Ibid.
101. (1970).
102. See endnote 206 in this list.
103. [1970] EA 620.
104. [1983] All ER, vol. 2.
105. [1976] All ER, vol. 2.
106. Cap. 16 (R.E. 2002).
107. (1981) TLR 149.
108. Ibid.
109. [1983] All ER, vol. 2.
110. Ibid.
111. [1973] EA 440.
112. Ibid.
113. (1978) LRT no. 27.

114. (1984) TLR no. 172.
115. (1982) TLR 318.
116. Ibid.
117. (Act No. 6 of 1967).
118. Ibid.
119. Section 35 of the PCCA, no. 11 of 2007, provides for presumption of corruption that where an advantage was offered, promised, or given; or solicited, accepted, or obtained—or agreed to be accepted or obtained—by a public official from a person or agent seeking to obtain a contract from public office, such advantage shall be deemed to have been offered, promised, or given; or solicited, accepted, or obtained—or agreed to be accepted—as an inducement or reward, unless the contrary is proved.
120. Cross and Tapper, *Cross on Evidence*, 110.
121. Ibid.
122. Ibid., 112.
123. S. L. Phipson, J. H. Buzzard, and M. N. Howards, eds., *Phipson on Evidence*, 10th ed. (London: Sweet & Maxwell, 1963), 91.
124. (1988) 2 S.C.R. 443, 466.
125. Ibid.
126. [1935] AC 462.
127. Ibid.
128. Ibid.
129. Cap. 329 (R.E. 2002).
130. Act no. 1 of 1985, cap. 343 (R.E. 2002).
131. Ibid.
132. Ibid.
133. Ibid.
134. Ibid.
135. Ibid.
136. Ibid.
137. Ibid.
138. See detailed discussion on elections in Tanzania in Samweli E. Chambua and Vincent Kihiyo, *Multiparty Elections and Corruption in Tanzania* (Dar es Salaam: University Press, 2002), 137.
139. Ibid, 220–221.
140. 352 U.S. 567, 567, IL. ED. 2d 563, 77s. Ct. 529 (1957).
141. Ibid.
142. Ibid.

143. Miscellaneous Civil Cause no. 71 of 2002 (Unreported, HCT, Dar es Salaam).
144. Ibid.
145. The Constitution of United Republic of Tanzania, 1977.
146. [1995] TLR 31. Judge Lugakingira (as he then was) held that *locus standi* is vested in every person in the capacity of an individual by virtue of articles 12–24 of the constitution.
147. CA Civil Appeal no. 64 of 2001 (unreported) that a juristic person may complain to before the HC seeking redress for violation of equality clause under the constitution.
148. Cap. 1 (R.E. 2002).
149. (1981) TLR. 140.
150. Ibid.

Chapter 4

Theories and Empirical Research on Reliability of Circumstantial Evidence

4.1. The Case for Circumstantial Evidence

In the previous chapter, we dealt with the analytical framework and the judicial interpretation of the law against corruption in Tanzania. Special attention was given to the relevant provisions of the PCCA.

In the present chapter, attention is devoted to the central theme of this study, namely, that circumstantial evidence is a potent tool in determining corruption cases. It is shown in this chapter that the traditional school of thought founded on common law has overly emphasised that direct evidence is better evidence than circumstantial evidence.

The findings of this study highlight arguments why the traditional common-law school of thought is not altogether correct, particularly where empirical evidence has demonstrated instances in which the terror of an eyewitness has caused the miscarriage of justice through over reliance on the *direct evidence paradigm*.

The law of evidence recognises the importance of both direct and circumstantial evidence during court trials in both civil and criminal cases. However, there has been a remarkable reliance on direct over circumstantial evidence among legal practitioners and laymen alike with respect to the efficacy and reliability of the two types of evidence. It is the central intention of this chapter to discuss and show how that overreliance could be levelled.

The research findings shown in tables 3 and 4 and chart 2, following them, demonstrate that the direct evidence paradigm is still strong in the perceptions of many respondents interviewed by the researcher. Eight sample locations were identified and the following tables sum up the actual perception of different people from all types of occupations.

The research findings corroborate the common-law understanding of the direct evidence paradigm that is perceived to be more reliable than circumstantial evidence.

On this basis, it is worth noting that circumstantial evidence has to be brought to the fore—to be understood and captured in its essence—in order to enhance the quality of prosecuting corruption cases that are

TABLE 3. Circumstantial evidence survey in Tanzania: 2005.

No.	District	No. of Respondents	Knowledge of What Corruption Is	Reliability of Direct Evidence	Reliability of Circumstantial Evidence
1	Newala	50	46	40	1
2	Tandahimba	30	23	27	1
3	Masasi	60	54	49	2
4	Lindi	67	50	52	2
5	Maswa	54	39	33	1
6	Lushoto	20	15	16	3
7	Tanga	15	10	9	2
8	Mwanza	30	20	24	1
	Total	326	257	250	13

Source. Research data.

Table 4. Percentage of respondents.

No.	District	Knowledge of What Corruption Is	Reliability of Direct Evidence	Reliability of Circumstantial Evidence
1	Newala	92	80	2
2	Tandahimba	77	90	3
3	Masasi	90	82	3
4	Lindi	75	78	3
5	Maswa	72	61	2
6	Lushoto	75	80	15
7	Tanga	67	60	13
8	Mwanza	67	80	3
	Average	79	77	4

Source. Research data.

Chart 2. Reliability of evidence.

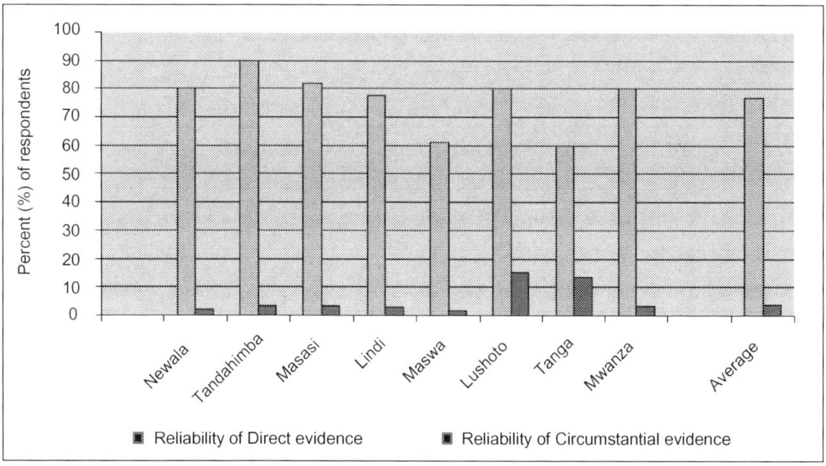

Source. Research data.

brought to the courts of law for adjudication. The preceding survey was conducted in eight geographically spread districts of Mainland Tanzania with the objective of gauging the perception of corruption by the general population. Four districts were selected from the southern parts of the country (Newala, Tandahimba, Lindi, and Masasi). Two districts from the lake zone (Maswa and Mwanza) and two districts from the northern coastal zone (Lushoto and Tanga). The following themes were covered: knowledge of what corruption is, and the relative reliability of direct and circumstantial evidence in the prosecution of corruption cases.

There were 326 respondents subjected to this empirical study, the results of which are tabulated in the preceding tables 3 and 4, together with the corresponding chart 2, which follows. Survey results and conclusions indicate that 79 percent of the respondents knew about corruption, which signifies a high level of understanding of corruption by the general public.

Regarding the relative reliability of evidence, direct evidence scored more highly (77 percent) than circumstantial evidence (4 percent). These results seem to correspond to the common-law traditional view that direct evidence is more reliable than circumstantial evidence since, without eyewitness proof, it is not possible to reach a fair conclusion.

It is against this backdrop that, in this chapter, our focus now turns to the bedrock of this study. We propose to demonstrate the potential efficacy of circumstantial evidence by using empirical evidence and research findings from several scholars on the subject of eyewitness evidence; it is demonstrated that authentication of writings, for example, can be proven by circumstantial evidence. The flaws of the eyewitness paradigm of direct evidence are exposed and subjected to scrutiny.

Attention is given to eyewitness error and judges' misconceptions of eyewitness testimony to amplify the fact that circumstantial evidence is as good as direct witness evidence, if not better in certain circumstances. In addition, it is shown in the chapter that judges mistake witness confidence as an indicator for eyewitness accuracy in determining the reliability and hence the admissibility of direct evidence. The testimony of an expert witness is also discussed and analysed in the light of the deficiencies identified in the testimony of eyewitness error. Empirical evidence provides substantial reason to doubt the assumption placed on the direct evidence paradigm, as is shown in this chapter.

At the end of this chapter, a survey of cases on the application of circumstantial evidence by the U.S. Supreme Court is examined for its wider application and a recognition of its utility, on the one hand, and East African Courts with limited application in murder cases, on the other. The U.S. experience is tapped into for the purposes of identifying the realities of the utility of circumstantial evidence in complex cases of white-collar crimes generally, which have a bearing on the proposed conclusion of this study as to its potential application in Tanzania. The correlation with corruption cases is evident because corruption is a white-collar crime, and its investigation to unearth the required evidence is very complex, particularly when one is dealing with high-profile or grand corruption cases.

The utility of circumstantial evidence becomes of apparent potential since the commission of corruption offences is highly shrouded in secrecy, and parties to the offence would rather remain silent—with their tracks untraceable—when the wheels of investigation move in search for the truth. Therefore, it is critical that circumstantial evidence is explored here at length to ensure that the so-called distinction between direct and circumstantial evidence is exposed, its weakness revealed, and a level playing field restored.

4.2. Direct Evidence

In judicial trials, whether criminal or civil, parties to the case have two possible ways to persuade the trier of facts or tribunal as to the proposition at issue. Firstly, the parties will present the thing itself to which persuasion is desired, and, secondly, the presentation of some independent facts by inference from which the persuasion is produced. On the first instance, Wigmore demonstrated direct evidence as follows: the instances are the production of a bloodstained knife, the exhibition of an injured limb, the viewing of the premises by the jury, or the production of a document.[1]

On the second instance, Wigmore informed that the distinction between the two classes depends on whether the basis of inference is the assertion of a human being as to the existence of the thing at issue or the basis of inference is any other fact. The one class is termed 'testimonial' or direct evidence, the other circumstantial or 'indirect evidence'.[2]

With reference to the first mode of production of evidence—or, put differently, producing persuasion—no question of relevance arises because *the thing* proves or disproves itself—*res ipsa loquitor*.[3]

Steven M. Tindall argued from common-law perspectives that direct evidence is evidence that, if believed, resolves a matter at issue without the need for an inference. Direct evidence is usually equated with eyewitness testimony where the witness actually saw or heard that which is intended to be proved. With circumstantial evidence, by contrast, additional reasoning is required to reach the proposition to which it is directed.[4]

This is where the distinction between direct evidence and circumstantial evidence has to be analytically clarified. The preceding survey has demonstrated clearly that the general belief is that the direct evidence paradigm is seen as more reliable than circumstantial evidence.

Common law distinguishes between two types of relevant evidence: direct and circumstantial. Direct evidence is defined as evidence that, if believed, establishes an essential element because no inferences other than those pertaining to the credibility of the eyewitness mediate between the evidentiary fact, the fact of consequence, and the essential element,[5] whereas for circumstantial evidence, the connection between evidentiary fact and an essential element is not so immediate and may require many intervening inferences.[6]

It is important, therefore, to carry out an analysis to establish whether the alleged difference between the two types of evidence is of substance. Allen et al. analysed further that there is no difference between direct and circumstantial evidence because both require inferential reasoning. Direct evidence establishes an essential element only if the jury or the court believes the eyewitness, and this requires inferential reasoning about the ability of the eyewitness to have observed the event correctly. Those standard issues of credibility must be resolved by the fact finder in order to evaluate any testimonial evidence, and they are the kinds of issues about which people use natural reasoning constantly in their everyday lives. Generally speaking, then, what distinguishes circumstantial from direct evidence is the length of the inferential chain.[7] Most importantly, the labels 'direct' and 'circumstantial' do not reflect the probative force of evidence. Circumstantial evidence can often be more reliable than direct evidence.

A fingerprint or blood spot found on a murder weapon, identified by fingerprint analysis or DNA testing as the defendant's, is an example of very accurate circumstantial evidence, and is probably more reliable than many eyewitnesses.[8]

The preceding analysis by the scholars referred to shows clearly that the so-called distinction between direct and circumstantial evidence has not, as a matter of fact, any probative force. Their distinction is a matter of degree and not of substance, and hence the view that direct evidence is more reliable than circumstantial evidence is of no merit or substance at all.

The common-law tradition seems to have treated direct evidence as superior to circumstantial evidence. However, the Tanzania Evidence Act (1967) does not provide for this. It is in fact the courts that have developed the interpretation of jurisprudence of the rules of evidence. Our study therefore makes the contribution that circumstantial evidence is an important tool or resource to be used in corruption cases, as discussed in the introductory chapter.

The sources for the law of evidence are (a) witness testimony, (b) documentary evidence, and (c) the thing, object, or exhibit. The production of the sources of the law of evidence is through direct and circumstantial evidence. The general approach to the admission of the hearsay exception—that is an out-of-court statement admitted into evidence to prove the matters they assert—is to admit such out-of-court statements presented by a witness only under certain conditions, assuming that they are otherwise unobjectionable. Such out-of-court statement is admitted through the testimony of a witness who overheard a conversation or through an exhibit that contains it—such as a document in which the statement is written or a tape or some other recording of it.

The correlation between direct and circumstantial evidence is a matter of degree and not of substance because, in the production of evidence in court, one may use either of the two or a combination of both. The linkage to hearsay evidence is only possible to the extent of the exception to the general rule of evidence that hearsay is no evidence. Hearsay is one person's statement that is offered to prove the matter asserted by the statement; it is a personal statement made at a time other than while the person is testifying at the hearing in which the statement is offered, and it is offered to prove the truth of the statement. Hearsay policy is to exclude such hearsay statements because there is no oath, no observation of demeanour, and no opportunity to cross-examine the hearsay declarant to determine whether there is sincerity, narration ambiguity, perception, or memory problems.

Res gestae, meaning 'things done', is often used to justify the admission of a broader context to an important incident. Courts admit some testimony that may not seem to have any obvious connection to any fact of consequence in the case, whereas circumstantial evidence is founded on clues, traces, and signs—the things we do not know; that is, we reconstruct an event that we did not actually witness. For example, we wake up one morning to find the ground outside is wet; we will probably infer that it must have rained during the night, even if we did not see or hear it rain. Whenever we form a belief that an event occurred—and we do so not on the basis of our own or someone else's perception of the event, but on the basis of clues or signs that suggest that the event must have occurred—we are relying on circumstantial evidence. The point here is that, while in the former case, we rely on past experience, in the latter, we do not. In corruption cases, circumstantial evidence includes disposition, motive, preparatory acts, knowledge, opportunity, suspicious behaviour, silence, or lies of the suspect.

4.3. Classification of Circumstantial Evidence

In one of his works, Wigmore, the professor of law of evidence respected worldwide, contended that the starting point of the classification of circumstantial evidence should be the proposition to be proved rather than the evidentiary fact offered.[9] That means the issue of relevance comes to fore, whether the claimed conclusion is a probable inference from the offered fact.

'Relevant evidence' means evidence having any tendency to make the existence of any fact that is of consequence to the determination of the action more or less probable than it would be without the evidence.[10]

Wigmore further expounded as follows:

> Since the purpose of using evidence is to confirm or deny a proposed conclusion, it is the conclusion to which evidence must be related in order to define the types of evidence in functional terms. This relationship is determined by the inference that can be properly drawn from the evidentiary proposition If the proposed conclusion is D Killed H; and the witness testifies, 'I saw D kill H', The evidence is direct because it is the basis of direct inference which coincided with the proposed conclusion; and the inference is the only relative to the proposed conclusion that can be properly drawn. Thus, the evidentiary proposition 'I saw D kill H' is consistent only with the proposed conclusion, 'D killed H'.[11]

On circumstantial evidence, Wigmore explained with clarity that the functional meaning of circumstantial evidence is determined in the same manner as the meaning of direct evidence by ascertaining the relationship of the evidentiary proposition to the proposed conclusion. If the proposed conclusion is 'D killed H', and the evidence is the proposition that 'D wrote H's wife a love letter', the evidence is consistent with the conclusion that 'D killed H'. Indeed, it will qualify as evidence, which must be relevant to the proposed conclusion in that it, just as direct evidence, will support an inference that coincides with the proposed conclusion.[12]

In *Commonwealth v. Harman*, Gibson, CJ,[13] held a position he shared with other traditionalists in that case—since no witness was produced who saw that act committed, he concluded that the evidence tendered was only circumstantial and, consequently, entitled to a very inferior degree of credit, if to any credit at all.[14]

But that is not necessarily the case. Drawing attention to reliability of circumstantial evidence, Wigmore propounded that a fact positively sworn to by a single eyewitness of blemished character is not as satisfactorily proved as a fact that is the consequence of a chain of other facts testified to by many witnesses of undoubted credibility, who may have not been at the scene of crime but are in position to relate to the court events about which, through inference, the court is able to draw conclusion regarding what actually happened.[15]

In the case of *Commonwealth v. Webster*,[16] Shaw, CJ, clearly brings out the advantages and disadvantages of both direct and circumstantial evidence. The advantage of positive evidence where there is direct testimony of a witness to the fact to be proved is that, if he speaks the truth, he saw it committed, and thus the only question is whether he is entitled to belief. The disadvantage is that the witness may be false and corrupt, and the case may not afford the means of detecting his falsehood.

In cases relying on circumstantial evidence, where no witness can testify directly to the fact to be proved, if the truth is arrived at by a series of other facts that, through experience, have been found so associated with the fact in question—that is in relation of cause and effect—they lead to a satisfactory and certain conclusion. An example is when footprints are discovered after a recent snow; it is certain that some animated being has passed over the snow since it fell, and from the form and the number of footprints, it can be determined with equal certainty whether they are those of a man, bird, or quadruped. Circumstantial evidence is therefore founded on experience and observed facts and the fact sought to be proved.[17]

The advantage is that the evidence comes from several sources, a chain of circumstances is less likely to be falsely prepared and arranged and falsehood and perjury are more likely to be detected and fail of their purpose. The disadvantages are that a jury has not only to weigh the evidence of facts, but also to draw just conclusions from them, and in so doing, it may be led—by prejudice, partiality, or by want of deliberations and sobriety of judgment—to make hasty and false deductions—a source of error not existing in the consideration of positive evidence.[18]

4.4. Traditional Meaning of Circumstantial Evidence

The traditional meaning of circumstantial evidence is simply evidence of circumstances. The question of relevance is again the operative one in this type of evidence.

Wigmore classified circumstantial evidence thus: for propositions of evidence, relevance exists in terms of inference. Evidence must be relevant to the proposed conclusion, and it is relevant only if it can support an inference that coincides with the proposed conclusion or the contradiction of the proposed conclusion. If a proposition of evidence is such that it can support inferences that coincide with both the proposed conclusion and its contradiction, it is consistent with either. This is always true of evidence of circumstances, and thus circumstantial evidence is a proposition consistent with either the proposed conclusion or its contradiction. The functional meanings of direct and circumstantial evidence thus suggested, then, are not radically different from the traditional meanings of the terms. They result primarily from a more refined analysis of the concepts than is usually accorded them. Thus, instead of classifying direct evidence on the basis of the relationship of the witness who gives the evidence to the fact, which is the basis of the evidence, and circumstantial evidence on the basis of the relationship of the evidence to the proposed conclusion, all evidence should be classified on the same basis. This basis is the relationship of the evidence to the proposed conclusion.[19]

On their part, Allen et al. further explained the meaning and application of circumstantial evidence as an inference in the deduction of fact that may logically and reasonably be drawn from another fact or group of facts established by the evidence. It is not necessary that facts be proved by direct evidence; they may be proved also by circumstantial evidence or by a combination of direct and circumstantial evidence. Both direct and circumstantial evidence are acceptable as a means of proof. Neither is entitled to any greater weight than the other. Further, each fact that is essential to complete a set of circumstances necessary to establish the defendant's guilt must be proved beyond a reasonable doubt. In other words, before an inference essential to establish guilt may be found to have been proved beyond a reasonable doubt, each fact or circumstance upon which such inference necessarily rests must be proved beyond any reasonable doubt.[20]

Sir Rupert Cross, an English writer, also reached the same conclusions regarding circumstantial evidence: if the only evidence that could be adduced were that directly from facts at issue, or direct evidence, many claims would fail for lack of adequate proof. At some stage, resort almost always has to be had to circumstantial evidence, which may be defined as any fact (sometimes called an 'evidentiary fact', 'factum probans' or 'factum probandum'). A typical instance is afforded by the statement of a witness at trial for murder that he saw the accused carrying a bloodstained knife at the door of the house in which the deceased was found mortally wounded.[21]

We can therefore state that circumstantial evidence is evidence that, if found to be true, proves a fact from which an inference of the existence of another fact may be drawn. We can thus draw the following lessons from the different scholars' views above on circumstantial evidence.

(a) Circumstantial evidence is evidence of circumstances, and thus circumstantial evidence is a proposition consistent with either the proposed conclusion or its contradiction.
(b) All evidence should be classified on the same basis. This basis is the relationship of the evidence to the proposed conclusion.

(c) A typical instance is afforded by a statement of a witness at trial for murder that he saw the accused carrying a bloodstained knife at the door of the house in which the deceased was found mortally wounded.

(d) In relation to corruption cases, a typical example is where one's standard of living is higher than the actual earning capacity, including official remuneration and other side income generated through lawful means. The circumstances an individual is found in, and his failure to justify the additional properties and other assets accrued, place circumstantial evidence at the helm of bringing to book those individuals who are engaged in corruption and earn their livelihood corruptly, or who cannot offer any explanation (unexplained property) to justify their possessions.[22]

4.5. Authentication of Writings and Circumstantial Evidence

The Tanzania Evidence Act provided for the proof of due execution of private documents in sections 69–75. Authentication, or identification, as it relates to circumstantial evidence, is a condition precedent to admissibility of writings, as to the fact at issue.[23] The relevance of a piece of writing to a particular issue raised in litigation will frequently be logically dependent upon the existence of some connection between that piece of writing and a particular individual. On the subject, McCormick wrote the following:

> There are various ways in which writings may be authenticated by direct evidence. Nevertheless, it will frequently occur that no direct evidence of authenticity of any type exists or can be found. Resort must then be had to circumstantial proof and it is clear that authentication by circumstantial evidence is uniformly recognized as permissible.[24]

In the authentication of ancient documents or writings under common law, it is sufficient if the party who offers it produces sufficient evidence that the piece of writing is thirty years old,[25] that it is unsuspicious in appearance, and further proves that the writing is produced from a place of custody natural for such a document.

Another application of circumstantial evidence is in the authentication of writings. Where a piece of writing purports to be an official report or record and is proved to have come from the proper public office where that report or record is kept, it is generally agreed that this authenticates the offered document as genuine.[26]

Disclosure of knowledge in replies to letters and telegrammes is another example where circumstantial evidence applies. Considerations concerning the reliability of mail are significant only to demonstrate that the likelihood that the purported author of the response did in fact receive the original communication. Thus, where receipt of the communication referred to in the reply can be established by other means, and the reply is timely received, these facts will be sufficient to authenticate.[27]

Modern technology makes commonplace the receipt of oral communications from persons who are heard but not seen, so that whatever the means of transmission, oral communications today will frequently be perpetuated in some form of recording. Where such is the case, the authentication of the communication is likely to be facilitated simply because otherwise unavailable proof of various kinds may be generated by use of recording. However, it must be constantly borne in mind that authentication does not necessarily equate with admissibility, and the recordings will often raise evidentiary problems other than authentication.[28]

Circumstantial evidence utility is seen in the preceding exceptions related to authentication of writings, and where the calling of attesting witnesses during trial has been dispensed with.

4.6. Weaknesses of the Direct Evidence Paradigm

Witnesses[29] are called to present evidence sufficient enough to arrive at a finding by which the court or jury can establish each element of its cause of action or of the crime charged. The witness must have a personal knowledge of the matters about which he will testify because of his own knowledge based on his own sensory perception.

The eyewitness or percipient witness who was there and perceived the events that took place, or who saw the thing that is the subject matter of the judicial inquiry, is the witness. In order for the court to have sufficient evidence to support a finding, the requirement of a witness that he or she had personal knowledge of the facts at issue is critical and essential. This eyewitness is part and parcel of the direct evidence paradigm that this study analyses in the context of the relationship and distinction, if any at all, between direct and circumstantial evidence.

Other means to produce evidence for the trier of facts are the use of exhibits, including real and demonstrative evidence;[30] documents of all kinds, including electronic and photographic; and data compilations and reproductions. All such exhibits must be shown to be what they are claimed to be before they can be admitted into evidence.[31]

Any exhibit that is submitted must be relevant to providing proof of the facts that are of consequence in the case. According to the relevance theory, Allen et al. contended that for the proponent to articulate a connection between the item and the parties or the litigated events in the case, this connection is typically what courts require the proponents to prove in order to identify or authenticate an exhibit. Although these terms are not defined, 'identification' usually refers to who authored a piece of writing, or whose voice was heard speaking; 'authentication' usually refers to genuineness of the connection between what the exhibit is and the specific facts of the case. Therefore, it follows from the preceding articulation of why tangible objects, photos, or documents are relevant.[32]

The U.S. Federal Rules of Evidence provide guidance to the meaning attached to the following phrase: the witness must have personal knowledge of that matter by evidence 'sufficient to support a finding'.[33] Allen et al. made it explicit that the proponents of a witness must produce evidentiary facts that the judge finds 'sufficient to support a finding' of personal knowledge. That is, a reasonable jury could find that it is more probable than not that the witness has personal knowledge and to satisfy the sufficiency standard; usually, all a proponent needs to do is to ask the witness whether the witness saw or heard the matters that are about to be described to the jury.[34]

By responding to the direct evidence paradigm in the context of an 'eyewitness testimony' as a classic example of direct evidence, Wells and Loftus carried out their scientific research and observed further that testimony by an eyewitness can be an event of profound importance. In one case, it can be the event that saves the community from the terror of future rapes or mugging by being the key evidence against their perpetrator. In another case, it can be the principal basis on which an innocent person is convicted of another's heinous crime. In other words, it has positive effects when it leads to the conviction of guilty people, but it has negative effects when it leads to conviction of the innocent.[35] To put it simply, an eyewitness may err in his testimony and may cause a conviction of an innocent defendant because the court tends to believe eyewitness testimony more easily than evidence by inference.

On his part, Brooke Whisonant Patterson clearly showed that the weakness of eyewitness evidence, which is frequently relied on and justified by the traditional common-law school of thought, is that jurors tend to overly believe eyewitnesses, mistake their confidence as an indicator of accuracy, are insensitive to many factors known to influence a witness' performance, and seem almost unaffected by cross-examinations and cautionary instructions. Jurors mistaking witness confidence for accuracy is a mounting crisis for courts. The external and inner-psychological effects on human memory contribute greatly to the inaccuracy of eyewitness evidence, an urgent problem that must be addressed.[36]

On the same issue of the weakness of the eyewitness paradigm, Stanley Z. Fisher articulated that the plight of men and women who have been convicted of serious crimes, incarcerated, and sometimes sentenced to death has recently come dramatically under national and international attention. A rising tide of prisoner exoneration, a significant number of which relied upon DNA testing, has revealed how miscarriages of justice can result from deficient practices of police interrogation and eyewitness identification.

Inadequate disclosure of exculpatory evidence, acceptance of unreliable 'junk science' and 'snitch' testimony, and ineffective assistance of counsel have taken place in states where the death penalty is permissible.[37]

Fisher, however, made reference to previous works by others—chiefly Edwin Borchard, Michael Radelet, Hugo Bedau, and Constance Putnam—whose works focused on studies of erroneous convictions dating from the early nineteenth century to the late twentieth century.[38]

Fisher showed through empirical studies that eyewitness misidentification has contributed disproportionately to wrong convictions in Massachusetts, just as it has elsewhere. Over half of the fifteen official exonerations involved mistaken eyewitness identification, as did the same proportion of the total number (thirty-three) of wrongful convictions. The demonstrated unreliability of eyewitness identification evidence in these cases necessarily raises doubts about the accuracy of other convictions in the Commonwealth based upon similar evidence.[39]

Fisher's work strengthens the thesis of this book, namely, that direct evidence in criminal trials is not necessarily a more reliable piece of evidence compared to circumstantial evidence.

Raymond Emson made it clearer that circumstantial evidence is an evidentiary fact from which an inference may be drawn, rendering the existence or nonexistence of a fact at issue more probable. The fact at issue is not proved by a witness relating what he or she directly perceived, so circumstantial evidence includes disposition, motive, preparatory acts, knowledge, opportunity, capacity, suspicious behaviour, silence, lies, and so on.[40]

Monika Jain drew the same conclusion in her commentary on eyewitness error, namely, that eyewitness error remains a substantial cause of wrongful convictions. With the fallibility of eyewitness testimony being so high, capital cases that rely on such testimony as evidence should require a quantitative evidentiary standard to be met in order for such evidence to be allowed at trial.[41]

This is what, in Baghdad's case, Judge Mwaikugile did not adequately consider. We have seen the respondents' perception of circumstantial evidence in tables 3 and 4 and chart 2 in this chapter that the public perception seems to indicate that circumstantial evidence is in some way an inferior form of evidence. Indeed, circumstantial evidence may be highly probative or even compelling evidence of what happened on a particular occasion. Emson put it more succinctly: in practice, the prosecution is unlikely to base their entire case on a single item of circumstantial evidence. The value of circumstantial evidence lies in its cumulative effect. That is, 'while a single item of circumstantial evidence may only slightly increase the likelihood that the accused is guilty, several items taken together may carry enough probative force to justify a conviction'.[42]

Frederick E. Chemay, another researcher on the same subject of eyewitness testimony, arrived at the same results in his study of eyewitness identification. The process known as 'unconscious transference', or the tendency to confuse a person seen in one situation with another person seen in a different situation, plays significantly in the eyewitness identification process. Chemay preferred the admission of expert testimony to increase the potential effectiveness of the oral argument in conveying to the jury or court the problems inherent in eyewitness evidence. The usefulness of a cognitive psychologist seems to depend on two factors: one, the significance of eyewitness evidence in the prosecution's case, and two, the likelihood of unreliability or misidentification. It would seem that expert testimony would be called for in aid of cases where the eyewitness evidence dominates the prosecution's case and where misidentification is all but certain.[43]

In his findings on eyewitness error, Chemay examined human memory. He contended that, contrary to the position taken by some, human memory does not operate like a camera, gathering every detail for recall exactly as it was perceived. Rather, images are instantly altered through the integration of new experiences and interpretations in an active, reconstructive process. A person can unknowingly integrate postevent information to fill gaps or replace forgotten or poorly remembered details, with imagination frequently playing a significant role. The result can be distorted by very incorrect recall.[44] Judges must be aware of this fact when the testimony is purely dependent upon the testimony of an eyewitness, because errors are a likely possibility.

Experimental psychologists have treated memory as a three-stage process: encoding, which involves the input of perceived information into the memory system; the point of acquisition at which perception registers in the various areas of the cortex and is initially stored; and storage, or retention, which is that part of the process during which the information is retained until when is to be recalled.[45] The lapse of time between encoding and retrieval is called 'retention interval'. Finally, the retrieval stage is what is commonly called 'remembering'—it occurs when the brain searches for the pertinent information, retrieves it, and communicates it.[46]

One important feature common to both perception and memory is that people are not conscious of these processes. They may be aware of the results, but research indicates that they do not realise how the processes of perception, encoding, retention, and retrieval can be manipulated to change the original information. This is a significant feature of perception and memory for those who must deal with eyewitness evidence.[47] The *Baghdad* decision should be viewed in this broader context in relation to circumstantial evidence, that is, that one needs to evaluate evidence in its cumulative effect to determine whether the evidence presented has sufficed or fulfilled the circumstantial evidence test.

Factors that affect the reliability of an eyewitness include witness, situational, or event factors, and recognition of faces factors. Witness factors are those that affect perceptions that are physical limitations to eyewitnesses' own senses. Each individual has unique upper limitations to his abilities to see, hear, smell, taste, and touch. Anything that causes the eyewitness to function beyond these limits will reduce the reliability of the eyewitness performance.

Chemay further explained that stimulus overload occurs when the senses are overwhelmed with too much information in too short a period of time, a condition that affects both perception and memory. The effect on perception is that the witness simply is unable to sense everything that happens and may misperceive some of the information, resulting in later storage of inaccurate and incomplete information. This phenomenon also raises the opportunity for confabulation, that is, the creation or substitution of false memories through later suggestion. Related to stimulus overload is the level of excitement, stress, and sensory arousal. Research indicates that very high and very low states of arousal reduce accuracy, while moderate levels may increase accuracy, contrary to the commonly held belief that high arousal or stress increases accuracy.[48] In other words,

> in a crime situation, the witness may be more concerned with personal safety, or safety of someone close to him, and if he is a witness or victim, he will focus intensely on some of the personally relevant cues, such as a weapon.[49]

Event or situational factors are those that relate to shorter observation of the object, which result in a less complete picture of perception and recall. Accuracy as the ability to remember and describe details diminishes because of situational factors. Facial recognition is also affected by what is known as 'unconscious transference'.[50] Chemay further elucidated the tendency to confuse a person seen in one situation with another one seen in a different situation. Recall of face depends on the particular face; some are more easily recalled than others, with uniqueness and attractiveness playing a role. Identification is affected by the race of the person observed—the accuracy of identification of members of one's race being higher than of members of other races. Operating singly and together, these factors can produce significant unreliability in eyewitness evidence.[51]

Another study supporting the same findings is that by Adele Bernhard who, in his research, interrogated mistaken eyewitness identification. The factors that contribute to wrongful convictions tend to be mistakes of fact, such as mistaken eyewitness identification, incorrect police hypothesis or careless police work, witness perjury, and false confessions, rather than errors in applying the law. As a result, improvements in criminal procedure laws and police investigatory techniques will at best reduce the frequency of wrongful convictions, not eliminate them altogether.[52]

The same is true for earwitness error. Using scientific findings and empirical data, Wells and Loftus concluded that earwitnessing and eyewitnessing are similarly and considerably error prone. This is not to say that voice identification should not be used as an aid to the prosecution or the defence, but it should not form part of any major part of the evidence presented in court.[53] The sophistication of corruption cases underscores the need to heed these research findings, more so in relation to a circumstantial evidence test, where detection through intelligence techniques and subsequent gathering of evidence require a clear understanding of what amounts to circumstantial evidence.

Psychologists also have important input to the whole understanding of the circumstantial evidence paradigm. Scientific studies on human memory error have found that human beings frequently describe from memory events that they have observed, and most people consider these descriptions to be accurate. However, scientific research on memory in the past few decades has revealed that people's memories are often inaccurate. These errors in memory are systematic and are especially likely to occur for the kinds of events that are reported in courtroom testimony. Attention is drawn to the memory gatekeeper. Our five senses are bombarded with vast amounts of external stimulation. In addition, we generate our own internal stimulation from our thoughts, feelings, and emotions. Any part of this stimulation creates a lasting impact so it can be remembered—this component of stimulation must be encoded into memory.[54]

Researchers have also convincingly demonstrated that the direct evidence paradigm is flawed through several weaknesses, as previously discussed, and therefore it has resulted in wrongful convictions and imprisonment as a consequence of erroneous identification by an eyewitness. It is recommended that courts should allow expert testimony relating to inherent problems of eyewitness identification to testify on such flaws of eyewitness memory.[55]

It is important here to note that an observer is qualified to testify because he or she has firsthand information or knowledge of the facts at issue. An expert has an added value over the knowledge of an eyewitness or observer and thus has something to contribute that is different from an eyewitness or observer of the facts at issue, particularly where eyewitness errors are imminent and could result in miscarriage of justice.

The *Chicago Tribune* carried a true story that, in September 1985, Dennis Brown heard the words that sent him to prison for rape. The victim took the stand and had no doubt about who had attacked her: 'I had his face this close for at least 20 minutes', she said, holding her hand inches from her nose, 'and he's the man'. Brown was convicted of aggravated rape and sentenced to life without parole. However, in October 1985, the thirty-six-year-old Brown walked out of the Louisiana state prison in Angola, having been exonerated by DNA evidence. After being locked up for nineteen years, more than half his life, an innocent man was set free.[56] This case illustrates the danger of relying on what used to be seen as the best evidence—a person who was present at the scene of the crime who can attest, 'I saw him do it'. Time and again, thanks to DNA evidence, we have seen that a victim can be absolutely sure in identifying her attacker but absolutely wrong altogether.

Faulty identifications are the single most common error generating bad convictions. Many of the mistakes occur during police identification parades, where witnesses try to pick out the perpetrator from a group of people or pictures. Experiments have shown that when confronted with several possible suspects at once, or a 'simultaneous' lineup, the witness is prone to choose whoever most resembles the actual criminal, even if the criminal is absent.[57]

Eyewitness testimony can be extremely useful in catching criminals, but it needs safeguards to make sure it does not nab the innocent, as the discussed scientific studies have shown or proved.

4.7. THE TESTIMONY OF AN EXPERT WITNESS

The preceding research findings have demonstrated with certainty that the 'eyewitness paradigm' is weak for reasons assigned thereto. In order to cure this anomaly, which has resulted in miscarriages of justice where the innocent have suffered penalties—including death sentences—that they did not deserve, the invocation of expert opinion becomes relevant to straighten the understanding of what actually happened with the aid of an expert in the field.

Since, in corruption cases, direct evidence is hard to come by, law enforcement agencies will resort to circumstantial evidence. This is where specialist or technical knowledge and information may be called upon to assist the court in determining the evidence presented before it. As a general rule, however, the court is not bound by an expert opinion. In corruption cases where undercover operations are used and where specialised knowledge or techniques are employed to uncover the most concealed corrupt transactions, the services of a technical expert may be called in to gather circumstantial evidence and produce it before the court. Technical or other specialised knowledge may become the subject of expert testimony, and the court may benefit from such evidence in order to understand what did take place. Circumstantial evidence may come from different sources and witnesses, among them an expert witness.

The Law of Evidence in Tanzania recognises and provides for opinion of experts. Section 47 of the law[58] stipulates the following:

> When a court has to form an opinion upon a point of foreign law, or science or art, or as to identity of handwriting or finger or other impressions, the opinion, upon that point of persons [generally called experts] possessing special knowledge or skill, experience or training in such foreign law, science or art or question as to identity of handwriting or finger or other impressions are relevant facts.[59]

Section 48 provides further that facts not otherwise relevant are relevant if they support or are inconsistent with the opinions of experts, when such opinions are relevant.[60]

Given the imperfection of direct evidence to which the traditional common-law proponents have adhered, the importance and reliability of circumstantial evidence is perhaps well articulated in this form in the

English case of *R. v. Exall*.[61] Sir. Jonathan Frederick Pollock, CB, said of circumstantial evidence that

> it is like the case of a rope composed of several cords. One strand of the cord might be insufficient to sustain the weight, but three strands together may be of quite sufficient strength. Thus it may be in circumstantial evidence; there may be a combination of circumstances, no one of which would raise a reasonable conviction or more than a mere suspicion; but the whole, taken together, may create a strong conclusion of guilt with as much certainty as human affairs can require or admit.[62]

On the subject of an expert witness in relation to circumstantial evidence, Paul C. Giannelli emphasised that securing the services of defence experts to examine evidence, to advise counsel, and to testify at trial is frequently critical in modern criminal litigation, and more so where circumstantial evidence is an issue at trial. Nonetheless, it was in 1985 that the U.S. Supreme Court, in *Ake v. Oklahoma*,[63] for the first time recognised a constitutional right to expert assistance.[64]

Allen et al. expounded further that expert witnesses present evidence based on knowledge acquired through specialised study or unusual training and experience that permits them to generate, piece together, or interpret data in a manner that would not be readily apparent to a fact finder. An expert can be useful at every stage of the fact-finding process.

a. Experts can generate evidentiary facts themselves. An example is a chemist who has analysed a substance in a case in which the chemical makeup of the substance matters, such as litigation over water pollution or a criminal drug charge. Another example is the medical worker who does blood or tissue analysis. Such individuals provide basic facts for the fact finder.
b. Experts can educate the jury regarding specialised or scientific information that is needed to draw inferences about evidentiary facts. For example, with respect to the safety of the construction of a car, an engineer may testify to the tensile strength of its

component metals. Another example is a medical specialist who educates the fact finder about the implications of the symptoms of a disease.

c. Most prevalent, and in our view least justifiable, experts may present inferences and conclusions to which fact finders may defer. A psychiatrist who testifies about the sanity of a criminal defendant is an example; a scientist who testifies that water pollution caused a person's health problems is another. A fact finder may have to rely on little more than a hunch when choosing to defer and accept as accurate the scientifically sophisticated conclusions of one of two conflicting experts.[65]

Nathan Benedict, another researcher, in relation to circumstantial evidence and the admission of scientific evidence by the U.S. courts with regard to fingerprints, stated that it is indisputable that, when properly employed, fingerprints can play a vital role in the justice system—both to implicate guilty defendants and to exonerate innocent suspects—to obviate the weakness of an eyewitness.[66]

His critical views were in relation to FBI investigators who so confidently misidentified the fingerprint of a suspect in relation to a bomb that ripped through three Madrid train stations, killing 191 people, which led to his incarceration for over two-week period as a misidentified defendant.[67] It is thus important, in the context of eyewitness weaknesses, to identify possible remedies such as the specialised knowledge or scientific application of evidence to confirm the existence or nonexistence of the fact at issue.

Walter G. Amstutz and Bobby Marzine Harges,[68] in their article on the evolution of the controversy of expert testimony based on the reasoning rendered by the U.S. Supreme Court in *Daubert v. Merrell Dow Pharmaceuticals, Inc.*,[69] characterised expert testimony as based not upon 'scientific' knowledge, but rather upon 'technical' or 'other specialized' knowledge.[70]

In their discussion on a narcotics-related case, for example, Amstutz et al. indicated that the prosecution, on the one hand, would want to use the expertise of a police officer, a veteran narcotics officer who has been trained and experienced in narcotics-related issues such as packaging, quantities, paraphernalia found near narcotics, proximity of weapons, ready cash on the scene, narcotics code language, and the amounts of drugs consistent with personal use to show the differences in the laws applicable to the case as well as established extrajudicial legal practices.

On the other hand, the defence would raise an objection based on the notions of improper foundation, relevance, prejudice, or improper qualification of the expert witness.[71] They consider five tests set out in *Daubert*[72] in relation to the testimony of an expert witness: (a) the testability of the officer's theory or technique; (b) whether that theory or technique has been subjected to peer review or publication, (c) the known or potential rate of error; (d) the existence and maintenance of standards controlling the technique; and (e) whether the methodology employed is generally accepted in the scientific community.[73]

The controversy to which *Daubert* refers has raised the question as to whether the principles pertaining to admissibility of scientific expert testimony apply as well to the admissibility of nonscientific expert testimony. In settling the controversy, the U.S. Supreme Court, in the case of *Kumho Tire Co. v. Carmichael*,[74] decided that the trial court's gatekeeping function regarding the admission of expert testimony applies to scientific experts as well as to nonscientific experts.

On the role of expert witness, Amstutz further clarified that when a witness is qualified as an expert, he or she may generally suggest inferences that should be drawn from the facts, including inferences embracing the ultimate issue in the case. However, it is important that the expert witness does not express a direct opinion concerning whether the defendant did or did not have the mental state or condition constituting an element of the crime charged. No expert witness should be allowed to testify in this respect. Such ultimate issues are matters for the trier of fact alone.[75]

Pasternak supported this view in that the trier of fact is the determiner of the ultimate issue of fact. It was for some time universally held that expert witnesses could only provide evidence of, and not state their opinions as to, the ultimate issues of fact. The development of common-law rule in this regard reflected concern with the usurpation of the province of the jury or court as the fact finder. On this basis, expert testimony that directly addressed and sought to make a determination of ultimate issues of fact was excluded.[76]

On the one hand, the exclusion of evidence is what may create the danger of unfair prejudice, confusion of the issues, bias, and misleading the court or the jury. The U.S. Federal Rules of Evidence,[77] on the other hand, makes admissible a broad array of testimony from a multitude of sources covering an enormous range of affairs. It includes scientific, technical, and medical experts, but its pragmatic phrase 'other specialized knowledge' extends the scope of the rule far beyond those confines. It includes skilled witnesses, such as bankers or landowners testifying to land values in condemnation proceedings, and ballistic and fingerprint evidence.[78] Given the complex nature of corruption cases, courts are invited to consider such modern trends to ensure that justice prevails, particularly where circumstantial evidence is an issue—hence the relevance of the U.S. experience in these new trends in the law of evidence.

On the testimony of an expert witness, Miles J. Vigilante noted further that a juror will give an expert witness greater attention and credibility than any other witness. Therefore, in order to adequately determine whether expert testimony is reliable, a trial court judge must have discretion in choosing what factors will be an accurate measure of reliability for the testimony of a particular expert. Expert testimony can be a valuable tool to a litigant when facing the complex issues of modern litigation. Complex litigation includes any cases involving transactions or occurrences, or requiring resort to forms of evidence beyond the experience of the typical jury. Included are cases involving corporate transactions, mergers and acquisitions, securities, sophisticated product liability issues, antitrust, intellectual property, and similar cases. It is difficult for the jury to evaluate facts of such complex cases intelligently without applying some scientific, technical, or specialised knowledge.[79]

Any knowledge that is not likely to be possessed by the fact finder qualifies any person with 'skill' to testify to it, and this means that if the skill was gained through experience rather than traditional formal study, it will be admissible in evidence. Allen et al. pertinently put it that the qualification need not include formal education in the subject matter. Federal Bureau of Investigation (FBI) agents have been permitted to testify to the structure of various criminal schemes based on their law enforcement experience. Farmers have testified to the likely value of their ruined crops, and so on. The crucial questions are whether the proposed witness has specialised knowledge, however obtained, and whether it would be helpful to the jury. Qualifying an expert involves a *voire dire* of the witness that brings out the person's expertise. If there is no reasonable doubt about the expertise, the opposing party may try to stipulate it. Wise counsel usually rejects the stipulation because they want the fact finder to hear the credentials of the witness. The opposing party can object to qualifying the witness as an expert, and can also *voire dire* the witness in an effort to show that the witness is not qualified or has nothing of relevance to add to the trial. The trial judge then decides if the person qualifies as an expert.[80]

Lubuva, JA, in the case of *Hilda Abel v. R.*,[81] expressed the position of expert testimony in Tanzania, namely, that 'courts are not bound to accept a medical expert's evidence if there are good reasons for not doing so'.[82] However, this does not mean that expert witnesses are not permissible but rather the court has to make a decision if such an expert qualifies to testify on specialised knowledge or experience. For this study, it is also important to consider witnesses with specialised knowledge on corruption matters to aid the court in assessing complex evidence. The same expression is found in the case of *Omari Ahmed v. R.*,[83] where Mwakasendo, JA (as he then was), on behalf of other Justices of the CA, stated that there must be some evidence connecting an accused with a theft other than the testimony of an expert who is uncertain. The trial court's finding as to the credibility of a witness is usually binding on the appeal court unless there are circumstances on an appeal court on record that call for a reassessment of their credibility.[84]

McCormick put it more conveniently: '[I]t seems eminently a case for discretion'.[85] The purpose of an expert witness is to give an opinion based on his or her professional qualifications, experience, and knowledge on the subject that is under scrutiny by the court. Experts are used, Amstutz et al. opined, to simplify complex and technical matters for the finder of facts. These complex and technical matters are usually beyond the knowledge of the average lay person. For example, in a product liability case, an expert may be called to testify that a particular drug can cause certain ailments. But in a medical malpractice case, a cardiologist may be called in to testify about the appropriate standards for cardiovascular medicine. Additionally, in a homicide case, a medical examiner may be called in to testify about the cause of death. In each of the above instances, the experts are said to base their testimony on science. In presenting the scientific evidence, the expert witness usually explains the date or test results, or explains the scientific principles that establish the reliability of the evidence.[86]

Having examined the general theory, classification, and traditional meaning of circumstantial evidence, the analysis thereof, the eyewitness error, and the expert testimony, it is important now to make a survey on how circumstantial evidence is applied particularly in white-collar crimes in the USA for analogous purposes, on the one hand, and in East Africa, on the other; the next step is to draw lessons from the survey in relation to circumstantial evidence as interpreted by the courts—the focus of this study.

4.8. The Application of Circumstantial Evidence

Corruption, money laundering, drug trafficking, terrorism, and other white-collar crimes are complex crimes that are difficult to investigate because their perpetrators are equally sophisticated and use numerous means to conceal the crimes. Our focus in this study is on corruption and the use of circumstantial evidence as a tool to bring it down to tolerable levels.

The standard of proof in corruption cases is the same as that in any other crime—that is, beyond reasonable doubt. However, corruption as a distinct crime has proved to be very difficult to prove unless investigation has been thorough and evidential rules have been complied with to convince the trier of facts of the case regarding the conclusion to the proposition. The primary focus of law enforcement agencies, and in this particular case the PCCB, is to ensure that the law reaches those corrupt core activities such as corrupt financial transactions and transfer of proceeds of a corruption crime to a safe haven where they are disguised transactions and converted into assets or properties through concealment or disguise of the sources of illicit funds or proceeds of corrupt transactions.

Thomas M. DiBiagio,[87] commenting on circumstantial evidence relating to the charge of money laundering in the context of white-collar crimes, stated that, typically, a money laundering charge is brought against a defendant on the basis of one of the following four fact patterns. First, the defendant is involved in drug trafficking and the money laundering charge arises from his participation in a transaction involving funds specifically and directly linked to a particular drug deal. Second, the defendant is involved in drug trafficking and the money laundering charge arises out of his participation in a transaction involving funds not traced to any particular drug distribution. Third, the defendant is not directly involved in the purchase or sale of narcotics, but is involved in a transaction involving funds specifically and directly linked to drug trafficking. Fourth, the defendant is not directly involved in the purchase or sale of narcotics but participates in a transaction involving funds that are circumstantially traced or linked to a narcotics enterprise.[88]

By analogy, the *Baghdad* case is an instance where cumulative effects of transactions that took place ought to be considered rather than looking at the revealed facts of the case in isolation. The seized documents—that is, copies of the certificates of offer and the notepads—are circumstantially traced and linked to Baghdad and public officers charged together with him in a corruption case.

George C. Austin, however, argued that there are such circumstances that cannot lie and that necessarily lead to a certain conclusion that the necessity of resorting to circumstantial evidence in many cases is obvious. Were it not so, crimes would go unpunished and wrongs unredressed. The most frequent necessity for its use arises in criminal cases for crimes that are secret.[89]

Austin stated further that to insuring correct inferences,

> the facts from which they are drawn must be carefully, precisely and minutely proved. They should be so proved as to lead to an irresistible conclusion, a conclusion that is the dictate of common experience and sound judgment. There probability is not enough. It must be a moral certainty, and that means, according to that, such a high degree of probability as will render a prudent man justifiable in acting under the circumstances the same as if they were absolutely certain. The probative force of circumstantial evidence depends upon the closeness of connection between the fact inferred and fact from which the inference is drawn.[90]

Considering screen writers and films documentaries correctly, Paul Bergman observed on the use of circumstantial evidence that films give audiences the impression that circumstantial evidence is inherently flawed, leading to irresistible and frequent miscarriages of justice. By contrast, direct evidence is inherently reliable.[91]

This is true even in Tanzania. My interviews with law students at the faculty of law, University of Dar es Salaam, show that out of 280 students—with the exception of 2 students, who were not clear in their answers—all reached a similar conclusion that circumstantial evidence is inherently imperfect and unreliable compared to direct evidence.[92] Research suggests that a majority of wrongful convictions are associated with mistaken eyewitness identification.[93]

Paul Bergman brought home the thrust of circumstantial evidence: the charge that verdicts based on direct evidence are more trustworthy than those based on circumstantial evidence is untrue because circumstantial evidence dominates every case, and while our justice system is committed to fair procedures, we must trust judges and jurors to draw factually correct inferences.[94]

Shaw, CJ, in the famous Webster case,[95] opined that circumstantial evidence, therefore, is founded on experience and observed facts and coincidences, establishing a connection between the known and proved facts and the fact sought to be proved. The advantages are that, as the evidence commonly comes from several witnesses and different sources, a chain of circumstances is less likely to be falsely prepared and arranged, and falsehood and seeing are more likely to be detected and fail of their purpose.[96]

Holland v. United States[97] dealt specifically with a circumstantial evidence controversy that circumstantial evidence in this respect is intrinsically no different from testimonial evidence. Admittedly, circumstantial evidence may in some cases point to a wholly incorrect result. Yet this is equally true of testimonial evidence. In both instances, a jury is asked to weigh the chances that the evidence correctly points to guilt against the possibility of inaccuracy or ambiguous inference. In both, the jury must use its experience with people and events in weighing the probabilities. If the jury is convinced beyond a reasonable doubt, we can require no more.[98]

The two cases of *Lloyd v. United States*[99] and *Panci v. United States*[100] applied the circumstantial evidence test that 'whether the jury might reasonably find that the evidence excluded every reasonable hypothesis except that of guilt and equally without wavering has applied it'.[101]

In another case, *McFarland v. United States*,[102] the defendant's motion for judgment of acquittal because of insufficient circumstantial evidence to convict had been denied, even though the government had been unable to produce evidence wholly inconsistent with his possible innocence. In sustaining conviction, the court held that the inferences to be drawn from circumstantial evidence are a matter for the jury to decide and not subject to review on appeal. It is not the function of an appellate court to weigh the evidence to decide whether it is substantial enough to establish a case from which the jury may infer guilt beyond a reasonable doubt.[103] The court concluded that it is necessary that the evidence be wholly inconstant with every conclusion except the guilt, provided the evidence is substantial enough to establish a case from which the jury may infer guilt beyond a reasonable doubt.[104]

In Baghdad's case, Judge Mwaikugile faulted the trier of facts and his findings that were ambiguous. But, reviewing the evidence on appeal, the issues should be on the application of the principle of circumstantial evidence to the facts of the case rather than on the findings of the trial court—and Judge Mwaikugile failed to distinguish the two, namely, the evidential principle of circumstantial evidence and its application, on the one hand, and the fact-finding role of the trial court, on the other.

Irene Merker Rosenberg and Yale L. Rosenberg observed correctly on the traditional common-law school of thought that early common law did, however, distrust circumstantial evidence, viewing it as inferior to direct testimony, fearing that its use might result in conviction of the innocent, and consequently allowing it only in exceptional cases, such as secret crimes.[105] This fear is apparent in Judge Mwaikugile, as evidenced in the *Baghdad* case.

In the case of *Commonwealth v. Webster*,[106] the defendant was a professor of chemistry at the medical college in Boston. He allegedly murdered a physician to whom he owed money; the authorities discovered parts of the victim's body in his laboratory. CJ Shaw of Massachusetts expounded on the requirement of proof beyond a reasonable doubt and on the limitation regarding circumstantial evidence that reasonable doubt, although not easily defined, is a doubt that leaves the minds of juries in that condition; they cannot say that they feel an abiding conviction to a moral certainty and of the truth of the charge. In the case of circumstantial evidence, great care and caution ought to be used in drawing inferences from proved facts. To that end, when such evidence is relied on, it is essential that the circumstances be taken as a whole, and giving them their reasonable and just weight, and no more, should to a moral certainty exclude every hypothesis but guilt.[107]

As already noted in *Holland v. United States*,[108] the Supreme Court unanimously held that there was no difference between the two types of evidence, and consequently, in federal court, there was no requirement that the trial judge charge the jury that the evidence must be such as to exclude every reasonable hypothesis but that of guilt.[109] This decision is very important in this study because it vindicates the thesis that circumstantial evidence is a reliable and potent tool to be applied in corruption cases and other complex white-collar crimes.

Rosenberg and Rosenberg further pointed out that over half of the states have eliminated the special charge, subsuming it within the reasonable doubt instruction. A minority of jurisdictions, however, still requires a charge that the circumstantial evidence must either exclude every reasonable hypothesis but that of guilt, or must be inconsistent with any reasonable theory of innocence.[110]

It suffices here to conclude that the U.S. jurisprudence on the subject is very useful in the context of Tanzania, particularly on the understanding of the application and efficacy of circumstantial evidence.

4.9. Application of Circumstantial Evidence in East Africa

In this section, case law in East Africa will be surveyed and the utility of circumstantial evidence analysed, particularly in murder cases, because there are no reported cases in the region that have employed circumstantial evidence in corruption cases other than Baghdad's case. Nonetheless, these cases are examined here for purposes of drawing analogy and understanding the application of circumstantial evidence.

The Ugandan case of *Simon Musoke v. R.*[111] is illustrative. The EACA—presided over by Sir Kenneth O'Connor, P. Forbes, and Gould in that case—considered the appropriate test to be applied in a circumstantial evidence case: in a case depending exclusively upon circumstantial evidence, the court must, before deciding upon a conviction, find that the inculpatory facts are incompatible with the innocence of the accused, and incapable of explanation upon any other reasonable hypothesis than that of guilt.[112]

The Kenyan case of *Sawe v. R.*[113] is instructive on circumstantial evidence: the trial judge in the case remarked that there were several facts that the prosecution had invited the court to hold as forming a series of circumstances leading to an inference or conclusion of the accused's guilt:

> I have accepted this invitation provided that as this is a case dependent upon circumstantial evidence the prosecution must show that these circumstances from which the inference of guilt is to be drawn are, in the first instance, proved beyond reasonable doubt. This simply means that the prosecution must prove on the required standard the existence of such fact.[114]

In evaluating the evidence on record against the ground of appeal by the appellant, the CA of Kenya concluded that the evidence did not irresistibly point to the appellant to the exclusion of all others within the meaning of *R. v. Kipkering Arap Koske and Another 16 EACA Report 135*, where it was held, *inter alia*, in order to justify the inference of guilt, that the inculpatory facts must be incompatible with the innocence of the accused, and incapable of explanation upon any other reasonable hypothesis than that of his guilt.[115]

The court concluded that the evidence did not satisfy the legal requirements of circumstantial evidence to warrant or justify the conviction. In another case of *Dhalay v. R.*,[116] adopting the laid-down principle of circumstantial evidence in the case of *Teper v. R.*,[117] the privy council said that it was also necessary, before drawing the inference of the accused's guilt from circumstantial evidence, to be sure that there were no other coexisting circumstances, which would weaken or destroy the inference.[118]

In *Khanja v. R.*,[119] as in *Ndirangu v. R.*,[120] the CA of Kenya held that circumstantial evidence against the appellant excluded coexisting circumstances, which would weaken or destroy the inference of guilt, and irresistibly pointed to the appellant as having committed the offences he stood convicted of the offence charged.[121]

The same views were expressed in *Mkendeshwo v. R.*,[122] reaffirming *R. v. Kipkering Arap Koske and Another*[123] and *Simon Musoke*,[124] that in order to justify a conviction based wholly on circumstantial evidence, the inculpatory facts must not only be incompatible with the innocence of the accused, and be incapable of explanation upon any other reasonable hypothesis than that of his guilt, but also the said fact must exclude coexisting circumstances, which may tend to weaken or destroy the inference of guilt.[125]

The case of *Chimera v. R.*,[126] decided by the CA of Kenya, pointed out clearly that it is a settled law that when a case rests entirely on circumstantial evidence, such evidence must satisfy three tests:

a. The circumstances from which an inference of guilt is sought to be drawn must be cogently and firmly established.
b. Those circumstances should be of a definite tendency unerringly pointing towards guilt of the accused.
c. The circumstances taken cumulatively should form a chain so complete that there is no escape from the conclusion that within all human probability the accused and none else committed the crime.[127]

The court concluded that in order to sustain conviction on the basis of circumstantial evidence, the evidence must be complete and incapable of explanation or any other hypothesis than that of guilt of the accused—circumstantial evidence that falls short of the required standard on all material particulars cannot in law form the basis for a conviction.[128]

The CA of Tanzania in the case of *Makungire Mtani v. R.*[129] held that the conclusion thus reached was that the t-shirt worn by the accused at the relevant time not only had bloodstains, but they were of human blood of group AB—the deceased's blood group. The accused was thus effectively linked to the killing of the deceased until he offered an explanation as to how he came to be stained with the deceased's blood.[130]

This case is relevant to the case of Baghdad in that there is an effective link between Baghdad and documents found in his home linking him with the allegations on the charge and other suspects he was charged with.

The case of *Protas John Kitogile and Another v. R.*[131] was decided by the CA based on circumstantial evidence, as it was held that the facts that only shortly after the murders were committed, the second appellant was found with a big cut wound, and that a trail of blood was traced from where he was found to the scene of the murders, were incriminating circumstances that led to the only reasonable inference that the appellant took part in the murders. And the fact that the second appellant gave a false account of how he sustained the injury went to strengthen this view.[132]

In another CA case, *Ally Bakari and Pili Bakari v. R.*,[133] the court—based on circumstantial evidence—held that

> where the evidence against the accused is wholly circumstantial to facts from which an inference adverse to the accused is sought to be drawn, it must be proved beyond reasonable doubt and must be clearly connected with the facts from which the inference is to be drawn.[134]

The case of *Nuhu Selemani v. R.*,[135] which dealt with voice identification in a murder case, was founded on circumstantial evidence. The CA reversed conviction of the appellant on the following basis:

> [T]he appellant had been convicted of murder based purely on circumstantial evidence. The first identification was that of the appellant's voice concerning what he had said to the deceased. The point was whether the circumstantial evidence in the case did irresistibly lead to the inevitable inference that it was the appellant who killed the deceased.[136]

In *Hamidu Mussa Thimotheo and Majidi Mussa Thimotheo v. R.*,[137] the CA, considering the circumstantial evidence presented during trial, could not agree with the appellants challenging the circumstantial evidence on which the conviction was based; the court held that the chain of circumstantial evidence linking the appellants to the death of their father was unbroken and therefore led to no other conclusion but that the appellants were responsible for the death of their father.[138]

The case of *Joseph s/o Kamiliango and 5 Others*,[139] decided by the CA, considered circumstantial evidence and held that the mere knowledge of the background and circumstances of the death of the deceased, coupled with the discovery of the dead body of the deceased, did not constitute sufficient circumstantial evidence to support a conviction of murder.[140]

The case of *Mariam Siri v. R.*[141] is perhaps the best judgment of all the previous ones, which expounded with clarity the meaning and application of circumstantial evidence. In this case, the appellant was charged with the murder of her husband, Yusuf Mohamed Yusuf. She was convicted by the HC (Judge Lugakingira) but appealed to the CA of Tanzania. The facts of the case can be summarised as follows. In November 1994, the husband, who resided in Dar es Salaam, took his annual leave and joined the appellant, who was his sixth wife, in Bagamoyo. Michael Joseph, his childhood friend, had a party at his residence and the deceased was invited. After the party, the deceased disappeared sometime after he got home. The prosecution case was that he was killed, criminally, by the appellant. In her defence, the appellant insisted that her husband did not leave home until 30 December 1984, and that when he did, he said he was going to Arabia, a trip he had been preparing for a whole year. On appeal, the defence counsel contended that the circumstantial evidence on record, such as it was, did not irresistibly establish that the appellant had killed her husband, and that it had not been proved that Yusuf Mohamed Yusuf was dead. The son of the deceased testified that his father did not visit him in the Lebanon where he was working. When the son returned to Tanzania and enquired after his father, the appellant's response was that she did not know where his father was. On another occasion, the son enquired of the appellant why the well was in disuse. She answered that it was filled with rubbish after a dog had fallen into it. The son became suspicious and a police inquiry commenced as a result. A male skull was found and a medical specialist in anatomy and a histologist concluded that it was, in fact, true. The evidence against the appellant was purely circumstantial in that there was no eyewitness, no confession, and no admission of guilt. Makame, JA, on behalf of his brethren, reasoned by asking the following question:

> You ask yourself if you are prepared and able to say with highest degree of certainty ordinarily attainable in human affairs whether, in the instant case, the skull Prof. Kaduri handled in court must

> have been that of the person alleged to be the deceased in this case. The allegation of death, the contention that it is the Appellant who caused her husband to die are so intertwined that one cannot usefully tackle one without necessarily dealing with the other. The dog in the well, the explanation as to where the alleged deceased was, and the circumstances in which he is allegedly left all crowd together and must be considered together in order to decide whether the Appellant's husband is dead and whether the human skull retrieved from the well was that of the Appellant's husband and whether he was killed, and to determine if he was killed, whether he was murdered, and by the Appellant.

The Court concluded that

> the circumstantial evidence leads to the inevitable conclusion that the death of the Appellant's husband was the result of the criminal act or contrivance of the Appellant. There is no alternative, which can with reasonable probability account for the murder.

The condition required in a conviction founded on circumstantial evidence was satisfied in this case. The doubt required to detract from the certitude necessary for convictions in criminal cases is only reasonable doubt, not fanciful doubt. Absolute certainty, almost impossibility, is not necessary in establishing criminal guilt. It is enough as in this case, that one feels certain that an accused person is guilty.

The preceding examination has shown that the reliance on direct evidence paradigm may sometimes and not necessarily present the reality of what indeed an eyewitness actually saw or heard. There is always a possibility of an eyewitness error.

Circumstantial evidence, as previously examined, provides a new way of thinking and the foundational basis for the same level of reliability—and sometimes even more so, as in DNA tests and the like—as direct evidence.

This study calls upon the courts, prosecutors, defence counsels, and other users of the criminal justice system to take a new and fresh look on the utility of circumstantial evidence, because it is a potent tool to assist the resolution of disputes contested in courts of law. There is always an engagement in various kind of analogical reasoning. Allen et al.

contended that some engagements involve cause and effect, some amount of filling in of the unobserved aspects of what you are observing by reference to what you have come to believe is commonly associated with what you presently are viewing; you rely on generalisations formed out of prior experience, and so on. These are tools that humans use to manipulate their environment, and, not surprisingly, they are the tools jurors use to resolve the disputes of historical fact before them. At the end of the day, when a consensus has emerged out of ringing the combined experience of the jurors to bear on the evidence presented at trial, the jurors look to the verdict options to determine who wins and who loses.[142]

Direct evidence is a visual perception that the witness was present at a historical event or occurrence. If a witness' testimony is not based on personal knowledge, then it is probably based either on speculation or on what someone else has said to the witness, which makes it disguised hearsay. The case for circumstantial evidence has been reconsidered and vindicated.

It is in this context that this study advances the case for circumstantial evidence to be applied in corruption cases as well, because, as examined in the preceding analysis, the traditional view of distinguishing between direct and circumstantial evidence diminishes the chances for corruption cases to be tried and tested in courts of law in Tanzania, especially where their foundational evidence is based on circumstantial evidence.

Endnotes

1. John Henry Wigmore and Peter Tillers, *Evidence on Trial at Common Law*, vol. 1A (Boston: Little Brown and Company), 944.
2. Ibid.
3. Ibid.
4. Steven M. Tindall, 'Note: Do as She Says: The Shortcomings of Justice O'Connor's Direct Evidence Requirement in Price WaterHouse v. Hopkins', *Berkeley Journal of Employment and Labor Law* 17 (2001): 332.
5. Allen, Kuhns, and Swift, *Evidence*, 147.
6. Ibid.
7. Ibid., 148.
8. Ibid.
9. Wigmore and Tillers, *Evidence on Trial at Common Law*, 1138.
10. Federal Rules of Evidence, 401–402.
11. Wigmore and Tillers, *Evidence on Trial at Common Law*, 948.
12. Ibid., 949.
13. 4 pas. St. 269, 271–273 (1846).
14. Ibid.
15. Wigmore and Tillers, *Evidence on Trial at Common Law*, 951.
16. 59 Mass. (5 cush.) 295, 311 (1850).
17. Ibid.
18. Wigmore and Tillers, *Evidence on Trial at Common Law*.
19. Ibid., 950–951.
20. Allen, Kuhns, and Swift, *Evidence*, 73.
21. Cross and Tapper, *Cross on Evidence*, 20.
22. See section 27 of the PCCA.
23. Exceptions are found in public documents, whether under seal or not, foreign public documents, certified copies of public records, official publications, newspapers and periodicals, trade inscriptions, acknowledged documents, commercial paper and related documents, and presumption under the act of parliament. See further sections 83–99 of the Evidence Act, no. 6 of 1967.
24. C. T. McCormick, J. W. Strong, K. S. Broun, et al., eds., *McCormick on Evidence*, 4th ed. (St. Paul MN: West Publishing Co., 1992), 2:44.
25. Section 99 of Tanzania Evidence Act, no. 6 of 1967, provides for twenty-year periods.
26. Ibid., 46.

27. Ibid., 50.
28. Ibid., 52.
29. Section 127 of Evidence Act, no. 6 of 1967—as amended by acts nos. 3 of 1971, 9 of 1980, and 4 of 1998—provides that '[e]very person shall be competent witness to testify unless the court considers that he is incapable of understanding the questions put to him or of giving rational answers to those questions by reason of tender age, extreme old age, disease (whether of body or mind) or any other similar cause'.
30. 'Demonstrative evidence' is that evidence that is prepared to show that the exhibit is a 'fair', 'accurate', or 'true' depiction of what it is claimed to portray; for instance, a murder weapon, a photo, recorded simulations, and construction of events—seeing is believing, and so forth.
31. Allen, Kuhns, and Swift, *Evidence*, 207–208. The authors also set out the foundational requirements for admissibility of evidence conforming to evidence sufficient to support a finding that the matter in question is what its proponents claims. (a) Testimony of witness with knowledge. Testimony that a matter is what it is claimed to be. (b) Nonexpert opinion on handwriting—the genuineness of handwriting, based upon familiarity not acquired for purposes of litigation. (c) Comparison by trier or the expert witness—specimens that have been authenticated. (d) Distinctive characteristics and the like—appearance, contents, substance, internal patterns, or distinctive characteristics, taken in conjunction with circumstances. (e) Voice identification, whether heard firsthand or through mechanical or electronic transmission or recording, by opinion based upon hearing the voice at any time under circumstances connecting it with the alleged speaker. (f) Telephone conversations indicating that a call was made to the number assigned at the time by the telephone company to a particular person or business. (g) Public record or reports that a writing authorised by law to be recorded or filed and in fact recorded or filed in public office, or purported public record, report, statement, or data compilation, in any form, is from public office where items of this nature are kept. (h) Ancient documents or date compilation—in any form, or condition, to create no suspicion concerning its authenticity. (i) Process or system to produce result that the process or system produces accurate results. (j) Methods of authentication provided by law or by the rules provided by the court pursuant to statutory authority.
32. Ibid. 208.
33. FRE 602 (U.S. Federal Rules of Evidence, as amended until 1 April 1997): witness may not testify to a matter unless evidence is introduced sufficient

to support a finding that the witness has personal knowledge of the matter. Evidence to prove personal knowledge may, but need not, consist of the witness' own testimony. This rule is subject to the provisions of rule 703, relating to opinion testimony by expert witness.

34. Allen, Kuhns, ad Swift, *Evidence*, 207–208.
35. Gary L. Wells and Elizabeth F. Loftus, *Eyewitness Testimony: Psychological Perspectives* (London: Cambridge University Press, 1984), ix.
36. Brooke Whisonant Patterson, 'The "Tyranny of the Eyewitness"', *Law & Psychology Review* 28 (2004): 195, is an account of Maurice Carter in prison, who, according to many witnesses in Benton Harbor, Michigan, he is innocent. Nearly three decades ago an all-white jury convicted this African American of shooting a white police officer despite key witnesses claiming that he was not the gunman. A new trial is contemplated to vindicate Carter's innocence.
37. Stanley Z. Fisher, 'Convictions of Innocent Persons in Massachusetts: An Overview', *Boston University Public International Law Journal* 12 (1994): 1.
38. Ibid. See also an extensive study by Wells and Loftus, *Eyewitness Testimony*.
39. Fisher, 'Convictions of Innocent Persons in Massachusetts', 1.
40. Raymond Emson, *Evidence*, 3rd ed. (New York: Palgrave McMillan, 2006), 11.
41. Monika Jain, 'Comment: Mitigating the Dangers of Capital Convictions Based on Eyewitness Testimony Through Treason's Two-Witness Rule', Journal of Criminal Law and Criminology 91 (2001): 761.
42. Ibid.
43. Frederick E. Chemay, 'Comment: Unreliable Eyewitness Evidence: The Expert Psychologist and The Defense in Criminal Cases', *Los Angeles Law Review* 45 (1985): 721.
44. Ibid.
45. Ibid.
46. Ibid.
47. Ibid.
48. Ibid.
49. Ibid. See also A. Trankell, *Reliability of Evidence: Methods for Analyzing and Assessing Witness Statements* (Stockholm: Breckmans, 1972), 16; Wells and Loftus, *Eyewitness Testimony*. A person's expectations and stereotypes can also affect both perception and memory, and what he perceives and encodes is, to a large extent, determined by cultural biases, personal prejudices, effects of training, prior information, and expectations induced by motivational states, among others.
50. Ibid.

51. Ibid.
52. Adele Bernhard, 'When Justice Fails: Indemnification for Unjust Conviction', *University of Chicago Law School Roundtable* 73 (1999): 73.
53. Wells and Loftus, *Eyewitness Testimony*, 123.
54. These researchers include Ralph Norman Haber and Lyn Haber, 'Experiencing, Remembering, and Reporting Events', *Psychology, Public Policy & Law* 6 (2000): 1057. See also Steven Penrod and Brian Cutler, 'Witness Confidence and Witness Accuracy: Assessing Their Forensic Relation', *Psychology, Public Policy & Law* 1 (1995): 817; Steven M. Smith, 'The Other Race Effect and Contemporary Criminal Justice: Eyewitness Identification and Jury Decision Making: Eyewitness Identification: Postdictors of Eyewitness Errors: Can False Identification Be Dangerous in The Cross-Race Situation?' *Psychology, Public Policy & Law* 7 (2001): 153; Richard C. Wydick, 'The Ethics of Witness Coaching', *Cardozo Law Review* 17 (1995): 1; Bryan K. Fair, 'Using Parrots to Kill Mockingbirds: Yet Another Racial Prosecution and Wrongful Conviction In Maycomb', *Alabama Law Review* 45 (1994): 403.
55. Ibid.
56. 'DNA Evidence', *Chicago Tribune*, February 17, 2005.
57. Ibid.
58. The Evidence Act.
59. Ibid.
60. (1866) 4 F & F 922 (Assize), 929.
61. Ibid.
62. 470 U.S. 68 (1985).
63. Ibid.
64. Allen, Kuhns, and Swift, *Evidence*, 732–733. See also U.S. FRE 702.
65. Nathan Benedict, 'Fingerprints and the Daubert Standard for Admission of Scientific Evidence: Why Fingerprints Fail and a Proposed Remedy', *Arizona Law Review* 46 (2006): 519.
66. Ibid.—Brandon Mayfield, an Algerian by origin and a Muslim attorney in Portland.
67. Walter G. Amstutz and Bobby Marzine Harges, 'Evolution Controversy: The Daubert Dilemma: The application of Daubert v. Merrell Dow Pharmaceutical Inc. to Expert Testimony of Law Enforcement Officers in Narcotic Related Cases', *Hawaii Law Review* 23 (2001): 67.
68. 509 U.S. 509, 593–594 (1993).
69. Ibid.
70. Ibid.
71. Ibid.

72. 526 U.S. 137, 141 (1999).
73. Amstutz and Harges, 'Evolution Controversy'.
74. Jeremy D. Pasternak, 'Sexual Harassment and Expertise: The Admissibility of Expert Witness Testimony in Cases Utilizing The Reasonable Woman Standard', *Santa Clara Law Review* 35 (1995): 651.
75. U.S. Federal Rules of Evidence (FRE 702): Testimony by Experts.
76. FRE 702 provides as follows: if scientific, technical, or other specialised knowledge will assist the trier of fact to understand the evidence or to determine a fact in issue, a witness qualified as an expert by knowledge, skill, experience, training, or education may testify thereto in the form of an opinion or otherwise, if (a) the testimony is based upon sufficient facts or data, (b) the testimony is the product of reliable principles and methods, and (c) the witness has applied the principles and methods reliably to the facts of the case. See Allen, Kuhns, and Swift, *Evidence*, 734–735.
77. Miles J. Vigilante, 'Screening Expert Testimony After KUMHO Tire Co. v. Carmichael', *Journal of Law & Policy* 8 (2000): 543–592; 526 U.S. 137 (1999).
78. [1993] TLR 246 (CA). See also *Agnes Doris Liundi v. R.* (1980) TLR 46.
79. Ibid.
80. [1983] TLR 52 (CA).
81. Ibid.
82. McCormick, Strong, Broun, et al., *McCormick on Evidence*, 137–161.
83. Ibid.
84. Thomas M. DiBiagio, 'Money Laundering and Drug Trafficking: A Question of Understand the Elements of the Crime and the Use of Circumstantial Evidence', *University of Richmond Law Review* 28 (1994): 255.
85. Ibid.
86. George C. Austin, 'The Value of Circumstantial Evidence', *Counsellor* 2, no. 8 (May 1898).
87. Ibid.
88. Paul Bergman, 'A Bunch of Circumstantial Evidence', *University of San Francisco Law Review* 30 (1995–1996): 985.
89. Third Year Law Students, Faculty of Law, University of Dar Es Salaam, August 2004.
90. Garry L. Wells and Eric Seelau, 'Eyewitness Identification: Psychological Research and Legal Policy on Lineups', *Psychology, Public Policy and Law* 765 (1995).
91. Paul Bergman, 'A Bunch of Circumstantial Evidence'.

92. 59 Mass. (5 cush.) 295, 511 (1850).
93. Ibid.
94. 348 U.S. 121 (1954).
95. Ibid.
96. 226 F. 2d 9, 13 (5th Cir. 1955).
97. 256 F. 2d. 308 (5th Cir. 1958).
98. Ibid.
100. 273 F. 2d 417 (5th Cir. 1960).
101. Ibid.
102. Ibid.
103. Irene Merker Rosenberg and Yale L. Rosenberg, 'Perhaps What They Say Is Based Only on Conjecture—Circumstantial Evidence, Then and New', *Houston Law Review* 31 (1994–1995): 1373.
104. 59 Mass. (5 cush.) 295 (1850).
105. Ibid.
106. 348 U.S. 121 (1954).
107. Rosenberg and Rosenberg, 'Perhaps What They Say Is Based Only on Conjecture'.
108. [1958] EA 715.
109. Ibid.
110. [2002] LLR 3808 (CAK).
111. Ibid.
112. Ibid.
113. [1997] LLR 514 (CAK).
114. [1952] AC 480
115. Ibid.
116. [1983] LLR 137 (CAK) See also *Musambi v. R.* [1983] LLR 147 (CAK).
117. [1997] LLR 3786 (CAK) See also *Simon Musoke v. R.* [1959] EA 715.
118. Ibid.
119. [2002] LLR 3700 (CAK).
120. [1949] EACA Report 135.
121. [1959] EA 715.
122. Ibid.
123. [1998] LLR 710 (CAK).
124. Ibid.
125. Ibid.
126. [1983] TLR 179 (CA).
127. Ibid.
128. [1992] TLR 51 (CA).

129. Ibid.
130. [1992] TLR 10 (CA).
131. Ibid.
132. [1984] TLR 93 (CA).
133. Ibid.
134. Ibid.
135. [1993] TLR 125 (CA).
136 . [1983] TLR 186 (CA).
137. Ibid.
138. The CA of Tanzania, Criminal Appeal no. 3 of 1990, decided by Makame, Ramadhan, and Mnzavas, Justices of Appeal (unreported).
139. (1983) TLR 186 (CA).
140. Ibid.
141. Court of Appeal Tanzania, Criminal Appeal No. 3 of 1990, Dar Es Salaam Registry (Unreported).
142. Allen, et al.

Chapter 5

Circumstantial Evidence and Entrapment: The U.S. Jurisprudential Experience

5.1. The Law on Entrapment: The Defence

Chapter 4 dwelt at length on theories and empirical research on the reliability of circumstantial evidence as opposed to the widely and passionately held view that direct evidence is more reliable than circumstantial evidence.

In this chapter, focus will be devoted to the USA's jurisprudence on entrapment cases for the purpose of drawing analogy with Tanzania's experience on the same subject. This is primarily because the research for this study found that the U.S. jurisprudence on entrapment cases is highly developed, and hence the researcher's choice of it. The defence of entrapment is not common in Tanzania, nor has it had its roots in the Commonwealth—hence the focus on the USA for the purposes of drawing its utility in Tanzania, where no efforts have been made to utilise this defence of entrapment.

The purpose of this chapter is to introduce the defence of entrapment in the Tanzanian jurisprudence, particularly where defendants are charged with corruption cases and other white-collar crimes where entrapment is an issue. The jurisprudence on entrapment draws a significant utility of circumstantial evidence, the heart of this book. Legal practitioners and the judiciary in Tanzania may find this theory on entrapment quite useful and effective, especially where the law enforcement officials or agencies charged with bringing down corruption in society ignore following professionalism and the laid-down ethical ethos in carrying out investigations.

Richard Lusalico saw entrapment as a criminal defence based upon a claim that law enforcement officials induced the accused to commit the crime charged. Insalaco et al. viewed this defence as relatively novel and unique to American law.[1] The genesis of entrapment defence was due to the following background. In the late nineteenth century, a flurry of legislation proscribed activities such as prostitution, homosexuality, gambling, and trafficking in obscene materials, narcotics, and liquor. Because such vice offences normally occurred in private and involved a willing victim who would not complain, the then prevailing methods of police detection were inadequate. To enforce the new statute, law enforcement agencies thus had to rely on informants and undercover agents to a much greater extent than ever before.[2]

Although entrapment has been in existence for the past half a century, courts have disagreed as to whether a defendant should be able to plead denial with entrapment as a substitute defence. In this chapter, the examination focuses on two contentious, opposing theories borne out of this disagreement by the courts: subjective and objective approaches.

In examining the defence of entrapment, the courts have set forth three questions to determine its application:

(a) Did the agent induce the accused to commit the offense charged in the indictment?

(b) If so, was the accused ready and willing without permission and was he awaiting any propitious opportunity to commit the offense?
(c) On the first question, the accused has the burden; on the second question, the prosecution has it.[3]

In Tanzania, Judge Mapigano dealt with the defence of entrapment in the case of *R. v. Stephen Dominic Mtetewaunga*,[4] which was discussed in chapter 3 of this book. The important facts in this case in relation to entrapment are that, following their (Swai and Mtetewaunga's) encounter the previous day at Lango la Jiji Bar, the next day (7 June 1986), Swai complained to the ACS and a trap was set up by ACS against the defendant (Mtetewaunga), and a sum of TSh 2,000 was given to Swai, being powdered and marked currency notes of TSh 100 denomination. Swai then went to the office of the defendant and, after a brief conversation, he handed over the money to the defendant. The next thing to happen was Swai got up and left without collecting the letter and. soon thereafter, ACS officers who were around to witness the transaction, stalked into the office of the defendant, apprehended and searched his person, and recovered the trap money. What is interesting in this case was that the day (7 June 1986) on which Swai went to the defendant's office was a Saturday, not a working day for public offices.

In his defence testimony, the defendant accounted that Swai was a drinking pal and regarded him as a friend. He denied ever soliciting a bribe from Swai and that he had directed his personal secretary to hand over to him the letter of reply to his complaint on the fateful day. When Swai entered his office, he asked him whether the secretary had given him his letter of reply and he had said he had been given the letter; Swai had then asked him if he was going to drop by at the club in the evening. He replied to say he had an appointment at Upanga, which he felt obliged to keep. Swai then produced the trap money and gave it to him, saying, 'Take this amount for your week end'. He received the money and pocketed it without counting it. He said he received the money in good conscience and that it never crossed his mind that there was anything wrong or sinister with the money. Judge Mapigano was of the view that the defendant received the money in the context of a brotherly relationship that then existed between them.

Judge Mapigano's findings on the case were as follows. The defendant was a public officer at the material time. Further, the defendant knew at the time that Swai had been concerned in a matter with himself as a public officer. For the words 'to have been concerned' show that obtaining an advantage would be an offence even if it is obtained after business or the proceedings are over.[5] What was more important in the defence of entrapment were the three questions that the court ought to ask and answer them in weighing the evidence before it. Did the agent induce the accused to commit the offense charged in the indictment? If so, was the accused ready and willing without permission and was he awaiting any propitious opportunity to commit the offense? On the first question, the accused has the burden; on the second question, the prosecution has it. These issues were not adequately answered in Mtetewaunga's[6] case to satisfy the defence of entrapment.

In his response to a number of objections to entrapment as unfair, Anthony M. Dillof[7] contended that the subjective version of entrapment defence has a two-part structure. In most courts employing the subjective version, a defendant wishing to assert entrapment must first establish by a preponderance of the evidence that a government agent 'induced' him to commit the crime he is charged with. If he is unsuccessful, the defence fails. If the defendant is successful in carrying this burden of proof, the burden shifts to the government to prove beyond a reasonable doubt that the defendant was 'predisposed' to commit the crime. If the government carries the burden of proof demonstrating predisposition, the defence fails. However, if at this point, the government fails to prove predisposition beyond a reasonable doubt, the defendant is acquitted on the grounds of entrapment.[8]

A person may not be convicted of a crime if he has been encouraged to commit it by a government agent under the appropriate circumstances. Only government inducement will qualify a defendant for entrapment. Where the government has played no significant role, the question of a predisposition does not arise. If the issue of predisposition arises then it is a question for the jury to consider the following factors relevant to whether a predisposition to the offence charged existed:

(a) The character or reputation of the defendant, including any prior criminal record;
(b) Whether the government initially suggested the criminal activity;
(c) Whether the defendant engaged in the crime for profit;
(d) The nature of government inducement; and, most importantly,
(e) Whether the defendant expressed reluctance to commit the crime, which had to be overcome through repeated government inducement.[9]

Theoretically, though the subjective and objective versions of entrapment are distinct, analysis of inducement and predisposition through case law, as is examined hereinafter, often overlap.[10] Anthony M. Dillof examined inducement at great length. According to him, inducement may be defined expansively as 'soliciting, proposing, initiating, broaching, or suggesting the commission of the offense charged'. It is clear that inducement requires more than merely the furnishing of an opportunity for crime. An offer to purchase drugs at market price, for example, is not an inducement. Nevertheless, inducement does not require that the government agent's conduct caused the defendant to commit the crime. Significantly, there is no formal requirement that the inducement offered by the government rise to a particular level of force, persuasiveness, or pressure. For example, entrapment has been found as a matter of law where a 1930s prohibition agent, after establishing that he and the defendant had served in the same army division, merely made repeated requests for illegal liquor to the defendant. Likewise, entrapment has been found as a matter of law based merely on repeated requests for narcotics by an acquaintance claiming to need them to assuage his addiction. Rather than focusing on the conduct of tempter, the requirement of inducement in practice seems to focus on the status of the tempter.[11]

In the case of *United States v. Hollingsworth*,[12] the issue of inducement was clearly brought out into a clear judicial picture. Arnold Hollingsworth, an Arkansas farmer and businessman, and William Pickard, an orthodontist, were convicted of money laundering by a jury. The two partners had established a corporation in the Virgin Islands, *Compagnie d'Investement de les Antilles Limittée* (CIAL), to conduct international banking. The business venture steadily lost money. To keep the corporation afloat, Pickard decided to acquire working capital by selling one of CIAL's assets, and he placed a classified ad in *USA Today* advertising the sale of a CIAL Grenadian banking license.

A U.S. customs agent, Rothrock, observed the ad and believed that an individual desiring to sell a banking license might be interested in money laundering. Over a period of time, Rothrock contacted Pickard on numerous occasions and continued to express his ambition to deposit large sums of cash. Pickard subsequently refused three times to assist Rothrock in depositing funds. Finally, Rothrock arranged a transaction with Pickard for a fee of US$2,045. Pickard agreed to deposit in a local bank a total of US$200,000 in increments. Rothrock and Pickard met in an Indianapolis hotel room to make the cash exchanges. During the last scheduled exchange, Pickard was arrested. So was Hollingsworth, at the same time, while in Arkansas, for his single trip to Indianapolis in lieu of Pickard. A jury convicted Hollingsworth and Pickard. On appeal, the U.S. CA for the seventh circuit reversed the conviction, holding that to survive the entrapment defence, the prosecution must prove that the defendant was both willing and ready to commit the crime before the government offered him the opportunity to engage in the prescribed activity.

Lori J. Rankin[13] provided another source of case law on entrapment and considered its implication against the Supreme Court interpretations. The Court addressed for the first time the issue of entrapment in the case of *Sorrells v. U.S.*[14] that enough evidence had been presented at trial to demonstrate that Sorrels had been induced by the government to commit the crime for which he had been convicted. The Court further noted that Sorrels had not possessed a prior disposition to commit the crime.

The court stated that law enforcement depends in part upon the governments ability to employ 'artifice and stratagem' to reveal criminal activity. The court noted that the law enforcement crosses the bounds of its authority when its officials implant in an innocent mind a disposition to commit the criminal activity. 'Common justice' requires that the defendant be afforded the opportunity to prove that he was induced by the government to commit a crime that was the 'product of the creative activity' of law enforcement officials.[15]

In *Sherman v. United States*,[16] the Supreme Court reaffirmed its holding in *Sorrells* that government activity that merely presents individuals with the opportunity or means to commit a particular crime does not constitute entrapment. The entrapment defence is based on a factual determination, and that entrapment occurs only when the crime is produced by the 'creative activity' of government agents.[17]

The court further observed that the government had failed to demonstrate that Sherman would have been 'ready and willing' to sell narcotics had the opportunity been presented without government inducement. The government agent had played on the weakness of an innocent party and beguiled him into committing crimes, which he otherwise would not have attempted.[18]

Fifteen years later, the Supreme Court, in *United States v. Russell*,[19] addressed the defence of entrapment, stating that 'the lower court had expanded the SORRELLS entrapment defence doctrine by focusing on government conduct rather than on the conduct and predisposition of the defendant'.[20]

Rankin noted further that the Supreme Court explicitly rejected such an expansion. Instead, the court reaffirmed the majority opinions in *Sorrells* and *Sherman* that the entrapment defence is available only when the government's deception actually implants the criminal's design in the mind of the defendant.[21]

Explaining the basics of the objective version of entrapment, Anthony M. Dillof stated that the objective version of the defence is simpler in structure than the subjective version. The sole and central issue is simply whether the government's conduct created a substantial risk such that an offence would be committed by persons other than those who are ready to commit it or, alternatively, by normally law abiding persons. In contrast to the subjective version of the defence, the defendant's characteristics, including any predisposition to crime, are irrelevant. The focus of the inquiry is how the police conduct at issue may affect a member of the public in the abstract, not the defendant in particular. Examples of government conduct found to have violated the objective standard including appealing to a close personal relationship with the defendant, forming a sexual relationship with the defendant, and offering excessive amounts of money.[22]

In the case of *Mathews v. United States*,[23] Mathews, a small business administration (SBA) employee responsible for providing aid to small businesses, was charged with accepting a bribe in exchange for granting SBA loans to a participating business. The district court denied Mathews' motion in trying to raise an entrapment defence, because Mathews refused to admit all of the elements of the charged offence, including the requisite mental state. Following his conviction, Mathews appealed to the U.S. CA for the seventh circuit, which upheld the lower court's ruling.

The sole issue before the Supreme Court was whether the district court had erred in refusing to instruct the jury regarding entrapment because the defendant had denied the charged crime. The Court held that, when sufficient evidence is presented at trial to allow a reasonable jury to conclude that the defendant was entrapped, the defendant is entitled to an entrapment instruction, even if the dependant denies an element of the crime.[24]

Rankin's analysis was that the *Mathews* court conclusion was that predisposition focuses upon whether the defendant was an 'unwary innocent', rather than an 'unwary criminal' who readily availed himself of the opportunity to perpetrate the crime.[25]

In the recent case of *Jacobson v. United States*,[26] Jacobson was convicted by a lower court for knowingly receiving, through the mail, magazines that depicted minors engaged in sexually explicit activity. The Supreme Court held that the government must establish that the defendant was predisposed to commit the crime prior to the government's approach. The government had overstepped the line between setting a trap for the 'unwary innocent' and the 'unwary criminal'. The government had failed to prove that Jacobson had been 'independently predisposed' to commit the crime for which he was convicted.[27]

Jacobson was targeted by the government sting operation following his legal mail-order purchase of two magazines that contained photographs of nude teenage boys. Within months after this purchase, congress had passed the Child Protection Act (1984), which prohibited the receipt through the mail of materials depicting minors engaged in sexually explicit activity.

The same month that the new law became effective, government agents found Jacobson's name on the mailing list of the bookstore from which he had previously ordered magazines. Over the next twenty-six months, the government agencies targeted Jacobson by establishing five fictitious organisations that purported to research consumer's sexual interest through surveys, to advocate free expression, and to sell 'stimulating' items to interested parties.

The government sent Jacobson various materials from these organisations on several occasions during its twenty-six-month investigation. Jacobson answered and returned surveys and briefs, and communicated with a government agent posing as a pen pal. After receiving a letter promising that the government could not view his mail, Jacobson ordered a magazine titled *Boys Who Love Boys*. He was arrested after a controlled delivery of his order.

A government search of Jacobson's home revealed the magazines that Jacobson had purchased prior to the Child Protection Act and the materials that the government had sent him during its investigation. Aside from the copy of *Boys Who Love Boys*, the government did not find any evidence demonstrating that Jacobson had used the mail for receipt of published materials.[28]

Rankin opined that the Jacobson opinion is significant for two reasons. First, the court expressly stated for the first time that to obtain a conviction when the defendant raises a valid entrapment defence, the government must demonstrate that the defendant was predisposed prior to government contact. Consequently, several courts and commentators have concluded that Jacobson established a new law regarding the entrapment defence.

Second, as the subject of this case note illustrates, at least one lower court has had difficulty in interpreting and applying Jacobson's mandate. This difficulty demonstrates courts' need to definitively articulate the defence and the applicable standard that lower courts should apply in determining whether a defendant was indeed entrapped, thereby making the governments' burden more difficult and making entrapment a more feasible defence for guilty defendants.[29]

The preceding cases reflect the position taken by the U.S. Supreme Court, as Rebecca Roiphe observed chronologically, as follows. In 1864 a New York trial court confronted a fairly run-of-the-mill entrapment defence. The judge, like most judges at the time, rejected the defence, admonishing that the great lawgiver overruled such tactics back when Eve complained, '[T]he serpent beguiled me, and I did eat'. The decades that followed witnessed an unprecedented retreat from this lofty precedent.[30]

At the end of the nineteenth century, as Rebecca Roiphe further explained, the machinery of the state had transformed so radically that the law could no longer protect individuals by securing a boundary around their person and their property. Serving as a neutral arbiter between one individual and the next proved not only insufficient, but also impossible. Notions of contractual relations, even stretched to their extreme, could not accommodate the modern state with its many tentacles reaching into realms of privacy that people never thought could be threatened. Sting operations conducted by state and federal detectives offered a fairly concrete example of how government had outgrown its neutral status. Thus, the state seemed both impersonal in its growingly distant, bureaucratic, and centralised form, ironically, and visible in officers' presence in the average citizen's daily life. Entrapment emerged as two visions of the state as one of many turn-of-the-century legal developments that subtly redrew the boundary between the individual and the government.[31]

On corruption, Rebecca Roiphe accounted that, throughout the country, the police gradually allied themselves with corrupt city politicians and grew increasingly ineffective at managing the escalating crime rates. There was also a kind of deliberate tolerance and, at times, an outright acceptance of vice. Ward bosses depended on police to manipulate the poles, provide patronage jobs, and grant favours for constituents. Police officers and their supervisors in turn were beholden to politicians for their jobs and coveted promotions. Officers in New York, for example, paid regular fees to Tammany leaders, which they then coupled by extorting money from saloons, gambling houses, and brothels. Thus, city politics operated in the shadow of the uneasy alliance between police, politicians, and the underworld.[32]

On police corruption, Roiphe reported further that, because police depended on revenue from crime just as politicians depended on votes and fees from the police, officers did not attempt to suppress crime or vice—they regulated it. Police in Chicago, for examples, facilitated illicit activity by dividing their beats between warring gangs of pickpockets. They staged arrests so that angry victims would feel vindicated, and then promptly released the culprit for a small fee. To further this symbiotic relationship, detectives developed a network of informers and maintained extensive relationships with the underworld—even conscientious detectives were so involved with the underworld that there was only a thin line between being guardians against crime and partners with criminals.[33]

Roiphe concluded that entrapment has gone through three different stages: First, the nineteenth-century private law model of entrapment; second, the emergence of the defence as a means of exonerating criminals who were created or planted by the state; and, finally, the academic push for an objective model of entrapment designed to deter government misconduct.[34]

It is further noted that, prior to 1870, no state or federal court recognised entrapment as a valid defence. The courts were influenced by a common law consent doctrine based on private law notions of contract.

5.2. Doctrine of Consent

Roiphe stated that the doctrine of consent dictates that if force (or lack of consent) is an element of a crime and the victim cooperates with authorities in capturing the perpetrator, then courts cannot convict, because the very act of entrapping the criminal negates a material aspect of the crime.[35]

After the Civil War, the court adopted the principles of the law of contract and agency, to the effect that, if a decoy was employed by the police to participate in the burglary with the consent of the owner, there was no burglary.[36] In the mid-nineteenth century, courts primarily expressed their approval of law enforcement tactics involving deceit and trickery to catch criminals.[37]

The current thinking of the courts focuses on whether criminal intent originates from the defendant. A successful defence has to prove that the government manipulated the defendant into committing a crime that he or she would not otherwise have consummated.[38]

In evaluating evidence pertaining to the actions of government officials and their informers, insofar as they were relevant in determining the origin of criminal design, the courts held that it is not proper, even during an investigation, to entice or persuade any one contrary to his or her own will or inclination, or to violate the laws of this state. If you find that the criminal design originated not with the accused, but was conceived in the mind of the officers of the state, and the accused was by persuasion or inducement lured into the commission of a criminal act, then it is proper to acquit.[39]

In the case of *Casey v. United States*,[40] the Supreme Court directed that the government could set decoys and lay traps, but it may not provoke or create a crime and then punish the criminal, its creature.[41]

In her comments, Roiphe distinguished the period when the courts applied subjective as well as objective tests in entrapment cases.

> The history of law enforcement and entrapment is useful because it illustrates that the defence emerged primarily as a way of

> redefining criminal responsibility and antinomy after the civil war. Most courts in the first decades of the defence reasoned that the accused simply was not guilty if government official manufactured the crime and moulded the criminal..., but the objective test follows logically only if the primary role of defence is to deter governmental misconduct and preserve the purity of the courts. The subjective test embodies the slightly different earlier concern about what exactly constitutes criminal responsibility: a person cannot be considered responsible if he did not act of his own free will, especially when the government has the power to undermine free will through its control over resources and information, and through its power of persuasion.[42]

On entrapment, Allen et al. argued that these defences recognise that virtually anyone can be induced to commit an otherwise illegal act when the ratio of potential benefit to potential harm (expected return, in the language of microeconomics) is high enough. The same logic applies to entrapment.[43]

5.3. Predisposition and Induced Acts

Allen et al. clarified the two tests in current use. The subjective test asks, was the defendant predisposed to commit the crime when he was approached by the government agent? The objective test asks, did the government's encouragement of crime exceed acceptable limits?[44]

Allen et al. countered the proposition that there are two versions of the test—the subjective and objective; that is—quite beside the point—the controversy presupposed the existence of a fictional entity, predisposition. Because a necessary ingredient of the subjective version of the test does not exist, the test, rather plainly, cannot be applied in any way that allows useful propositions to be asserted about the existence of predisposition, except to assert its nonexistence. Because predisposition does not exist, no one is, under any circumstances, 'predisposed' to commit the crime; alternatively, everyone, under every conceivable circumstance, is predisposed to commit the crime. Such is the consequence of using false propositions in one's analysis and, in any event, the point is that 'predisposition' cannot sort anyone from anyone else and thus is useless as a tool designed for just that purpose.[45]

Allen et al. justified their reasoning that everyone else, it is assumed, has a price; the price may be quite high because, for example, a person puts a high value on her good name, but it exists nonetheless. If this assumption is true, then everyone—except saints—is predisposed to commit crimes. But, that in turn means that predisposition cannot usefully distinguish anyone from anyone else. The only salient question is whether a person's price has been met, not whether he has one, since by hypothesis everyone but the saintly does. The real point is that talk of predisposition is meaningless and commits an existential fallacy. A person who takes the bait has had his price met; a person who does not, has not. But the person who does not take the bait almost surely would take a higher bait. The failure to take this one is evidence of his price, but nothing to do with predisposition.[46]

When individuals are induced to commit acts, and those acts actually cause specific harm—such as in the case of violence—entrapment is not available. Such persons are blameworthy even if induced. Entrapment is largely about human frailty in the context of markets—monetary and emotional; it is about the corrupting effect of riches beyond one's reasonable expectations. In other words, to use Allen's analogy, everyone has a price dictated by the market.[47] In response to Allen's critique of the two versions of entrapment, Anthony M. Dillof argued as follows:

> Allen's argument for the acquittal of the entrapped applies with equal force to cases of government and private entrapment. A defendant accepting an above-market criminal solicitation does not indicate a real world propensity to crime whether the offer was made to a government agent or private citizen. Allen, however, is not embarrassed by this implication of his theory. According to Allen, cases of private entrapment will be highly unlikely. To overlap the market price is, in Allen's view, tantamount to a charitable donation.[48]

Kenneth M. Lord, another researcher on entrapment, asked the same question that is so fundamental to the doctrine of entrapment, vis., 'Why should society exculpate those committing crimes at the behest of the government, but not those beguiled into criminal activity by someone else?[49]

The judiciary in the U.S. has developed two tests: the objective form of entrapment defence emphasises the nature of the government's actions, while the subjective form focuses on the defendant's state of mind.[50]

The objective test focuses on the conduct of the government actor, rather than on the defendant's predisposition or culpability: if the government engaged in conduct that was illegal or inappropriate, then courts applying the objective standard may find that the defendant was entrapped, regardless of other considerations.

Kenneth M. Lord's analysis of the hybrid approaches to entrapment showed that, although it has its benefits, the composite hybrid approach has its own weakness. He contended that, while the various creators of the composite hybrid approach presumably aspired to maximise the fairness and benefits associated with the entrapment defence, they merely succeeded in negating the benefits of the individual subjective and objective approaches. The primary societal benefit of the subjective standard is that those who would not commit a crime on their own are not punished for committing it at the behest of the government. However, this benefit is significantly diminished under the composite approach when an additional burden is placed on the defendant to prove that the police used improper or egregious methods to coerce her behaviour. One of the principal advantages of the objective standard is that it avoids some of the difficulties of the subjective standard—there is no need to introduce prejudicial evidence of the defendant's reputation or past behaviour, and there is greater equity of treatment between predisposed and nonpredisposed defendants. These advantages, too, are lost under the composite hybrid approach because the defendant is still required to answer the subjective inquiry concern.[51]

On his part, Anthony M. Dillof was of the contrary view: there are benefits of entrapment and conviction because theorists distinguish between general specific deterrence—the deterrence of a punished person who learns the hard way that crime does not pay—and general deterrence of the members of the general population who learn the lesson through observation of examples. Entrapping and convicting a nondisposed individual would send an enormously powerful message that the government is aggressively enforcing a given prohibition. Quantifying the net effects of any proposed rule of law has always been the bane of utilitarianism. Still, as a broad proposition, it is hard to doubt that punishing more will deter more. Such an effect is particularly important in the prevention of so-called victimless crimes, such as narcotics trafficking and prostitution, where the traditional law enforcement techniques are less effective. Any convictions—even those of nondisposed individuals—advance the cause of general deterrence. Furthermore, the police have an inherent interest in not expending resources where there will be no net reduction in crimes. It may therefore be presumed that the police would only engage in entrapment where they had reason to believe significant deterrence would result. Entrapment requires a high degree of subtlety and precision.[52]

5.4. ENCOURAGEMENT

Jonathan C. Carlson wrote on the subject of entrapment that the most objectionable feature of encouragement is that, by using it, the government is no longer in a neutral position vis-à-vis its citizens and the choice that they make. Rather than giving an individual full freedom to comply with the law, and thereby respect individual autonomy and the ability to avoid crime, by offering encouragement, the government tries to persuade the individual to violate the law. By manipulating the arrays of choices facing the individual, encouragement saps the individual's ability to resist crime and to avoid punishment. Encouragement circumvents the requirements of the act restrain the state's intrusive powers.[53]

However, Anthony M. Dillof responded strongly to Carson's autonomy of the individual, arguing that the primary purpose of criminal law is to establish an incentive system to influence the choices people make and to guide their conduct. Deterring a person from an immoral act is surely a legitimate interference with an individual's decision making. However, a person who is entrapped is fully culpable for his conduct—being enticed into crime by an appealing officer is not analogous to brainwashing, precisely because we believe a person should be able to resist such pressures. This culpability implies that decision to engage in criminal conduct in light of the inducement was autonomous.[54]

Dillof expressed entrapment as an unfair enterprise in abstract forms, that a government's practice of imposing burdens in order to achieve a general social good is fair only if the burdens are imposed pursuant to allocating such burdens generally among those expected to benefit from the practice.[55]

However, the government practice will be unfair if it violates that principle. Nonetheless, entrapment is justified, as expounded by Dworkin's views that it is not always incoherent to invite someone to do the very act that one is trying to get them to avoid doing. Consider a parent trying to teach a child not to touch a stove. In the case of a particularly recalcitrant child, the most effective technique might be to encourage the child to touch the stove in one's presence. The slight pain now will teach the child to avoid the greater pain later.[56]

Dillof responded to the critique against the government's entrapment with the following analogy:

> Taxation provides a particularly germane example. It is unfair and improper for the government to select a person to be taxed based on a morally arbitrary characteristic, for example, being seated at the end of a bar in a local nightclub. However, it is neither unfair nor improper for the government to impose a tax based on a morally relevant characteristic, such as net income. This is true even if it is morally arbitrary that a person happens to possess that characteristic, for example, by winning a large promotion prize based on random drawing. Likewise it is unfair and improper for the government to target for entrapment the person who happens to be seated at the end of a bar in a local nightclub,

> while it is acceptable to prosecute and convict someone who others have arbitrarily selected, perhaps through location at a nightclub, to have the morally relevant characteristic of criminal culpability.[57]

On the one hand, Carlson explained the justification for police entrapment by saying that, to secure the trust and cooperation of the criminals whose activities they seek to uncover, government undercover operatives must be prepared to cultivate a target over a period of time, to make repeated overtures to that target, and to offer some inducement to the target as the price of the agents' admission to the criminal activity. Consequently, police solicitation and inducement of criminal conduct are believed to be necessary in order to investigate and stop crimes that are committed in secret among willing participants.[58]

On the other hand, Carlson reflected on the use of agents provocateurs in this way: the use of agents provocateurs to obtain evidence against individuals by inducing and participating in criminal acts is a feared tool of government oppression, used historically by repressive regimes seeking to suppress their political opponents. Such a tactic also creates grave risks of leading otherwise law abiding persons into crime. The combination of an ongoing relationship between the undercover agent and his target, the necessity for the government to offer inducements to secure action by the suspected criminal, the police officer's natural desire for professional success, and the use of informants of uncertain reliability is a mixture with potential for abuse.[59]

Thus, entrapment defence should be understood as a tool with many functions but a single goal—repairing the damage that encouragement causes to the criminal law's commitments to justified punishment and personal freedom.[60]

On the same topic of entrapment, David J. Elbaz concluded that entrapment defence is a tool of compromise because, on the one hand, government involvement in unlawful activities and provocation of crime may be the only effective way to detect various crimes. On the other hand, the use of government agents to induce and participate in criminal acts can be considered oppressive and may lead to harm within society.[61] The gravest harm occurs when these tactics lead an ordinary law abiding person into crime. The entrapment defence exists to directly prevent this harm and indirectly to prevent other associated types of harm.[62]

Elbaz anchored his argument on entrapment from an economist's point of view that an economic account of crime demonstrates that a rational actor will engage in a crime when expected benefits outweigh expected costs. Under efficient sanctions, the costs of a crime marginally outweigh its associated benefits, and rational actors will not choose to engage in the crime. Entrapment strategies can, however, affect both the costs and benefits of crime. When used in a limited and careful manner, entrapment strategies are a useful enforcement tool and can be an effective method of increasing deterrence levels. The economic approach suggests that efficiency can help to delineate the proper limits of entrapment tactics. Entrapment strategies are likely to be inefficient in two principal circumstances. The first circumstance is whenever government tactics sharply increase the benefits ordinarily associated with a crime. In this situation, a target rationally responds to the extraordinary inducement and commits the crime, yet the commission of crime under these circumstances offers unreliable evidence that the target would have committed such a crime under ordinary circumstances. The second circumstance is when the government agents squander resources in an effort to sharply decrease an individual's probability of conviction.[63]

This approach insists that entrapment strategies should apply only where the tactics use reliable evidence that a target would engage in the crime under ordinary circumstances and such tactics yield a marginal increase in deterrence levels. If an entrapment yields neither result, it is inefficient, and entrapment defence should be considered applicable.

The same conclusions were reached through the model penal code, and the minority of the Supreme Court justices in *Sorrells*[64] that have favoured the objective approach to entrapment: the defence of entrapment was intended to control undesirable police conduct, not to free an otherwise innocent defendant; the court had inherent authority to forbid government entrapment without relying on a fictional statement about legislative intent; and a defendant's predisposition had nothing to do with whether particular police conduct was permissible.[65]

Karis A. Hastings proposed, however, that the inconsistency rule must focus on balancing society's interest in the truth-finding function of criminal trials against the need to protect the interests of criminal defendants. There is justification for prohibiting a defendant from both denying the crime and pleading entrapment. Such a prohibition is essential to the truth-seeking function of criminal trial and to deterring the commission of perjury by criminal defendants. It simply denies the defendant the opportunity to present two defences that cannot both be true.[66]

Allen et al. convincingly replied to all their critics by arguing that the discussion in the cases of whether the defendant was a willing participant or the government implanted the criminal design in the defendant or created the crime verge on the silly. The defendant is always 'willing' (otherwise there would be no need to rely on entrapment—duress would do) and, to our knowledge, the government has never physically opened the brain of a defendant and 'implanted' anything. Perhaps the government implants criminal designs psychologically but, again, if so, it is always so, for the government always plays a causal role in the act. In all cases of police involvement, and thus of potential entrapment, the act would not have occurred as it did but for the involvement of the police—a tautology if ever there was one. Nor does the objectivity test avoid this point, simply because it pragmatically operates upon the assumption of the existence of predisposition as a real thing. Without predisposition as a sorting mechanism, the objective test is rootless.[67]

Allen et al. concluded that government-encouraged criminal conduct will not be punished unless either (a) the encouraged conduct injured or seriously threatened to injure the interests protected by the law in question, or (b) the defendant initiated the criminal act or transaction in response to an opportunity to commit the crime that was neither uncommon nor excessive.[68]

5.5. Practice of Entrapment Law in the U.S. and Its Relevance to Tanzania

It is appropriate to conclude the analysis by saying that the law on entrapment in the U.S. is a rich exposition of the subject matter, for which Tanzanian legal practitioners and courts should borrow a leaf of experience to see how it can be applied in corruption cases and other white-collar crimes, especially in relation to circumstantial evidence.

Nonetheless, the point that this study is making is that the defence of entrapment should be used by the defence counsel or the accused charged with corruption cases in appropriate situations, to challenge the use of such excessive means by the investigators in tracking down criminals who commit crimes of such serious magnitude. Innocence of defendants must be seen to be preserved in any civilised and democratic society, because it is one of the fundamental and tenets of the rule of law, which guarantees fairness and justice in the dispensation of criminal proceedings.

ENDNOTES

1. Richard C. Insalaco and Peter G. Fitzgerald, 'Note: Denying the Crime and Pleading Entrapment: Putting the Federal Law in Order', *University of Michigan Journal of Law Reform* 20, no. 2 (1986–1987): 567.
2. Ibid.
3. Ibid.
4. *Mtetewaunga*, Judge Mapigano made reference to the case of *Ramadhan Masoud v. R.* (1974) LRT 31, 114.
5. Ibid.
6. Ibid.
7. Anthony M. Dillof, 'Unravelling Unlawful Entrapment', *Journal of Criminal Law and Criminology* 94, no. 4 (Summer, 2004): 828.
8. Ibid., 832.
9. Ibid., 833–834.
10. Ibid.
11. Ibid.
12. 9F.3d 593 (7th Cir. 1993), 1994 U.S. App. LexisNexis 588 (7th Cir. 10 Jan 1994).
13. Lori J. Rankin, 'Entrapment: A Defense for the Willing, Yet Unready Criminal?', *University of Cincinnati Law Review* 63 (1994): 1487.
14. 287, U.S. 443.
15. Ibid.
16. 356 U.S. 369 (1958).
17. Ibid.
18. Ibid., 376.
19. 411 U.S. 423, 433 (1973).
20. Ibid.
21. Rankin, 'Entrapment'.
22. Dillof, 'Unravelling Unlawful Entrapment', 836.
23. 485 U.S. 58, 62 (1988).
24. Ibid.
25. Rankin, 'Entrapment'.
26. 1125. Ct. 1535 (1992).
27. Ibid.
28. Ibid.
29. Rankin, 'Entrapment'.

30. Rebecca Roiphe, 'The Serpent Beguiled Me: A History of the Entrapment Defense', *Seten Hall Law Review* 33 (2003): 257. See also *Board of Commissioner of Excise v. Backus*, 29 How. Pr 33 (N.Y. Sup. Ct.1864).
31. Ibid.
32. Ibid.
33. Ibid.
34. Ibid.
35. Ibid.
36. Ibid. See Eggington's case, 2 East's P.C. 666 (1801), where the court noted that when a property owner cooperates with authorities in capturing a burglar, he essentially assents to the entry, thereby negating trespass, an essential element of the crime.
37. Ibid. See *Board of Commissioners of Excise v. Backus 29 How*. Pr. 33 (N.Y. Sup. Ct. 1864): the court reasoned that because Backus was guiltier than the commissioners, the two were not in *pari delicto*, and the court ought not to shield the guiltier from the consequences of his act.
38. Ibid.
39. 276 U.S. 413, 416–417 (1928).
40. Ibid.
41. Roiphe, 'The Serpent Beguiled Me'.
42. Ronald J. Allen, 'Clarifying Entrapment', *Journal of Criminal Law and Criminology* 89, no. 2 (Winter, 1999): 407.
43. Ibid.
44. Ibid., 588.
45. Ibid.
46. Ibid., 413.
47. Dillof, 'Unravelling Unlawful Entrapment', 857.
48. Kenneth M. Lord, 'Entrapment and Due Process: Moving toward a Dual System of Defences', *Florida State University Law Review* 25 (Spring, 1998): 463.
49. Ibid.
50. Lord, 'Entrapment and Due Process'.
51. Dillof, 'Unravelling Unlawful Entrapment'.
52. Jonathan C. Carlson, 'The Act Requirement and The Foundation of The Entrapment Defense', *Virginia Law Review* 73 (1987), 1011, 1063.
53. Dillof, 'Entrapment and Due Process'.
54. Ibid.
55. Ibid.
56. Ibid.

57. Carlson, 'The Act Requirement'.
58. Ibid.
59. Ibid. See also John Rawls, *A Theory of Justice* (Cambridge, MA: Belknap Press, 1999), 3. On the one hand, retributive justice in the context of criminal justice system justifies harsh treatment of an actor as an intrinsically morally appropriate or permissible response to actor's wrongful conduct towards his victim. 'Interactive justice', on the other hand, asserts that a three-place relationship involves wrongdoer, victim, and government; whereas 'distributive justice', though most likely inapplicable in criminal realm, propound that a social system will be deemed just to the extent that its institutions maximise the welfare of the least well-off members of society, that is, raise the tail end of the wealth distribution curve.
60. David J. Elbaz, 'Note: The Troubling Entrapment Defence: How About an Economic Approach?', *American Criminal Law Review* 36 (Winter, 1999): 117.
61. Ibid.
62. Ibid.
63. 287 U.S. 453.
64. Ibid. See also Insalaco and Fitzgerald, 'Note: Denying the Crime and Pleading Entrapment', 567.
65. Karis A. Hastings, 'Note: Entrapment and Denial of the Crime: A Defence of Inconsistency Rule', *Duke Law Journal* 866 (1986).
66. Allen, Kuhns, and Swift, *Evidence*.
67. Ibid.
68. Ibid.

Chapter 6

The Use of Covert Operations in White-Collar Cases and Its Rationale: An Investigative Perspective

6.1. White-Collar Crimes

The investigation of complex crimes such as corruption and other white-collar crimes demands the use of covert tactics to be able to penetrate and expose criminal syndicates. The evidence that is normally brought to fore after the application of covert operation techniques is by and large circumstantial evidence, given the complexity and secrecy surrounding the commission of corruption offences.

In this chapter, attention is given to such use of covert operations in complex crimes, especially white-collar crimes, such as embezzlement, fraud, computer crimes, money laundering, business crimes, export control crimes, narcotics, and corruption. They are not violent crimes and thus, seemingly, victimless.

For an embezzlement to occur, for example, the embezzler must have, first, a nonsharable financial problem; second, the knowledge necessary to commit the crime; thirdly, the use of a suitable rationalisation to adjust the contradiction between his or her actions and the normative standards of society.[1]

For a successful prosecution of corruption cases, undercover operations are essential and demand criminal profiling. Criminal profiling is a high-profile investigative technique. Therefore, a criminal profiler should have some understanding of psychology, the study of individual behaviour; sociology, the study of group behaviour, groups being comprised of individuals; *criminalistics*, a general term for the scientific study of the recognition, collection, and preservation of physical evidence as it relates to law; and forensic pathology, a branch of medicine that applies the principles and knowledge of the medical sciences to problems in the field of law.

Criminal profiling in the context of undercover and covert investigations should unfold a lot of circumstantial evidence and is thus relevant to this study, because the means to acquire circumstantial evidence is through covert operations and undercover techniques.

In 1939 Edwin H. Sutherland introduced to the world the idea of white-collar crimes in the academic world; this occurred during his presidential address to the American Sociological Society in Philadelphia, and he defined a white-collar criminal as 'a person with high socioeconomic status who violates the laws designed to regulate his occupational activities'.[2]

Another definition of white-collar crime provides that it is the illegal abuse of power by the upper-echelon businessmen in the service of their corporations, by high-ranking politicians against their codes of conduct and their constituents, and by professional persons against the government and against their clients and patients.[3] Gilbert Geiz viewed white-collar crimes as crimes by the powerful, upper-world crime, crimes in the suites, organisational crimes, and abuse of power.[4]

Susan Shapiro further defined white-collar crime by stating that it ought to refer specifically and only to the violation of trust by which persons are enabled to rob without violence and burgle without trespass.[5]

Looking at it from a sociological point of view, one may draw a reasonable conclusion that, as a symbolic construct to an individual behaviour, motivation is explained in terms of the way actors of crime define themselves and the social situation they face. That is to say, people choose the course of action that they believe will bring them the most pleasure and the least pain.

Greed motivates crime even after need is satisfied. Wealth actors who have their needs satisfied with want to accumulate goods for exchange rather than for use. Accumulation of goods for exchange enables the constitution of illegitimate opportunity for the rich that cannot be constituted for the poor.[6]

6.2. Covert Operations

In this chapter, focus is devoted to the use of covert investigation as a convenient tool used by specialised law enforcement agencies around the world to gather the needed evidence for both restraint and preventive purposes or deterrence, or both, for the purposes of the prosecution of offenders, particularly of offences relating to organised crime such as corruption.

The use of covert tactics, especially undercover investigations, is geared towards infiltrating criminal networks that are hard to crack through normal investigative tactics and techniques to gather evidence that is, by and large, circumstantial.

The undercover investigation is quite old, stretching as far back as 1895.[7] Different countries vary significantly in their attitudes towards the legitimacy of undercover investigations and in their approaches to regulating them.

Jacqueline E. Ross revealed the worries of critics of relying on undercover agents in the following manner:

> What worries Western European critics are not that these methods are foreign, but rather that they are all too familiar and rooted

> in only recently discredited practices. Europeans associate undercover agents with a long history of internal spying by state security services which used agents provocateurs to infiltrate and radicalize dissident political movements, occasionally inciting acts of violence to discredit these movements. The term 'agent provocateur' itself comes from France, which adopted the use of undercover tactics on a significant scale in the seventeenth century and perfected these techniques during the revolutionary era of Napoleonic rule, and the subsequent ascendancy of centralized state power. These techniques were widely used and abused as a form of social control throughout the nineteenth century; undercover infiltrations have become associated as much with the suppression of political deviance as with the control of crime. At the end of the Second World War, Western European democracies nominally renounced undercover activity as a crime-fighting tool, while continuing to use such methods freely in the service of national security.[8]

Ross further cautioned that limiting the coercive powers of the police and their ability to conduct warrantless searches invites development of proactive alternatives, including undercover agents, informants, and electronic surveillance.[9]

Covert operations in corruption cases[10] becomes the necessary tool because, as alluded to in chapter 1 of this book, the offence of corruption does not normally leave any traces or clues for investigators to mount an operation to follow up corrupt transactions because the perpetrators of such crimes operate in secrecy and conspiracy as one of their *modi operandi* not to reveal what happened. This causes the investigative function of law enforcement agencies to resort to infiltration devices to uncover the crime before it is committed, so as to preserve the required evidence to prove the corrupt conspiracy before the court of law.

Covert operations therefore would require a choice between infiltration and secret forms of surveillance, such as wiretapping or ambient microphones. That is unlike electronic surveillance, which does not alter the target's environment, beliefs, and perceptions.

Ross explained the rationale of undercover operations thus: undercover operations may alter the target's criminal opportunities and incentive structure or manipulate his conduct, creating a risk that the investigation may encourage his criminal actions. Unlike undercover investigations, electronic surveillance avoids the risk of affecting the conduct of the target, but at the cost of intruding more deeply into his personal affairs. Accordingly, a legal system that permits covert tactics may use undercover infiltration as a substitute for electronic surveillance, or may make greater use of electronic surveillance than undercover infiltration.[11]

Slobogin contended further that a lie is a statement meant to deceive. Like many other people, the police lie occasionally; some police, like some other people, lie routinely and pervasively. Police lie to protect innocent victims, as in hostage situations, and they tell placebo lies to assure or placate worried citizens. They tell lies to project nonexistent authority and they lie to suspects in the hope of gathering evidence of crime. Some of the lies are justifiable. Some are reprehensible. They lie to catch a criminal.[12]

In Tanzania, the PCCA controls and regulates abuse by PCCB officers when carrying out their mandate of detection and investigation. Section 13 (1) and (2) of the PCCA provide as follows:

(1) Any person being an officer of Bureau who maliciously or without lawful cause procures arrest prosecution, seizure of property of another person or the exercise of powers vested in the Bureau by this Act against such person commits an offence.

(2) Any person who contravenes subsection (1) shall on the conviction be liable to a fine not exceeding one million shillings or to imprisonment for the term not exceeding six months or to both.

Over and above the provisions of subsections 1 and 2 of this section, the government can also have recourse to subsection 3 of the same section to recover any loss, cost, or damage suffered by reason of an officer of the bureau. Therefore, these subsections provide for ethical considerations, especially in the collection of information and evidence in order to employ circumstantial evidence in corruption cases.

Slobogin referred to undercover work as deceptive because it involves outright lies. An undercover agent presents a fake identity and fabricated history, denies any involvement with the police, and engages in any number of other lies. He may pose as a priest, a prisoner, or a member of the mafia; in playing such roles, lying is inevitable and extensive. The whole business of using lies in undercover operations is essentially the efficacy of catching a criminal.[13]

Most countries surveyed by Gary T. Marx, Den Boer, and Cyrille Fijnaut show that they limit undercover investigations to crimes that are serious enough to warrant the intrusiveness of covert operations and that they may not be effectively investigated by less intrusive means.[14]

There is a shift of emphasis to use trained agents rather than citizen informants, particularly where the law enforcement agency uses covert tactics in a targeted fashion in response to intelligence, which suggests that a crime is being committed, rather than using 'reasonable suspicion' on information received about commission of a particular crime.[15]

The use of informants and undercover tactics—particularly in money laundering, corruption, and other crimes of a serious nature—makes it possible for the defendants not to discover the identities of those who are collaborators in the investigation itself.[16] Ross discusses the use of undercover tactics among different state agencies as follows:

> The confluence of undercover tactics available to the police and the intelligence branches may also lead to a blurring of the distinction between political and criminal policing. Criminal enforcement agencies gradually shift from gathering evidence to gathering intelligence, as infiltration becomes an end in itself. As criminal investigators, adopt undercover tactics, the police and the state security services become more alike.[17]

The sophistication of criminal rackets, particularly white-collar crimes, has necessitated law enforcement agencies all over the world to adopt the alternative methods of preferring covert operations than overt investigation in serious criminal syndicates.

Ross further put forward a comparative view on the use of covert tactics between Europe and the USA.

> While covert tactics have come to pervade policing in the United States, the Western European democracies have largely confined these powers to highly specialized forces (within state security agencies and regular police alike). Undercover operatives often work in secrecy and isolation from the mainstream of criminal enforcement. The Netherlands, for example, formed interregional serious crimes teams to operate in isolation from the rest of the force. Gradually shifting their emphasis from evidence gathering to intelligence acquisition, they came to merge many of the functions of criminal policing and national security. In so doing, they successfully avoided the traditional controls of police management and the judiciary, on the one hand and the oversight apparatus that monitors security and intelligence services, on the other.[18]

The research that has been conducted by Dennis Tollborg showed, for example, that Swedish law authorises use far more intrusive covert tactics against socially marginal people, particularly 'immigrant groups and shadowy political groups with low social legitimacy', than against coteries of military officers, politicians, and policemen whose crimes are particularly of serious consequences.[19]

The covert penetration of criminal syndicates and organised criminals is a potent tool for obtaining inside information about secret criminal networks and therefore makes it easier to prosecute high profile crimes that have posed and continue to pose a great risk and danger to society's social, political, and economic fabric.

6.3. Surreptitious Search

In order for a law enforcement agency to search premises through covert means, the court must be involved to issue a search warrant. A surreptitious search is generally understood as a search of property without the consent or knowledge of the owners or occupants of the property. They are known as secret searches.[20]

A warrant that would allow law enforcement agents to enter premises covertly and search for the targeted materials or objects of an investigation is an unusual search warrant. In a normal search, the court has to agree on condition that the agents seize the items described on the warrant and leave a copy of the warrant on the premises.

This would allow the law enforcement officers to arrest the suspect based on the identified items seized. Search warrants are normally issued *ex parte* upon an application by the law enforcement agency showing probable cause to believe that a crime has been or is being committed and the evidence of the crime can be found at the specified location.

The warrant application must describe location as accurately as possible, the evidence to be seized and its expected location. The law enforcement officer must leave a receipt for the items seized at the premises searched and promptly return an inventory of those items to the issuing official.[21]

For a covert search, agents would often execute the search secretly at a given location, protecting the integrity of investigation and avoid any notice or detection from the suspects who might destroy the needed evidence. In the U.S., the Supreme Court has repeatedly upheld warrantless intrusions to avoid imminent destruction in the case of *Chambers v. Maroney*.[22]

Walker, however, opined that where the Court has allowed the police to dispense with a warrant, the evidence in question was usually vulnerable to relatively immediate destruction. While the same immediacy is absent when the suspects are away from the premises, similar logic would support the warrant-backed entry to preserve a record of evidence that is highly mobile because it could easily be disassembled and dispersed, or that reliable police reports indicate that it will be relocated in the near future.[23]

A court should require that a less immediate risk of destruction be balanced by an even greater certainty of eventual destruction than would be needed for that court to uphold a warrantless search.[24]

Covert search allows law enforcement agencies to protect public safety where there are imminent threats, such as toxic chemicals used in illicit drugs, potential violence, or any variety of significant danger to public safety.

Walker suggested that courts should weigh the government's claimed rationale carefully before issuing covert warrants. Any warrant requires probable cause to believe the suspected crime-related objects are at the place to be searched. Before issuing a warrant for a covert search, a magistrate should also require proof of a substantial risk of destruction of evidence or of the danger to agents or the public, and a more-than-conclusory statement in the application that no alternative measure will satisfy the need.[25]

Konovalov also echoed the same justification for using covert operations and search by stating the following:

> Certain types of searches or surveillance depend for their success on the absence of premature disclosure. The use of a wiretap, or a bug, or a pen register, or a video camera would likely produce little evidence of wrongdoing if the wrongdoer knew in advance that their conversations or actions would be monitored. When non-disclosure of the authorized search is essential to its success, neither Rule 41 nor the Fourth Amendment prohibits covert entry.[26]

The Court has also dispensed with the requirement of notice in a covert search, where there is a belief that the destruction of evidence is likely. Under this exception, law enforcement agencies are excused from the usual notice requirement when they are reasonably acting to prevent the destruction or disposal of items mentioned in a warrant.[27]

In a normal investigation of crimes, a search warrant is a traditionally recognised means of protecting fundamental privacy interests by permitting the target of investigation to surrender his or her privacy interests under the process of law.

Konovolav summarised the importance of notice in protecting the innocent persons under covert operations as follows:

> Notice is generally seen as minimizes the chance of entry of the wrong premises by mistake and the consequent subjecting of innocent persons to the shock, fright or embarrassment attendant upon

> an unannounced police intrusion. Notice is also seen as decreasing the potential for violence in search because startled householders are made aware of the nature of the search. Notice may protect against the unnecessary destruction of private property by the searching officers, since a householder with notice may voluntarily admit an officer executing a warrant.[28]

Surveillance therefore minimises and eliminates the fear that law enforcement agencies will search the wrong premises or property and without the owner's knowledge or consent. In the modern age of electronic surveillance, law enforcement agencies are required to show that the information gained from the electronic surveillance cannot be gained from any other more conventional form of surveillance.

In the USA, Congress has imposed a maximum limit for the amount of time that can pass before the target of the surveillance is notified of the covert undertaken.[29] In Tanzania, the PCCA imposes such limitation to the PCCB and other officers in similar line of duty—for example, where an officer of the bureau intentionally abuses his position in the performance of or failure to perform his duties in violation of the law.[30]

The Law of Evidence in Tanzania recognises evidence gathered through undercover operations to include information retrieved from computers or electronic systems, records obtained through surveillance, information from means that preserve information (facsimile, electronic transmission), and audio or video recordings of acts or behaviour.

The 2007 amendment to the Law of Evidence,[31] section 40A provides as follows:

> (a) [A]n information retrieved from computer systems, networks or servers; or
> (b) the records obtained through surveillance of means of preservation of information including facsimile machines, electronic transmission and communication facilities;
> (c) the audio or video recording of acts or behaviours or conversation of persons charged shall be admissible in evidence.

The new amendment will add to the improved quality of investigated corruption cases, and the application of circumstantial evidence in corruption cases will be improved tremendously.

The common law and the U.S. Supreme Court do not, however, consider that notice to surreptitious search to be constitutionally required under the privilege against self-incrimination. Konovolav was of the opinion that, over time, courts have recognised three exceptions where notice was not required: 'the danger to person' exception, the 'destruction of evidence' exception, and the 'useless gesture' exception.[32]

The Supreme Court has also recognised the common-law exception to the notice requirement where there is a belief that the destruction of evidence is likely. Under this exception, officers are excused from the usual notice requirement when they are reasonably acting to prevent the destruction or disposal of items named in a warrant. In some situations, the Court has broadened the scope of potential uses for this exception and has even upheld warrantless searches in order to avoid the imminent destruction of evidence.[33]

Notice to the defendant is not constitutionally mandated in carrying out covert operations to either detect a crime or prevent its occurrence, and, as such, notice is one of the factors that should be balanced in deciding a constitutional challenge of a search. There is always the need to balance competing interests in effective law enforcement, on the one hand, and individual security and privacy, on the other.

Law enforcement agencies need not announce their purpose before carrying out the otherwise legitimate undercover operation, if such notice would provoke the escape of the suspect or the destruction of critical evidence. It must be emphasised, however, that during surreptitious search warrants, no property should be taken or disturbed during the search, because that is not the reason or rationale for surreptitious search anyway.

Building the case for the relationship between notice and privacy, Konovalov contended that surreptitious search warrants invariably avoid concerns about the unnecessary destruction of property because the warrants often expressly state that the property is not to be disturbed during the search.[34]

It is fair to draw the conclusion that surreptitious searches are valid as long as they are legitimately conducted by law enforcement agents to infiltrate organised criminals for the purposes of gaining valuable information in ongoing criminal investigations. As Konovolav advised,

> [F]or surreptitious searches to be used legitimately, however, a sufficient legal justification for their use must exist. Without question, surreptitious search warrants are effective tools for law enforcement agents to gain valuable information for the purposes of ongoing criminal investigations.[35]

Slobogin came to the same conclusion on the justification for undercover investigations by law enforcement agencies when he stated that, where active undercover operations are contemplated, judicial authorisation should be obtained. The police should not be able to use such techniques unless the public, in the form of the judge, decides that good reason to do so exists and that methods that are more straightforward are not likely to work.[36]

On the other hand, the U.S. Supreme Court considered the constitutional implications of surreptitious interrogations by law enforcement agencies in the case of *Illinois v. Perkins*,[37] stating that 'surreptitious interrogations do not inherently compel suspects to incriminate themselves. Thus, undercover agents are not required to inform incarcerated suspects of their rights before interrogation'.[38]

This decision by the Supreme Court is viewed by some[39] to have gone out of the way, contrary to the famous decision handed in *Miranda v. Arizona*,[40] that suspects be advised of their rights prior to custodial interrogation, because custodial interrogations inherently compel individuals to incriminate themselves.

Young-sook Kim showed that custodial interrogation consists of questioning initiated by law enforcement officers after a person has been taken into custody or otherwise deprived of his or her freedom of action. The procedural safeguards required by *Miranda* include warnings to suspects that they have to remain silent, that anything they say may be used against them, and that they have the right to consult with an attorney.

The *Miranda* court also established a Fifth Amendment right to counsel, concluding that the presence of counsel during questioning reduces the likelihood that police will coerce the suspects into confessing.[41]

The reasoning behind *Perkins*[42] is that *Miranda*[43] warnings do not require undercover officers posing as inmates to administer warnings to incarcerated suspects prior to questioning. Perkins believed that he was speaking with fellow inmates; viewed from a suspect's perspective, Perkins was not coerced—he voluntarily offered the incriminating information; thus the *Miranda* warnings were not required because covert interrogations do not inherently amount to compulsion.[44]

In the U.S., the Attorney General's Guidelines on FBI Undercover Operations, issued on 5 January 1981 regulate the conduct of FBI agents in carrying out undercover operations.

Goldwasser explained how to carry out an undercover operation, which, in my opinion, is very instructive to the Tanzanian law enforcement agencies.

> Before an undercover operation may be authorized, the guidelines require that a Special Agent in Charge (SAC) of an FBI field office make a written determination setting forth facts and circumstances sufficient to establish that the operation will be an effective means of obtaining evidence, and that it meets the requirements applicable to FBI investigation in general.
>
> Importantly, the SAC must determine that initiation of the operation meets a factual predicate requirement—which 'facts or circumstances reasonably indicate that a federal crime has been, is being, or will be committed'. The guidelines permit inducements to be offered to an individual during the course of an ongoing operation even where there is no reasonable indication that the individual has engaged or is engaging in the illegal conduct under investigation.[45]

These guidelines are not judicially enforceable, because the U.S. Supreme Court has held that, unless compliance is mandated by the Constitution or federal law, responsibility for remedying violations of self-imposed guidelines rest solely with the executive branch.[46]

It is also important to note that the success of undercover investigations depends upon maintenance of a cover that should not be disclosed because premature public disclosures in an undercover investigation will jeopardise its success if the general public learns—for example, through the press—of the investigation. In an undercover operation, wiretaps, audio and video tapes, visual surveillance, electronic tracking devices, and pen register are often used to supplement the agents' testimony about the interplay between agents and targets of investigation.[47]

It is important to remember that infiltrating criminal organisations is possible only because undercover agents and informants that the government uses to gain access to inside knowledge from the vantage point of a participant in a crime. The decoy operations are used by law enforcement for the purposes of gaining access to criminal activities that otherwise in normal investigation are not accessible.

6.4. Rationale for Covert Investigations

The rationale for using undercover infiltration of criminal gangs is that covert infiltration is a special, powerful weapon against organised crime because it reveals structures of hierarchy, divisions of responsibility, and many otherwise inaccessible details about the inner workings of secretive organisations. It has been widely deployed against a variety of legitimate enterprises, such as stock exchanges, in which illegitimate practices secretly coexist with lawful ones.

But the cost of obtaining inside knowledge is that the investigator must be an insider. To be an insider, the investigator must be a participant (either as victim or an accomplice). By participating, the investigator affects the course of events. Indeed, the better an investigator positions herself to learn firsthand about the doings of a criminal gang, the more she risks altering what she seeks to observe.[48]

Another advantage to infiltrate criminal syndicates for the purposes of evidence may be to corroborate the evidence of an informants' testimony, disclosure of a defendant's financial records, and wiretapped conversations. Investigators are unlikely to catch officials taking bribes unless agents offer the cash themselves.[49]

Ross further reasoned as follows.

> Electronic surveillance counts as 'search' and therefore implicates the target's Fourth Amendment rights. Infiltration does not. According to Supreme Court, offenders assume the risk of betrayal by their societies, including the danger that such associates will turn out to be informants or undercover agents. Infiltration therefore infringes no reasonable expectation of privacy. As a result, investigators need not to establish probable cause or even reasonable suspicion as a predicate for infiltration. If undercover agents or informants tape-record conversations targets; this does not count as electronic surveillance and therefore requires no judicial authorization. Since the target is allowed to infiltrate and testify about the resulting conversations, he is equally free to record them. The recording will count as the functional equivalent of his testimony. Prosecutors therefore use covert agents as a substitute for, rather than auxiliary to, phone telephone tapping and bugs.[50]

Ross's cautionary opinion is valid in that infiltration should be used as a means of proving independent crimes and rules should be in place to prevent the government from using the infiltrator's actions to supply the *actus reus* of a crime.[51]

Bridges noted the effect of organised crime and corruption as being the fact that the money and power of organised crime are increasingly used to infiltrate and corrupt legitimate business and labour unions and to subvert and corrupt our domestic process; organised crime activities in the USA weaken the stability of the nation's economic system, harm innocent investors and competing organisations, interfere with free competition, seriously burden interstate and foreign commerce, threaten domestic security, and undermine the general welfare of the nation and its citizens.[52]

In an effort to curb organised crime, the USA introduced the Racketeer Influenced and Corrupt Organizations (RICO) law as part of the Organized Crime Control Act in 1970 and as part of broad measure to fight syndicated crimes.[53]

This law brings four types of attack on syndicated criminal operations. Firstly, the government may bring criminal actions carrying stiff penalties for RICO violations. Secondly, any interest obtained through, or with proceeds from, racketeering, or of any interest claim affording a source of influence over any enterprise whose operation or control the defendant shares through a pattern of racketeering. Thirdly, the government can bring civil actions for divestment or restriction on investment or enterprise activity. Fourthly, RICO provides private parties with an express damage remedy. A losing defendant must pay treble damages automatically. This treble-damages award is supposed to provide an incentive for individuals to bring the mob to court.[54]

Bridges summarised the advantages that RICO brings to the government.

> Civil RICO provides government with three advantages not available in a criminal prosecution: First, the government gets to put evidence of the whole racketeering operation before a jury unimpeded by Federal Rules of Evidence 404 (b), which limits the admissibility of evidence of other crime, wrongs, or acts. This advantage gives the jury a broader perspective of the case and expands the scope of allegations plaintiff can take to a jury and of discovery that can be demanded of defendants. This benefit also accrues to private plaintiff. Second, the preponderance-of-the evidence standard of proof in civil actions is much easier to meet than the criminal standard. Third, the government can appeal adverse civil verdicts under RICO. To avoid civil prosecution of RICO claims, the statute expressly allows the government to stop defendants convicted of RICO offences from re-litigating the issues of those offences; private plaintiffs may also take advantage of collateral estoppels to prove predicate crimes that resulted in convictions.[55]

RICO is a lynchpin introduced by government through Congress, as a full-scale attack on organised crime. Michele L. Jacobins argued that prominent in the RICO arsenal of weapons was the sanction of personal forfeiture designed to deter the growth of organised crime by preventing convicted 'racketeers' from continuing to use their ill-gotten gains in illegal activities.

The 1970 act also contained a provision that enabled trial courts to enter *ex parte* restraining orders against forfeitable property, thereby depriving defendants of access to their property upon indictment.[56]

In the course of prosecuting organised crime offences, the prosecution will provide background material about the target group. Such material may consist of informant information, prior electronic surveillance tapes, transcripts of related accomplice testimony at previous trials, and physical surveillance summaries.[57]

The Supreme Court has imposed procedural due process requirements as follows:

> Most significantly, notice and an opportunity to be heard both of which must occur at a meaningful time and in a meaningful manner. Because the due process is meant to protect against arbitrary deprivations of property, the 'meaningful time' to be heard is usually before the deprivation of property. Some extraordinary situations, however, may justify postponing notice and hearing until after seizure is necessary to secure an important government or general public interest. In addition, the person initiating the seizure must be a government official responsible for determining, under the standards of a narrowly drawn statute that it was necessary and justified in the particular instance. Examples of extraordinary situations justifying postponement are the collection of the internal revenue, meeting the needs of a national war, and protecting people from misbranded drugs and contaminated food. In no instance, however, may the opportunity to be heard be denied entirely.[58]

There is a registered agreement by courts in the USA that, before the court could issue a final restraining order in a RICO prosecution, the government had the burden of demonstrating the probability that a jury would both convict the defendant of RICO violations and find the property at issue subject to forfeiture under RICO. To satisfy the burden of proof during hearing, the prosecution had to produce additional evidence other than the indictment to enable the court assess independently the strength of government's case.[59]

The rationale for preventing the defendant's pretrial disposition of assets to escape forfeiture was the postindictment restraining order. However, the U.S. congressional reaction to a court imposition of due process requirements was captured in the Senate report on the subject matter.

> Certain recent court decisions have required the government to meet essentially the same stringent standards that applies to the issuance of temporary restraining orders in the context of civil litigation and have also held the Federal Rules of Evidence to apply to hearings concerning restraining orders in criminal forfeiture cases. In effect, such decisions allow the courts to entertain challenges to the validity of the indictment, and require the government to prove the merits of the underlying criminal cases and forfeiture counts and put on its witnesses well in advance of trial in order to obtain an order restraining the defendant's transfer of property alleged to be forfeitable in the government to assure the availability of assets after conviction—quite difficult.[60]

Essentially, the Senate report advocated for the legal position that the use of an indictment is sufficient both to enter and to sustain a restraining order until the completion of trial. A contrary view was taken in the case of *United States v. Rogers*[61] that the 1984 amendments required postrestraint evidentiary hearing.[62]

Michele L. Jacobins was of the view that the *Rogers* court violated the clear intent of Congress. Its strained reading of the statute and legislative intent no doubt reflected its discomfort with the section's due process problems and was an attempt to avoid striking down the section as unconstitutional.

However, while it is permissible, and perhaps preferable, for a court to reach a strained interpretation in order to uphold a statute's constitutionality, a court cannot construe a law to mean that which was clearly not intended by the legislature.[63]

The due process and standard of proof at postrestraint hearings is well articulated in the decision of the U.S. Supreme Court in *Mathews v.*

Eldridge,[64] which called for the weighing of three factors: (a) the private interest affected, (b) the risk of error created the state's chosen standards and the probable value of any alternative safeguards, and (c) the countervailing government interest supporting use of the challenged standard, including fiscal and administrative burdens imposed by using a substitutive procedure.[65]

It is important to note, however, that a legislative scheme cannot be accommodated by the courts at the expense of an individual's constitutional right to due process of law.

6.5. Foreign Corrupt Practices Act (FCPA)

On the issue of bribery, the U.S. Congress passed this law (FCPA) in 1977 in order to criminalise conduct relating to the bribing of foreign government officials.[66] In 1989 the U.S. government began an effort to influence trading partners at the Organization for Economic Cooperation and Development (OECD) to criminalise the bribery of foreign public officials.

Ellen S. Podgor wrote that, under a voluntary disclosure of the Securities Exchange Commission, more than four hundred companies admitted making questionable or illegal payments in excess of US$300 million to foreign government officials, politicians, and political parties. Therefore, FCPA was intended to stop these types of illegal payments to restore the reputation of U.S. companies conducting business abroad.[67]

The efforts by the U.S. to convince its OECD trading partners brought about the OECD convention against bribery of foreign officials.[68] The convention provides for extradition of offenders to the convention.

In Tanzania, the EOCCA regulates white-collar crimes.[69] The first schedule to the act contains economic offences, which include offences under the PCA other than an offence under section 4 of that act.

It is fair to conclude that the preceding analysis has been able to demonstrate the importance of the use of covert and undercover operations and their rationale in the investigative process, particularly on the gathering of circumstantial evidence by drawing experiences from the USA, where such techniques have been tested in courts of law and the latter had issued directives on how to moderate the process against the defendants. Finally, in Tanzania, the EOCCA and the PCCA regulate white-collar crimes, and the Evidence Act provides for the admissibility of evidence including covert derived evidence of which circumstantial evidence is found, particularly corruption.

Endnotes

1. V. Branham and S. B. Kutash, *Encyclopedia of Criminology*, 1949.
2. Schlegel and Weisburd, eds., *White-Collar Crime Revisited* (Boston: Northeastern University Press, 1992), 31.
3. Branham and Kutash, *Encyclopedia of Criminology*, 511.
4. Schlegel and Weisburd, *White-Collar Crime Revisited*, 43.
5. Ibid., 346. That means such persons manipulates norms of disclosure, disinterestedness, role stealing, misappropriation, self-dealing, corruption, and the role conflict.
6. Ibid., 81. Consider several theories of crimes, such as the structural dimension (law and culture), organizational theory, poverty-power, and crimes (inequalities increases crimes).
7. *Grimm v. U.S.*, 156 U.S. 604 (1895). See Katherine Goldwasser, 'After ABSCAM: An Examination of Congressional Proposals to Limit Targeting Discretion in Federal Undercover Investigations', *Emory Law Journal* 36 (1987): 75n34. An undercover operation is an investigation by a law enforcement agency where an employee of the agency, or someone acting at the agency's discretion, conceals from other persons his/her relationship with the agency to carry out instructions on a specific target of crime under investigations. These operations range from relatively simple, short-term investigations using a single undercover agent, who may pose, for example, as an elderly person, vulnerable to criminals; to long-term and more complex investigations using a number of undercover agents in the form of established businesses that are vulnerable to extortions by local public officials or organised crime, equipped with a device that permits video and audio taping of conversations and transactions inside the establishment, and operated over a period of time. The characteristic of it all is the use of deception by law enforcement authorities.
8. Jacqueline E. Ross, 'Management and Control of the Modern Business Corporation: Review: Trade-off in Undercover Investigations: A Comparative Perspective', *University of Chicago Law Review* 69 (2002): 1501.
9. Ibid.
10. This applies to all white-collar crimes as well and is not limited to corruption cases as such.
11. Ross, 'Management and Control'.

12. Christopher Slobogin, 'Deceit, Pretext, and Trickery: Investigate Lies by the Police', *Oregon Law Review* 76 (1997): 7775.
13. Ibid.
14. See Gary T. Marx, *Undercover: Police Surveillance in America* (Berkeley: University of California Press, 1988), 35, 49; C. Fijnaut and G. T. Marx, eds., *Undercover: Police Surveillance in Comparative Perspective* (The Hague: Kluwer Law International, 1995); Gerald M. Caplan, ed., *ABSCAM Ethics: Moral Issues and Deception in Law Enforcement* (Cambridge, MA: Ballinger Pub. Co., 1983), 43, 59.
15. Schlegel and Weisburd, *White-Collar Crime Revisited.*
16. The use of concierges, trusted persons, telegraph operators, observers, consultants, agents of influence, workplace personnel departments, building commandants, doormen, watchmen, hotlines, and so forth.
17. Ross, 'Management and Control'.
18. Ibid.
19. Referred to in Ross, 'Management and Control': on one hand, the Swedish Terrorism Act provides the police with virtual carte blanche in wiretapping deportable and incarcerated aliens, while placing significant limitation on the application of similar measures against citizens. See Fijnaut and Marx, 256–258. On the other hand, the USA has not hampered its undercover investigations by concerns about agent complicity or constraints on which the investigation may target.
20. Paul V. Konovalov, 'On a Quest for Reason: A New Look at Surreptitious Search Warrants', *Hastings Law Journal* 48 (1987): 435.
21. John Kent Walker, Jr., 'Covert Searches', *Stanford Law Review* 38 (1987): 545. See also 4ule 41 of the U.S. Federal Rules of Criminal Procedure and title 3 of the Omnibus Crime Control and Safe Streets Act of 1968.
22. 399 U.S. 42, 48–51 (1970).
23. Walker, 'Covert Searches'.
24. Ibid.
25. Ibid.
26. Konovalov, 'On a Quest for Reason', quoting the Ninth Circuit decision in *U.S. v. VILEGAS*, 700F, supplement, 99.
27. Ibid., the case of *Katz v. U.S.*, 389 U.S. 347 (1967).
28. Konovalov, 'On a Quest for Reason'.
29. Ibid.—ninety days. See also 18 U.S.C. 2518 (1) (c) (1996).
30. Section 31 of the PCCA, no. 11 of 2007, criminalised the abuse of position.
31. The written laws (miscellaneous amendments), act no. 11 of 2007.
32. Konovalov, 'On a Quest for Reason'.

33. Ibid. See *Chambers v. Moroney* 1030, 304 (N.Y. Sup. Ct 1833), *Warden v. Hayden*, 387 U.S. 294, 298–300 (1967).
34. Konovalov, 'On a Quest for Reason'.
35. Ibid.
36. Ibid.
37. 110 S. Ct. 2394 (1990).
38. Ibid.
39. Kathryn Young-sook Kim, 'Self-Incrimination, Compulsion, and the Undercover Agent: Illinois v. Perkins', *Washington Law Review* 66 (1991): 605, notes that *Perkins* imprudently carved out an exception to *Miranda's* per se rule requiring that custodial interrogations be preceded by warnings. *Perkins* fails to uphold the Fifth Amendment privilege against self-incrimination by allowing police to use covert tactics that may compel a suspect to confess.
40. 384 U.S. 436 (1966).
41. Kim, 'Self-Incrimination, Compulsion, and the Undercover Agent', 605.
42. 110 S. Ct. 2394 (1990).
43. 384 US. 436 (1966).
44. Kim, 'Self-Incrimination, Compulsion, and the Undercover Agent'.
45. Katherine Goldwasser, 'After ABSCAM: An Examination of Congressional Proposals to Limit Targeting Discretion in Federal Undercover Investigations', *Emory Law Journal* 36 (1987): 75.
46. Ibid. See also *U.S v. Caceres*, 440 U.S. 741, 749–756 (1979).
47. Goldwasser, 'After ABSCAM', 75.
48. Jacqueline E. Ross, 'Valuing Inside Knowledge: Police Infiltration as a Problem for the Law of Evidence', *Chicago–Kent Law Review* 79 (2004): 1111.
49. Ibid.
50. Ibid.
51. Ibid.
52. Andrew P. Bridges, 'Private RICO Litigation Based Upon "Fraud in the Sale of Securities"', 18 Georgia Law Review 18 (1983): 43.
53. Title 9 Public Law no. 91–452, 84 Stat. 922 (1970).
54. Bridges, 'Private RICO Litigation'.
55. Ibid.
56. Michele L. Jacobins, 'Note: RICO Post-Indictment Restraining Orders: The Process Due Defendants', *New York University Law Review* 40 (1985): 1162.
57. John C. Jeffries, Jr., and John Gleeson, 'The Federalization of Organized Crime: Advantages of Federal Prosecution', *Hastings Law Journal* 46 (April 1995): 1095.

58. 384 US. 346 (1966).
59. Ibid.
60. Ibid.—general statement regarding the RICO forfeiture amendment.
61. 602 F. Supp. 1332 (D. Colo. 1985).
62. Ibid.
63. Jacobins, 'Note: RICO Post-Indictment Restraining Orders'.
64. 424 U.S. 319 (1976).
65. Ibid.
66. In 1988 there were amendments to the act, which changed the focus of illegality from the status of the recipient to the purpose of the payment. Scandals that occurred in the U.S. in the mid-'70s revealed that companies admitted making payments in excess of US$300 million to foreign officials, politicians, and political parties. 'Slush funding' from illegal campaign contributions were made and illegal bribes were being paid to foreign officials. These scandals involving U.S. companies to public officials in Japan, Italy, and Mexico. This led to tarnishing the reputation of American companies throughout the world.
67. Podgor, *Understanding International Criminal Law*, 29.
68. Organisation for Economic Cooperation and Development Convention on Combating Bribery of Foreign Public Officials in International Business Transactions. Thirty-three member states signed the convention on 17 December 1997.
69. [Cap. 200 R.E. 2002], section 57 (1)—these crimes include hording commodities; leading organised crime; hoarding of money; fraudulent schemes; games and artifices; theft of public property; conveying or possession of goods suspected of having been stolen or unlawfully acquired; unlawful sale of designated goods; authorisation of unlawful supply of designated authority goods; occasioning loss to a specified authority; prohibited, restricted, and uncustomed goods; interfering with a necessary service under the National Security Act (cap. 47); using firearms; offences against conservation of wildlife; unlawful prospecting; and offences in relation to gemstones, diamonds, theft of mail matter, possession of arms, and ammunition.

Chapter 7

Summary and Conclusion

7.1. Summary

This study has argued for the use of circumstantial evidence in white-collar crime cases in Tanzania, particularly corruption, which has become endemic. There is enormous potential to such use because of its efficacy and potential for increasing detection and corruption prosecuted cases in court.

The study has identified the anomaly of the traditional common-law approach to evidence, which has emphasised the reliability and accuracy of direct evidence over circumstantial evidence. This emphasis has been tested on the ground and data has shown that such belief and emphasis is founded on the traditional common-law understanding, which has been shaken by the weaknesses of the eyewitness paradigm.

In this study, it has been clearly demonstrated through scientific and empirical research that there is a need to maximise the understanding and potential use of circumstantial evidence, which has proved to be of equal force as, if not sometimes better and more reliable than, direct evidence in combating white-collar crimes and, in particular, corruption.

The distinction made by the traditional common law between direct and circumstantial or indirect evidence has been overtaken by the reality of the consequences due to eyewitness terror and the emergence of scientific discovery of the DNA forensic testing. We have shown that there is really no distinction other than the fact that the two types of evidence are differentiated only in degree—not in substance—in their reliability and accuracy in evidential analysis, as shown in chapter 4 of this study.

In chapter 1, the book set the stage by introducing the major highlights of the study and the methodology adopted to articulate the outcome of the book. Chapter 2 dove into a thorough discussion of the Tanzania scenario in tackling the perspectives of corruption from policy orientation, legal framework, and government strategies as background material to the central thesis of this book: the case for circumstantial evidence.

In chapter 3, the book focused exclusively on the anatomy of the anti-corruption law in Tanzania and its application, particularly the interpretation given by courts to offences prescribed by that law. The study also demonstrated several weaknesses manifested by the law; it also offered many recommendations for remedy by examining best practices elsewhere in the SADC and international instruments against corruption to which Tanzania is a signatory and to which the country acceded through their ratification. In that chapter, the book also showed the need to strike out *takrima* provisions from the electoral law because of its offending proposition and we make comparisons with the U.S. Supreme Court's interpretation on similar frequency of the offending section of the law.

For chapter 4, the study specifically analysed the contentious distinction between direct evidence and circumstantial evidence. The analysis took the form of empirically tested case studies, which were then applied on the results of sampled field research in selected geographical areas of Tanzania. The results would seem to have testified to the soundness of the position that the traditional common-law approach to evidential significance of the two types of evidence, which, on balance, has often been misinformed and favoured direct evidence as the most reliable type of evidence compared to circumstantial evidence.

It was, however, also demonstrated there that the informed view that has been tested scientifically with verifiable data has elevated circumstantial evidence from its perceived inferior status to be at par and sometimes in a more advantageous status than direct evidence, as eye witness error has proven to be the case, especially where many inmates in prisons are released after the DNA evidential presentation vindicated the victims of given eyewitness errors based on the direct evidence paradigm.

Chapter 5 the study introduced entrapment as a defence in corruption and other white crime cases and showed how Tanzania is yet to set a strong foot on the ground; it also revisited the application of entrapment in the U.S. for comparative purposes and the extent to which it should be of greater utility and relevance to Tanzania, particularly for defence lawyers and accused persons confronted with similar situations.

In chapter 6, the study dwelt exclusively on the use of covert operations in dismantling the white-collar crime networks, examining covert operations from an investigative perspective. The study then explored the rationale for the use of undercover and other surreptitious techniques, including electronic surveillance and other related techniques employed by advanced and sophisticated law enforcement agencies in penetrating entrenched criminal rackets within and outside the borders of a country. It also showed how effectively gathered circumstantial evidence can be very useful in bringing to justice criminals of organised crime, along with the use of such evidence by the courts. The amendment to the Evidence Act is another positive step that will assist law enforcement agencies in Tanzania to employ covert operations in corruption cases and, in particular, electronically gathered evidence, which will enhance the quality of circumstantial evidence presented to the courts of law.

The study used the experience obtained in the U.S. because of its comparative advantage in this area and for its advanced techniques in unearthing organised white-collar criminals. Their experience, if translated into use within the context of Tanzania, would go a long way to tackling the escalating wave of organised crime and systemic corruption as shown in chapters 1 and 2 of this study.

7.2. Conclusion

This book presented the design and findings of a study whose main aim was to determine the effectiveness of existing legal frameworks (legislative and interpretative) in detecting, investigating, and prosecuting corruption in Tanzania. Specifically, robust but balanced discussion is presented on the fundamental problem of overreliance on *direct evidence* as opposed to *circumstantial evidence* in gathering evidence and prosecuting and securing convictions in corruption cases. Support was then given to a plea for the conscious privileging by of circumstantial over direct evidence, the effect of which would be to advance the deterrence effect of anticorruption prosecutions, particularly with a view to increasing the success of prosecuted corruption cases brought to the courts of law for judicial dispensation.

The study advanced the legitimate claim that circumstantial evidence is a potent tool that law enforcement in Tanzania should take advantage of in countering the growing trends of white-collar crimes and corruption, in particular. Circumstantial evidence is a tool that has been tested elsewhere, and there is no reason why it should not work in Tanzania with the necessary modifications to suit the realities and circumstances of Tanzania.

References

Books

Allen, R. J., R. B. Kuhns, and E. Swift. *Evidence: Text, Problems and Cases*. 3rd ed. New York: Aspen Law & Business, 2002.

Allot, A. N. 'The Chain of Evidence in Criminal Trials, in Criminal Trials'. In *The Magistrate in the Commonwealth Basic Principles and Practice*, edited by Margaret Rogers and Jane Kellock. London: Commonwealth Magistrates' and Judges' Association, 1979.

Campos, J. E., and S. Pradhan, eds. *The Many Faces of Corruption: Tracking Vulnerabilities at the Sector Level*. Washington, DC: The World Bank, 2007.

Caplan, G. M. *ABSCAM Ethics: Moral Issues and Deception in Law Enforcement*. Cambridge, MA: Ballinger Pub. Co., 1983.

Chaligha, A., B. Mattes, and A. Dzenga. *Public Perceptions on Democracy and Governance in Tanzania*, May 2004 (Unpublished).

Chambua, S. E., and V. Kihiyo. *Multiparty Elections and Corruption in Tanzania*. Dar es Salaam: University Press, 2002.

Cross, R., and C. Tapper. *Cross on Evidence*. 7th ed. London: Butterworths, 1990.

Doig, A., and S. Riley. 'Corruption and Anti-Corruption Strategies: Issues and Case Studies From Developing Countries'. In *Corruption and Integrity Improvement Initiatives in Developing Countries*, edited by S. J. Kpundeh, I. Hors, UNDP, and OECD. New York: UNDP, 1998.

El-Ayouty, Y., K. J. Ford, and M. Davies, eds. *Government Ethics and Law Enforcement*. New York: Praeger Publishers, 2000.

Emson, R. *Evidence*. 3rd ed. New York: Palgrave McMillan, 2006.

Branham, V., and S. B. Kutash. *Encyclopedia of Criminology.* 1949.

Government of the United Republic of Tanzania. *The National Anti-Corruption Strategy and Action Plans for Tanzania*. Dar es Salaam: Government Printers, 1999.

———. *National Vision 2025*. Dar es Salaam: Government Printer, 2005.

———. *Poverty Reduction Strategy II.* Vice President's Office, August, 2004.

———. *Tanzania at the Turn of the Century*. A World Bank Country Study. Washington DC: The World Bank, 2001.

———. *Tanzania's Third Phase Government Fight Against Corruption: A Brief on Achievements and Challenges 1995–1999*. Dar es Salaam: Government Printer, 1999.

Halsbury's Statutes of England and Wales. 4th ed. London: Butterworths, 1985.

Hoseah, E. G. *Essays on Combating Corruption in Tanzania and the Basic Legal Principles*. Dar es Salaam: Ecoprint, 1999.

International Labour Organization. *A Fair Globalization: Creating Opportunities for All*, World Commission on the Social Dimensions of Globalization. Geneva: International Labour Organization, 2004.

International Monetary Fund. *Good Governance: The IMF's Role*. Washington, DC: International Monetary Fund, 1997.

James, S. H., P. E. Kish, and T. P. Sutton. *Principles of Bloodstain Pattern Analysis: Theory and Practice.* Boca Raton: CRC, 2005.

Klitgaard, R. *Controlling Corruption*. Berkeley, CA: University of California Press, 1998.

Lal, R., and D. Lal. *The Law of Evidence.* 21st ed. Reprint. New Delhi, India: Wadwa and Company Nagpur Publishers, 2006.

MacLean, Robert M. *Public International Law*. 4th ed. London: HLT Publications, 1995.

Marx, G. T. *Undercover: Police Surveillance in America*. Berkeley: University of California Press, 1988.

———. 'Undercover: Some Implications for Policy'. In *Undercover: Police Surveillance in Comparative Perspective*, edited by C. Fijnaut and G. T. Marx. 313–321. The Hague: Kluwer Law International. 1995a.

———. 'Undercover in Comparative Perspective: Some Implications for Knowledge and Social Research'. In *Undercover: Police Surveillance in Comparative Perspective*, edited by C. Fijnaut and G. T. Marx. 323–337. The Hague: Kluwer Law International. 1995b.

McCormick, Charles T., John W. Strong, Kenneth S. Broun, et al., eds. *McCormick on Evidence*. 4th ed. St. Paul, MN: West Publishing Co., 1992.

Muganda, A. *The Prevention of Corruption Act: Its Weaknesses and Suggested Amendments* (Unpublished, 1995).

Narayan-Parker, D., et al. *Can Anyone Hear Us? Voices of the Poor*. New York:, Oxford University Press for the World Bank, 2000.

Nyerere, J. K. *Freedom and Unity*. Dar es Salaam: Oxford University Press, 1966.

Palmer, A. *Proof and the Preparation of Trials*. Sydney: Lawbook Co., 2003.

Phillips, S. M. *Famous Cases of Circumstantial Evidence*. Boston: Estes & Lauriat, 1874.

Phipson, S. L., John H. Buzzard, Richard May, and M. N. Howard, eds. *Phipson on Evidence*. 10th ed. London: Sweet & Maxwell, 1963.

Podgor, E. S. *Understanding International Criminal Law*. Newark, NJ: LexisNexis, 2004.

Rawls, John. *A Theory of Justice*. Rev. ed. Cambridge, MA: Belknap Press, 1999.

Rose-Ackerman, S. *Corruption and Government: Causes, Consequences and Reform*. New York: Cambridge University Press, 1999.

Schlegel, K., and D. Weisburd, eds. *White-Collar Crime Reconsidered.* Boston: Northeastern University Press, 1992.

Trankell, A. *Reliability of Evidence: Methods for Analyzing and Assessing Witness Statements*. Stockholm: Beckmans, 1972.

UNDP. *Governance for Sustainable Human Development.* UNDP Policy Document. New York: UNDP, 1997.

Wells, G. L., and E. F. Loftus. *Eyewitness Testimony: Psychological Perspectives*. London: Cambridge University Press, 1984.

Wigmore, J. H., and P. Tillers. *Evidence on Trial at Common Law*. Vol. 1A. Boston: Little Brown and Company, 1983.

Williams, R. *Political Scandals in the USA*. Edinburgh: Keele University Press, 1998.

World Bank. *Governance: The World Bank's Experience*. Washington, DC: World Bank, 1994.

ARTICLES AND JOURNALS

Allen, R. J. 'Clarifying Entrapment'. *Journal of Criminal Law and Criminology* 89, no. 2 (Winter, 1999): 407–431.

Amstutz, W. G., and B. M. Harges. 'Evolution Controversy: The Daubert Dilemma: The Application of Daubert v. Merrell Dow Pharmaceutical Inc. to Expert Testimony of Law Enforcement Officers in Narcotic Related Cases'. *Hawaii Law Review* 23 (2001): 67.

Austin, G. C. 'The Value of Circumstantial Evidence'. *Counsellor* 2, no. 8 (May 1898).

Bank of Tanzania. *Monthly Review*, August 2008.

Bardhan, P. 'Corruption and Development: A Review of Issues'. *Journal of Economic Literature* 35, no. 3 (September 1997): 1320–1346.

Benedict, N. 'Fingerprints and Daubert Standard for Admission of Scientific Evidence: Why Fingerprints Fail and a Proposed Remedy'. *Arizona Law Review* 46 (2004): 519.

Bergman, P. 'A Bunch of Circumstantial Evidence'. *University of San Francisco Law Review* 30 (1995–1996): 985.

Bernhard, A. 'When Justice Fails: Indemnification for Unjust Conviction'. *University of Chicago Law School Roundtable* 6 (1999): 73.

Bridges, Andrew P. 'Private RICO Litigation Based Upon Fraud in the Sale of Securities'. *Georgia Law Review* 18 (1983): 43–82.

Campos, J. E., D. Lien, and S. Pradhan. 'The Impact of Corruption on Investment: Predictability Matters'. *World Development* 27, no. 6 (1999): 1059–1067.

Carlson, J. C. 'The Act Requirement and the Foundation of the Entrapment Defense'. *Virginia Law Review* 73 (1987): 1011–1108.

Chand, Sheetal K., and Karl O. Moene. 'Controlling Fiscal Corruption'. *World Development* 27, no. 7 (1999): 1129–1140.

Chemay, F. E. 'Comment: Unreliable Eyewitness Evidence: The Expert Psychologist and The Defense in Criminal Cases'. *Los Angeles Law Review* 45 (1985): 721.

Daily News, 6 February 1978.

De Koker, L., B. A. K. Rider, and J. J. Henning, eds. *Victims of Economic Crime*. Transactions of the Centre for Business Law, 31. Bloemfontein, South Africa: UOVS/UOFS, 1999.

DiBiagio, T. M. 'Money Laundering and Drug Trafficking: A Question of Understanding the Elements of the Crime and the Use of Circumstantial Evidence'. *University of Richmond Law Review* 28 (1994): 255.

Dillof, A. M. 'Unravelling Unlawful Entrapment'. *Journal of Criminal Law and Criminology* 94, no. 4 (Summer 2004): 827–896.

'DNA Evidence'. *Chicago Tribune*, 17 February 2005.

Elbaz, D. J. 'Note: The Troubling Entrapment Defense: How About an Economic Approach?' *American Criminal Law Review* 36 (Winter, 1999): 117.

Fair, B. K. 'Using Parrots to Kill Mockingbirds: Yet Another Racial Prosecution and Wrongful Conviction in Maycomb'. *Alabama Law Review* 45 (1994): 403.

Fisher, S. Z. 'Convictions of Innocent Persons in Massachusetts: An Overview'. *Boston University Public International Law Journal* 12 (2002): 1.

Gerald, D. 'The Serpent Beguiled Me and I Did Eat: Entrapment and the Creation of Crime'. *Seten Hall Law Review* 44 (1985): 17–39.

Goldwasser, K. 'After ABSCAM: An Examination of Congressional Proposals to Limit Targeting Discretion in Federal Undercover Investigations'. *Emory Law Journal* 36 (1987): 75–147.

Goodling, N. A. 'Nigeria's Crises of Corruption—Can UN Global Programme Hope to Resolves the Dilemma?' *Vanderbilt Journal on Transnational Law* 36 (May 2003): 99.

Haber, Ralph N., and L. Haber. 'Experiencing, Remembering and Reporting Events'. *Psychology, Public Policy & Law* 6 (2000): 1057–1097.

Hastings, K. A. 'Note: Entrapment and Denial of the Crime: A Defense of Inconsistency Rule'. *Duke Law Journal* 866 (1986).

Hellman, J., and D. Kaufmann. 'Confronting the Challenge of State Capture in Transition Economies'. *Finance and Development* 38, no. 3 (September 2001). http://www.imf.org/external/pubs/ft/fandd/2001/09/hellman.htm (accessed December 4, 2008).

Insalaco, R. C., and Peter G. Fitzgerald. 'Note: Denying the Crime and Pleading Entrapment: Putting the Federal Law in Order'. *University of Michigan Journal of Law Reform* 20, no. 2 (1986–1987): 567.

Jacobins, Michele L. 'Note: RICO Post-Indictment Restraining Orders: The Process Due Defendants'. *New York University Law Review* 40 (1985): 1162.

Jain, M. 'Comment: Mitigating the Dangers of Capital Convictions Based on Eyewitness Testimony Through Treason's Two-Witness Rule'. *Journal of Criminal Law and Criminology* 91 (2001): 761–790.

Jeffries, J. C., Jr., and J. Gleeson. 'The Federalization of Organized Crime: Advantages of Federal Prosecution'. *Hastings Law Journal* 46 (April 1995): 1095.

Joseph, H. K. 'The Upright and the Low-Down: An Examination of Official Corruption in the United States and the People's Republic of China'. *Syracuse Journal of International Law and Commerce* 27 (Summer, 2000).

Kaufmann, D. 'Corruption: The Facts, Foreign Policy'. *Foreign Policy* (Summer 1997).

Kim, K. Y. 'Self-Incrimination, Compulsion, and the Undercover Agent: Illinois v. Perkins'. *Washington Law Review* 66 (1991): 605–622.

Konovalov, P. V. 'On a Quest for Reason: A New Look at Surreptitious Search Warrant'. *Hastings Law Journal* 48 (1987): 435.

Leff, N. 'Economic Development Through Bureau of Corruption'. *American Behavioural Scientist* 8.

Lord, K. M. 'Entrapment and Due Process: Moving Towards a Dual System of Defences'. *Florida State University Law Review* 25 (Spring, 1998): 463.

Mauro, P. 'Corruption and Growth'. *Quarterly Journal of Economics* 110 (1995), 681–712.

Msuya, E. 'Mawaziri waache kuwalinda wabadhirifu'. *Rai Newspaper*, 5–11 July 2007.

Nichols, P. M. 'Colloquy: Regulating Transnational Bribery in Times of Globalization and Fragmentation'. *Yale International Law Journal* 24 (Winter, 1999): 257.

Onyango-Obbo, C. *The East African*, no. 409, September 2002.

Omar, A., L. Young, and A. Swamy. 'The Causes and Consequences of Corruption'. *Annals of the American Academy of Political and Social Science* 573 (2001): 42–56.

Soopramanien, R., W. Paatii Ofosu-Amaah, and K. Uprety. *Combating Corruption: A Comparative Review of Selected Legal Aspects of State Practice and Manor International Initiatives.* Washington, DC: International Bank for Reconstruction, 1999. 2–3.

Patterson, B. W. 'The "Tyranny of the Eyewitness"'. *Law & Psychology Review* 28 (2004): 195–204.

Pasternak, J. D. 'Sexual Harassment and Expertise: The Admissibility of Expert Witness Testimony in Cases Utilizing The Reasonable Woman Standard'. *Santa Clara Law Review* 35 (1995): 651.

Patterson, B. W. 'The Tyranny of the Eyewitness'. *Law and Psychology Review* 28 (2004): 195–204.

Penrod, Steven, and Brian Cutler. 'Witness Confidence and Witness Accuracy: Assessing Their Forensic Relation'. *Psychology, Public Policy & Law* 1 (1995): 817–845.

Polinsky, A. M., and S. Shavell, 'Corruption and Optimal Law Enforcement'. *Journal of Public Economics* 81 (2001): 1–24.

Rankin, L. J. 'Entrapment: A Defence for the Willing, Yet Unready Criminal?' *University of Cincinnati Law Review* 63 (1994): 1487.

Richards, E. L. 'Federal Election Commission v. Colorado Republican Federal Campaign Committee'. *American Business Law Journal* 40 (2002): 83.

Roiphe, R. 'The Serpent Beguiled Me: A History of the Entrapment Defense'. *Seten Hall Law Review* 33 (2003): 257.

Rosenberg, I. M., and Y. L. Rosenberg. 'Perhaps What They Say Is Based Only On Conjecture—Circumstantial Evidence, Then and New'. *Houston Law Review* 31 (1994–1995): 1373.

Ross, J. E. 'Management and Control of the Modern Business Corporation: Review: Trade-off in Undercover Investigations: A Comparative Perspective', *University of Chicago Law Review* 69 (2002): 1501.

———. 'Valuing Inside Knowledge: Police Infiltration as a Problem for the Law of Evidence'. *Chicago–Kent Law Review* 79 (2004): 1111–1149.

Salbu, S. R. 'Battling Global Corruption in the New Millennium'. *Law and Policy International Business* 31 (1999): 1–12.

Slobogin, C. 'Deceit, Pretext, and Trickery: Investigative Lies by the Police'. *Oregon Law Review* 76 (1997): 7775.

Smith, S. M. 'The Other Race Effect and Contemporary Criminal Justice: Eyewitness Identification and Jury Decision Making: Eyewitness Identification: Postdictors of Eyewitness Errors: Can False Identification Be Dangerous in The Cross-Race Situation?' *Psychology, Public Policy & Law* 7 (2001): 153.

Svensson, J. 'Eight Questions About Corruption'. *Journal of Economic Perspectives* 19, no. 3 (Summer, 2005): 19–42.

Tanzanian Affairs 79 (September 2004).

Tindall, S. M. 'Note: Do as She Says: The Shortcomings of Justice O'Connor's Direct Evidence Requirement in Price WaterHouse v. Hopkins'. *Berkeley Journal of Employment and Labor Law* 17 (2001): 332.

Unzicker, B. 'From Corruption to Cooperation: Globalization Brings a Multilateral Agreement against Foreign Bribery'. *Indiana Journal of Global Legal Studies* 7 (2000): 655–686.

Vigilante, Miles, J. 'Screening Expert Testimony After KUMHO Tire Co. v. Carmichael'. *Journal of Law & Policy* 8 (2000): 543–592.

Walker, John K., Jr. 'Covert Searches'. *Stanford Law Review* 39 (1987): 545.

Walker, R. C. 'Circumstantial Evidence in Homicide Cases'. *Virginia Law Register* 20 (1915): 721–732.

Wells, G. L., and E. Seelau. 'Eyewitness Identification: Psychological Research and Legal Policy on Lineups'. *Psychology, Public Policy and Law* 765 (1995).

Wydick, R. C. 'The Ethics of Witness Coaching'. *Cardozo Law Review* 17 (1995): 1.

RESEARCH AND OTHER PAPERS

Economic and Social Research Foundation (ESRF) and Front Against Corrupt Elements in Tanzania (FACEIT). *The State of Corruption in Tanzania, Annual Report 2002*. October 2002.

Government of the United Republic of Tanzania. *The Presidential Commission of Inquiry Against Corruption*. Washington, DC: World Bank/ Development Agency, November 1996.

Hansard, 23rd Session, Vol. 4, 1958.

Hansard, 35th Session, Parliamentary Debate on the Budget 17th May, 1960.

Hansard, Parlimentary Debate, 7th Sitting, 20th April, 2007.

Holle, J. *The Role of Parliament in Eradicating Corruption in Tanzania* (Bachelor of Laws research paper, University of Dar es Salaam, 2003).

ICAC. *Independent Commission Against Corruption Annual Report 2002/2003*. Port Louis, Mauritius: ICAC, 2003.

Johnston, M. 'Cross-Border Corruption: Points of Vulnerability and Challenges for Reform'. In *Corruption and Integrity Improvement Initiatives in Developing Countries*, edited by S. J. Kpundeh, I. Hors, UNDP, and OECD. New York: UNDP, 1998.

Kaufmann, D. *Empirical Frontiers and the Case for Collective Action: The Role of Bilateral Donors in Fighting Corruption, Improving*

Governance and Controlling Corruption. Maastricht, the Netherlands: World Bank Institute, 25–27 April 2000.

Kikwete, J. M. *Speech by President of the United Republic of Tanzania When Inaugurating the Fourth Phase Parliament*. Dar es Salaam: Government Printer, 2005.

Kilonzo, A. *Administrative Irregularities as the Principal Agent of Corruption and Mismanagement of Government Funds in Tanzania* (Bachelor of Laws research paper, University of Dar es Salaam, 2003).

Kpundeh, S. J., I. Hors, UNDP, and OECD, eds. *Corruption and Integrity Improvement Initiatives in Developing Countries*. New York: UNDP, 1998.

Lambsdorff, J. G. 'The Economics of Corruption Handout'. In *The Institutional Economics of Corruption and Reform: Theory, Evidence, and Policy*, edited by J. G. Lambsdorff. New York: Cambridge University Press, 2007.

Langseth, P., and R. Stapenhurst. *National Integrity System Country Studies*. EDI Working Papers, Washington, DC: Economic Development Institute of the World Bank, 1997.

Longino, F. *Understanding and Preventing Corruption in Tanzania*. Master's thesis in criminology, University of Cambridge, 2001.

Masatu, M. (2004), *Fighting Corruption in Tanzania: A Critique of the Law and the Administration of the Anti-Corruption Institutions*. Master's thesis, University of Dar es Salaam, 2004.

Mndolwa, E. B. *Auditors Role in the Fight Against Corruption and Enhanced Good Governance*. Open lecture to Accounting Association, Faculty of Commerce and Management, University of Dar es Salaam, 22 February 2003.

———. *Liquidation Law and Practice in Tanzania Mainland: Is There Room for Improvement?* MBA dissertation, Institute of Development Management, Mzumbe, 2002.

Planning Commission. *The National Framework on Good Governance: The Steering Committee Good Governance*, December 1999 (Unpublished).

Rutashobya, L. *Fiduciary Risk Assessment For the Provision of Direct Budgetary Support in Tanzania.* Unpublished report Submitted to DFID Tanzania, May 2004.

Shaidi, L. P. *The Problem of Corruption in Tanzania.* Master's thesis, University of Dar es Salaam, 1975.

Transparency International. *Global Corruption Report 2004.* London: Pluto Press, 2004.

UN Department of Economic and Social Affairs and UN Development Programme. *The Challenges of Restoring Governance in Crisis and Post-Conflict Countries*, 7th Global Forum on Reinventing Government Building Trust in Government, 26–29 June 2007, Vienna, Austria. New York: United Nations, 2007.

United Nations Office on Drug and Crime. *Proceedings Document on Strengthening Judicial Integrity and Capacity in Indonesia*, Kendari, 7–8 October, 2004.

United Republic of Tanzania. *The Presidential Commission of Inquiry Against Corruption in Tanzania.* 2 vols. WB/ODA, Washington, DC: World Bank/Overseas Development Assistance, 1996.

———. *The State of Corruption in Tanzania.* Dar es Salaam: Front Against Corrupt Elements in Tanzania (FACEIT)/ Prevention of Corruption Bureau (PCB), 2002.

Index

Made in the USA
Monee, IL
12 November 2026

5c7e2bee-d504-44ee-b7fb-a5cfe9af6333R01